Reading Disability

READING DISABILITY

A Human Approach to Learning

THIRD EDITION, REVISED & EXPANDED

FLORENCE G. ROSWELL

AND

GLADYS NATCHEZ

Foreword by Katrina de Hirsch

Basic Books, Inc., Publishers   New York

Library of Congress Cataloging in Publication Data

Roswell, Florence G
    Reading disability.

    Includes bibliographical references and index.
    1. Reading disability.   I.   Natchez, Gladys, joint
author.
LB10.50.5.R6   1977   428'.4'2   76-55874
ISBN: 0-465-06849-9

TO OUR FAMILIES

In this much dark, no
light is little

MARK VAN DOREN

Contents

CONTENTS

Part III
Treatment

Appendixes

Illustrative Examples

ILLUSTRATIVE EXAMPLES

Foreword

IN A FIELD beset by emotional controversies and evangelical fervor, *Reading Disability* is a much-needed and highly desirable book. It does not press a theory. It does not assume that children's difficulties with printed words are necessarily the result of intrapsychic conflict or that significant neurophysiological factors are easily separable from a child's total social and emotional experience. It does take cognizance of the complexity of the problem and the multidimensional aspects of maturation. The authors' respect for the individual rhythm of growth and their insight into the problems of the classroom teacher, who all too often feels threatened by the "expert," demonstrates an awareness and wisdom which is lacking in much of the literature on the subject.

The chapter on diagnosis is exemplary of the authors' fortunate handling of the problems. Their recommendations that reading tests be evaluated qualitatively in addition to quantitatively, that trial lessons be part of the diagnostic procedure, and that the child be given a sympathetic explanation as to his specific strengths and weakness after tests are completed are as yet by no means standard procedure. Of utmost importance also is their emphasis on involving the pupil in searching for the remedial measures most appropriate to his needs. Beyond the wealth of practical suggestions which should be immensely helpful to remedial therapists and teachers, the book has a spirit of warmth and empathy. It is this spirit which is so essential in handling children with reading problems.

KATRINA DE HIRSCH
Consultant, Language Pathology,
New York State Psychiatric Institute

xi

Preface to the
Third Edition

IN PLANNING the third edition we tried to find a balance between quantitative and qualitative approaches to a child's functioning. We believe with Thorndike that "reading is thinking," and we would add it is also feeling and reaction—not a word-calling process. Thus, we search to uncover some of the more elusive aspects of children's reading problems. Rather than rely mainly on test scores and teaching techniques, we observe the children's responses during typical learning situations. We are interested in sparking students with whom we work so that they can at least keep pace with their school requirements and start to expand their lives in the areas of knowledge and literature. In this way they have a chance to capture the joy and excitement that are intrinsic to the art of reading.

Accordingly, the focus of the book is on the human aspect. We recognize the need for standardized tests but question their unending proliferation. We agree with the necessity of test scores but question giving them great weight. We believe in the judicious teaching of reading skills but question the emphasis on mechanical competency which stresses separate entities. We use many of the methods and techniques offered in teaching reading but question their efficacy when they are used routinely. Instead of a predetermined scheme, we look for children's reactions and the hidden aspects of their functioning. These often uncover the kernel of the problem. During treatment sessions we try to foster their natural curiosity—rather than squash it with rote methodology.

In the following chapters we present procedures for the diagnosis and treatment of children with reading difficulties. We show how we might integrate the viewpoints of the family, teacher, reading specialist, psychologist, and others connected with the child. We portray the teaching that we have used with students of all ages, ranging from the non-reader to those at college level who experience difficulties with reading and have related language disorders.

The talents of the students we discuss have ranged from mediocre to exceptional, but for the most part they have been able to come to terms with their limitations and to appreciate their strengths. Thus they have been able, with some degree of confidence, to choose the route they wish to take at different stages.

We are pleased to announce the addition of several new chapters. Chapter 3, "The Neurological Basis of Reading Disability," was written by Dr. Martha Denckla. She is director of the Learning Disabilities Clinic at Children's Hospital Medical Center in Boston.

Ruth G. Nathan, who has had wide experience in the field as a reading specialist and college instructor, wrote Chapter 11, "High School and College Students with Marked Comprehension and Expressive Writing Difficulties."

The authors contributed a new chapter, "The Psychological Basis of Reading Disability," Chapter 4.

References and articles have been updated. Representative tests including recent revisions have been listed as well as new materials suitable for pupils at all levels who have reading problems.

We express our gratitude to colleagues, teachers, parents, and students who have continued to expand our understanding of the multifaceted problems in reading disability. Any examples in the cases we present have been used to describe general rather than unique problems. If many readers are reminded of similar individuals in their own experience, we will consider our examples realistically drawn.

Part I

Basic Considerations

1

An Introduction to
Reading Disability

READING DISABILITY signifies disharmony in the life of a child. The disharmony may arise from a variety of problems related to psychological, physical, educational, environmental, and other difficulties, or from the interaction that occurs among them.

It is the purpose of this book to examine the complex causes of reading disability and to suggest methods for diagnosis and treatment. Frequently the various disciplines approach the problem from their own particular bias. Here we are attempting to combine pertinent theory and methodology from each area with a view toward assessing the problem in as wide a scope as possible.

The number of children who cannot cope with school has been increasing. Gibson and Levin[1] report that at least 15 percent of American schoolchildren have reading difficulties. Other authorities have estimated that the number of children with inadequate reading skills is significantly higher in cities than in other areas of the country.[2,3] Whatever the percentage, most educators agree that the number of children who read less effectively than they should—and could—is far too high.

1. E. Gibson and H. Levin, *The Psychology of Reading* (Cambridge, Mass.: MIT Press, 1975), p. 486.
2. J. Carrol and J. Chall, eds., *Toward a Literate Society* (New York: McGraw-Hill, 1975), p. 61.
3. H. Goldberg and G. Schiffman, *Dyslexia* (New York: Grune & Stratton, 1972), p. 15.

What Is a Reading Disability?

A child has a reading disability when there is a significant discrepancy between his reading level and his intellectual potential as measured by standardized tests. Quantitative evaluation, however, is always used with caution because test scores alone do not provide accurate appraisal of a process as complex as reading.

The word *dyslexia* is often used loosely in connection with reading disorders. There are differing opinions among professionals regarding this ambiguous term. Although it is sometimes used to describe a specific condition involving some degree of neurophysiological dysfunction, it is more generally considered to be synonymous with the term *reading disability*. According to a glossary published in mimeographed form by the Interdisciplinary Committee on Reading Problems, *dyslexia* is defined as "a disorder of children, who despite conventional classroom experience fail to attain the language skills of reading, writing, and spelling commensurate with their intellectual abilities."[4]

Learning disability is another term that has become popular in recent years. It also is ambiguous. The concept developed around deficit brain functions, particularly lesions, and low intelligence. Today designations include *perceptual deficits* and *minimal neurological dysfunction* as the root of the problem.[5] According to many authorities,[6] there can be no precise definition as yet. Myklebust suggests, however, that we need to view children with learning disability from a clinical vantage point. He considers that they "have a dysfunction in the brain that [is] not manifested in gross neurological abnormalities but often [causes] serious deficits in learning and adjustment and in the actualization of what might be high or even very high intellectual potential."[7]

4. The Interdisciplinary Committee on Reading Problems (Washington, D.C.: Center for Applied Linguistics, 1969).

5. S. Sapir and A. Nitzburg, eds., *Children with Learning Problems* (New York: Brunner/Mazel, 1973), pp. xiv, xv.

6. J. Wepman, pp. 155–56, R. Rabinovitch, p. 146, Marian Vernon, p. 114, in Natchez, *Children with Reading Problems* (New York: Basic Books, 1968).

7. H. Myklebust, "Learning Disorders—Psychoneurological Disturbances," *Rehabilitation Literature* 25 (1964): 355 ff.

Varied Characteristics of Children with Reading Disability

Children with reading disability do not fall into set categories. They are found in all age groups, all ranges of intelligence, and all cultural groups, and they have all types of physical and personality components. Pupils who read poorly grow up in diverse environments; they may live with understanding or punitive parents, in happy or broken homes. Some may be affected by these conditions; others remain untouched. In some instances, a child with reading problems shows severe emotional difficulty at the outset; sometimes the maladjustment manifests itself only after the appearance of poor achievement. But all children with reading disability manifest some disequilibrium in their lives.

Attitudes toward Early Learning Experiences

Let us consider briefly how these characteristics may develop. The infant has great potential for healthy growth despite possible minor handicaps, but he depends on those around him for nurture. Parents are likely to allow the youngster more freedom in his early years than later on. Rarely will they insist, for instance, that an infant go to sleep or awaken at a given hour. Undoubtedly they also recognize their limitations in imposing an arbitrary timetable on walking and talking. Even if they try to hurry him along for their own purposes, they soon resign themselves if he fails to respond. At this time they seem willing to accept his innate physiological and psychological pattern. As one youngster put it, "After you are born, you have about five years of relaxation; but once you reach the age of five, your parents decide your life for you." The initial acceptance and indulgence may have a significant influence on the fact that the rapidity of learning in the early years is rarely equaled later on.[8]

Take parents' attitudes toward their child's early speech as one example, and contrast it to their reactions toward his beginning efforts in reading. The first sound that a child makes may be the famous nonsense syllable *da da*. Proud Papa undoubtedly considers himself crowned king,

8. J. Bowlby, *Child Care and the Growth of Love* (Harmondsworth, Middlesex, England: Penguin Books, 1973), pp. 36–37.

5

and the accomplishment is greeted accordingly. Soon the baby catches on to the language around him. When he can respond to a game of "Peek-a-Boo," it sometimes gains him the amount of applause accorded a prima ballerina. The rate at which other words soon appear is even more startling. According to various estimates, vocabulary growth progresses from approximately a dozen words at one and a half years of age to anywhere from 2,000 to 6,000 and higher for the first grade child.[9] But vocabulary growth is only one source for wonder; phrases, sentences, grammatical structure, meaning, and thought are all learned spontaneously in varying degrees by most children during their first few years.[10,11]

All this time parents usually allow the child to talk in his own way and at his own rate. They are not likely to ask the pediatrician how many words their child should be saying. And with regard to mispronunciation, he can probably repeat the words *wi bwed* for *rye bread* over and over to the accompaniment of delighted giggles from parents and friends.

Repercussions of Reading Difficulty

Although talking tends to proceed according to the child's natural urges, reading seems to be in the province of adult prescription. When a child is slow in reading, parents and teachers become alarmed. When will he learn? How will he manage at school? What about college?—and if it happens that he misreads *where* for *whom* there is no laughter. Instead, adults wonder whether he will have a serious reading problem. If he continues to progress slowly, their apprehension mounts. No matter how they try to disguise it, this anxiety is communicated to the child. This in turn can increase his own doubts and uneasiness.

Perhaps parents become anxious because they feel they must guide the child's learning. Since reading does not "come naturally," maybe the adults feel that it is *their* success or failure that is at stake. For instance, when the child mistakes one word for another, they often blame them-

9. I. Lorge and J. Chall, "Estimating the Size of Vocabularies of Children and Adults: An Analysis of Methodological Issues," *Journal of Experimental Education* 32 (1963): 147–57.

10. D. Johnson, "The Language Continuum," in S. Sapir and A. Nitzburg, eds., *Children with Learning Problems* (New York: Brunner/Mazel, 1973), ch. 24.

11. K. de Hirsch, "Language Deficits in Children with Developmental Lags," in *Psychoanalytic Study of the Child* (New Haven, Conn.: Yale University Press, 1975), pp. 92–126.

selves. If he does not learn easily, they begin coaxing him. The child senses their uneasiness and becomes bewildered. He does not wish to incur displeasure. Nor does he wish to face ridicule from his classmates. But disapproval over slow progress is in the air—in the community. He begins to feel desperate.

It is hard for the child under these conditions to feel assured that some individuals simply need more time than others and that he will learn to read eventually. Indeed, he is usually convinced of the opposite. He must be stupid. Silently he asks himself, "What *is* wrong with me?"

On the other hand, school experiences can reverse a child's doubts and shakiness. If the child finds adults who encourage him to proceed at his own pace, to risk making mistakes, to discover for himself, he can overcome some of his mistrust. If he begins to feel valued for his individuality rather than forced into preconceived standards, he has a chance to grow toward understanding.

This presupposes that school personnel consist predominantly of cooperative, constructive people. It assumes also that they generally recognize many of the intricacies involved. They do not depend solely on any one theory or methodology. They do not use tests to evaluate only one aspect of the child's functioning. One-sidedness in approach detracts from seeing the child in his full array of strengths and limitations.

Unfortunately investigations which examine each entity singly have encouraged a limited viewpoint. Due to the exigencies of research, studies are rarely sufficiently extensive to include the interplay of major forces. Reporting findings in only one area, significant though they may be, can distort the picture because in any child some, any, or all components may be acting in concert or conflict.

Overview of Research

Indeed, if we look back at the historical picture, we can see how each separate element received primary importance at one time. The very first workers in 1905 were German and French ophthalmologists and neurologists who concerned themselves with eye movements, brain mechanisms, and what are now termed perceptual problems. A short time later, between 1910 and 1916, studies centered on reading in the classroom and environmental influence. At this time, interest also focused on theories behind learning to read.[12] Later, between 1935 and 1955, investigators directed their first serious attention to the relationship between personality traits and reading achievement. In recent years, emphasis has turned back to cultural and perceptual disorders.[13] Piaget,[14] with his original thinking, has recently investigated children's developmental processes in a new light. Thus we can see that the pendulum swings during the years, with each area enjoying the spotlight at different periods. At the present time studies on personality problems as related to reading are startlingly scarce. Without perspective, one would imagine that causation has been considerably narrowed. But we know that to consider any one deficiency as the major cause of a learning disorder is to assume causality and ignore coincidence.

Thus, in treating children with reading disability, we cannot rely on any one methodology; so far there is insufficient evidence to substantiate the use of any one procedure. There are so many unknowns that we cannot rely on any single solution, no matter how excellent the research. For example, despite the fact that authorities differ as to the level of intelligence necessary for acquisition of beginning reading skills, Montessori was able to engender learning even among mongoloids. We consider that certain levels of perceptual integration are required during the initial stages of reading; yet we find many children with deficits in these areas who are able to compensate sufficiently to learn. It seems that there are many data that we have accumulated regarding children's reading problems and many that still remain unclear. The more we delve, the more we recognize that we are still trying to clarify the significance of dynamic interplay which unfolds in unique ways for each child.[15]

Throughout this book we propound our ideas and experiences with children regarding the diagnosis and treatment of reading disability. Part I considers the ramifications of causation, diagnostic techniques are elaborated in Part II, and treatment procedures in Part III. We evaluate each child in as much depth as possible and plan treatment accordingly. Because the aim of instruction is to liberate the child to learn and to

12. W. Gray, "Summary of Investigations Relating to Reading," *Supplementary Education Monographs,* No. 28 (Chicago: University of Chicago Press, 1925).

13. T. Ingram, *The Nature of Dyslexia,* Department of Child Life and Health (Edinburgh, Scotland: University of Edinburgh, 1969).

14. J. Piaget, *The Grasp of Consciousness* (Cambridge, Mass.: Harvard University Press, 1976).

15. A. Korner, "Individual Differences at Birth: Implications for Early Experience and Later Development," *American Journal of Orthopsychiatry* 41, no. 4 (July 1971).

grow, practices are based on each pupil's individual requirements and qualities. In cases where we have been specific, we have not meant the description to be duplicated. We hope rather that the techniques cited will be used as a guide.

We recognize that there is still much that is not known in the area of causation and treatment of reading disability, and so we continue to question, to investigate, and to try to deepen our understanding.

2

Causes of
Reading Disability

READING DISABILITY is rarely caused by a single isolated factor. It is more likely to be an integral part of some inconsistency or imbalance in the forces governing the child's whole life. Such major forces include the child's innate constitutional makeup as it affects his growth and intellectual capacity, as well as the environment in which he develops. The interplay of these forces influences his social and emotional growth. The child brings this whole pattern with him to any situation, which of course includes learning.

Thus, investigation of causation is extremely complicated. In most cases, many factors are found together in various combinations. The most common include constitutional, psychological, neurological, intellectual, educational, and cultural. It is the interaction among them that is hardest to discern and yet yields the most reliable data on the child's learning problem. The psychological and neurological factors, however, are so complex and so significant that for purposes of clarity we have described them in two separate chapters—Chapter 3, "The Neurological Basis of Reading Disability" by Martha Denckla, and Chapter 4, "The Psychological Basis of Reading Disability" by the authors. Here we try to describe the major causative factors and show their influence on each other.

Constitutional and Physical Factors

Constitutional factors include all that we are born with. The idionsyn-cracies and commonalities of our natures influence the paths that we follow and the way that we learn. Physical ailments, for instance, even those of a minor or temporary nature, affect efficiency and reading performance. Consider, for example, how an adult's powers of concentration are reduced by hay fever, a cold, or even an irritating rash. Children are generally less well equipped to overcome such discomfort. Such factors as lack of sleep and even inadequate clothing can also make it difficult or impossible for a child to profit fully from school instruction.

Obviously some physical factors are of more importance than others in causing reading disability and need special medical attention. For example, inadequate nutrition,[1] defects in hearing, speech, or vision, brain damage, and endocrine or neurological dysfunction are particularly pertinent.[2] Adequate vision is so essential that it will be discussed below.

Vision

Research investigators differ as to the incidence of visual disorders in children with reading disability. Recent studies indicate that there is little relationship between visual ability and the interpretation of reading symbols. One such study, carried out at the Wilmer Institute in Baltimore, found no statistically significant difference in frequency of eye disorders among a group of 200 children with reading problems in comparison with a normal control group of the same size.[3] These findings have been corroborated by other studies.[4,5] However, they should not be interpreted to mean that eye difficulties can be ignored. There is general agreement that visual dysfunction may cause a degree of discomfort and

1. J. Cravioto, "Nutritional Deprivation in Psychological Development Studies in Man," in *Deprivation-Psychological Development*, Pan American Health Organization (Scientific Publication 134, 1966).
2. D. Hammill and N. Bartel, *Teaching Children with Learning and Behavior Problems* (Boston, Mass.: Allyn & Bacon, 1973), particularly the chapter "Assessing and Training Perceptual-Motor Problems."
3. H. K. Goldberg, "Vision, Perception and Related Facts in Dyslexia," in A. H. Keeney and Virginia T. Keeney, eds., *Dyslexia* (St. Louis: C. V. Mosby Co., 1968), pp. 90–109.
4. G. E. Park, "Functional Dyslexia vs. Normal Reading: Comparative Study," *Journal of Learning Disabilities* (1969), pp. 74 ff.
5. M. Preston, J. Guthrie, and B. Childs, "Visual Evoked Responses in Normal and Disabled Readers," *Psychophysiology* 11 (1974): 452–57.

fatigue which leads to unevenness and slowness in handling the printed page, strong resistance, and even general avoidance of reading. Therefore, if a child's visual efficiency seems to be impaired in any way, it is essential that he be referred to an eye specialist for examination.[6]

Emotional Factors

Rarely can emotional difficulties be isolated in order to determine precisely how they interfere with learning. The fundamental issues and theories with regard to the functioning and malfunctioning of personality are still in their infancy. Furthermore, personality factors exist as only one feature in a much more complex and intricate amalgam of physical, environmental, familial, and social forces.

In general, however, there are three major ways in which emotional disturbance arises in children with reading disability. First, a child who suffers emotional upset and conflict as he is growing up may face the school situation with heightened anxiety or similar psychic disturbances. In many cases, distracting, unconscious conflicts can diminish his concentration in class. The disturbance can be so overwhelming that he learns little.

Consider a child as he grows up in his family. If his parents accept his uniqueness, if he feels welcome and trusted, he has a chance to develop self-respect and confidence. At an early age he may know who he is and what he wants within the family circle and beyond.[7]

On the other hand, the child may find himself with people who are damaging, who lack faith in him and feel that he is hopeless. They coerce and criticize him in order to force him to do their bidding. The child can sense whether the surrounding atmosphere tends toward respect for his individuality or leans in the opposite direction. According to the leeway he experiences, he can develop his particular uniqueness. The more restrictions that he endures, the more will he mold himself in response to others and risk becoming alienated from himself.[8]

In addition, although the child may be fairly free from emotional

6. We are indebted to Dr. Herman K. Goldberg for his guidance and comments regarding visual factors as related to reading disability.

7. H. Searles, *The Non-Human Environment* (New York: International Universities Press, 1973), part I.

8. E. Erickson, *Insight and Responsibility* (New York: Norton, 1970), chapter 3.

maladjustment at the outset, it may evolve as a direct outgrowth of his frustration with schoolwork. Consider two children who have a similar emotional disturbance and similar reading problems. One is placed in a class where there is some provision in the curriculum to meet his needs and he is given individual attention; the class is composed of pupils not too far ahead of him in achievement, and he is able to make progress. The other child is placed in a class where the pupils are beyond his range of achievement; the teacher feels that she should not be expected to cope with such deviant functioning. She has no time to give him special treatment. Although neither of these atmospheres is aimed at curing the basic problem, it is likely that the first child will become better able to cope with schoolwork and may even develop a stronger ego through academic accomplishment, while the other is likely to recede more and more into negative patterns of defense.

Finally, both conditions can be present and reinforce each other. That is, a pupil's negative reactions from poor schoolwork can cause emotional difficulties or increase any that were already present. The personality disturbance then heightens the reading problem and creates a vicious circle. It is this cyIclical nature that makes it so difficult to determine whether or not emotional disturbance is at the root of the trouble. Yet in terms of treatment, it is important to attempt a distinction. According to Silver,[9] observation and data need to be collected on the intrapsychic, the interpersonal, the family, and environmental systems in which the child lives, in order to do justice to understanding the problem. Thus the etiology of the personality maladjustment and its relation to reading disability needs to be explored to the extent possible.

Neurological-Developmental Factors as Related to Reading Disability

Maturational Factors

The process of slow maturation is extremely complicated, and research is still needed before its implications can be fully understood. In general, maturation refers to the multifarious facets of a child's growth

9. L. Silver, "Acceptable and Controversial Approaches to Treating the Child with Learning Disabilities," *Pediatrics*, March 1975.

in such areas as height, weight, responsiveness, control of behavioral reactions, intelligence, perception, and integrative capacity, which is the ability to organize stimuli into an ordered pattern. Development of certain of these factors is crucial to learning and is described at length in Chapter 3.

However, before any discussion of maturational factors proceeds, it is important to clear up a misconception. Because deviant growth is frequently intertwined with emotional disturbance, one factor can easily be mistaken for the other. For example, a slowly developing child may incorrectly be considered emotionally immature if no account is taken of the rate of his physiological development. Or a child who has not yet attained the physiological growth necessary for learning to read may be mislabeled "emotionally disturbed."

Obviously individuals will show a variety of growth rates as they develop. Irregularities differ in degree from extremely mild to severe, embracing all types of neurological dysfunction.[10] In between are a number of variable conditions which are difficult to identify or categorize, yet they influence an individual's functioning in many ways.

Each particular stage of physiological development affects the tasks that an individual can master. When discrepancies in growth processes occur, they affect these and other tasks in different ways, depending on the nature and severity of the irregularity. Whether developmental factors can be influenced by training is being studied by many investigators.[11,12,13]

Extremely Slow Maturation

Children who reach the second, third, and fourth grades or even higher without acquiring the basic word-analysis skills because of slow maturation generally show deviant development in many areas. These difficulties may be a part of a general language disorder, so that a child may show difficulty in forming words, in expressing himself both orally

10. Many terms are used in referring to delay in maturation, such as *maturational lag, developmental lag,* or *delayed development.* In their most severe form, they are referred to as brain damage, organic injury or disease, dyslexia, irregular functioning, or disturbance of the central nervous system.

11. A. Silver, R. Hagin, and M. Hersh, "Reading Disability: Teaching through Stimulation of Deficit Perceptual Areas," *American Journal of Orthopsychiatry* 37 (1967): 744–52. Also see materials for diagnosis and treatment by Silver and Hagin, *Search and Teach* (New York: Walker Educational Books, 1976).

12. E. Koppitz, *Children with Learning Disabilities: A Five Year Follow-up Study* (New York: Grune & Stratton, 1971).

13. P. Myers and D. Hammill, *Methods for Learning Disorders: An Appraisal of Perceptual-Motor Training* (New York: Wiley, 1976), pp. 375–85.

and in written work, in figuring out words, and in reading. The language disorder may persist for many years so that these pupils may have difficulty not only in conceptualizing but in spelling and other subjects as well. Foreign languages in particular could be extremely difficult for them to learn. There is often evidence of poor motor coordination, general awkwardness, restlessness, hyperactivity, perceptual problems, and difficulty with integration of sensory modalities.

Sometimes these children have trouble controlling their impulses. They may show outbursts of temper; they may not be able to sit quietly for any length of time; they may be quick to shove or push. Finer muscle integration can also be affected and cause poorly formed or illegible handwriting. There may be, in addition, a residual ambidexterity and a tenuous establishment of left to right progression which is so essential to speaking, reading, or writing in accurate sequences. Hence the well-known reversal errors that these children make.

Maturational Factors Interfering with Word Analysis

Children who have persistent trouble with word recognition usually show varying difficulties with visual and auditory discrimination, blending separate sounds together, and establishing sufficient dominance and directionality to analyze words into proper letter sequences. They often understand words and passages that are read to them, but they simply cannot read comparable material independently. In addition, many children have difficulty in retrieval of words, often referred to as *anomia*.[14] This means that when they cannot produce a particular word on demand, let us say the word *subway*, they use a circumlocutory process to describe it—that is, "that train that goes underground."

Visual Discrimination. Reading requires instant recognition of printed symbols. Many symbols differ only in minute details. Some letters are exactly alike except that they face in opposite directions, such as *b* and *d*, *p* and *q*, *u* and *n*, *b* and *p*. Numbers present similar problems, as *6* and *9*, *81* and *18*. A child with immature perceptual functioning in all probability will have difficulty discriminating among them. Insufficient visual discrimination and poor spatial orientation[15] also interfere with recognizing words.

14. M. B. Denckla, "Research Needs in Learning Disabilities," *Journal of Learning Disabilities* (1973): 43–51.

15. It has not been established whether difficulty in distinguishing such symbols is due to visual discrimination, directional confusion, or spatial orientation. The latter factors are discussed in the section "Dominance and Directional Confusion," this chapter.

Auditory Discrimination. Inadequate perceptual functioning also makes it difficult for children with delayed maturation to detect differences in sounds of letters even though they have adequate hearing. Thus a child who cannot tell the difference between the beginning sounds of such words as *fin* and *sin*, or hears no distinction between *beg* and *bag*, will find it virtually impossible to learn to read when taught by a method requiring him to associate sounds with letters.

Blending Ability. Children with developmental lag show great difficulty not only in distinguishing separate sounds, but in blending them to form words. This apparently requires a high degree of neurological integration. Extensive research has been carried out to discover the nature of this difficulty, but no clear evidence has so far emerged.[16]

For instance, if a teacher pronounces slowly a simple word such as *s-a-t*, enunciating clearly and being careful not to put extraneous vowel sounds between the letters, the pupils with severe disability cannot put the sounds together so that they recognize aurally the word *sat*. When these pupils are taught by a phonic approach, which requires synthesizing sounds to form words, they have difficulty. Even if they have developed sufficient auditory discrimination to associate letters and sounds correctly, they cannot synthesize them easily to decipher unknown words. It is disheartening to observe them struggling unsuccessfully with this procedure. Exhorting them to put forth more effort, sending home report cards with "U" for unsatisfactory, drilling the child over and over again, all merely aggravate the problem. (Alternate methods which may be used are discussed in Chapters 8 and 9. The cases of Frank and Lloyd in Chapter 12 describe such children in detail.)

Dominance and Directional Confusion. To complicate further the acquiring of academic techniques, children with irregular functioning will perhaps show difficulty in establishing dominance and directionality. This can interfere with their learning to read. Lateral dominance and directional confusion have for many years been in the forefront of discussion on reading disability. Harris[17] defines lateral dominance as "the preferred use and superior functioning of one side of the body over the other." A person who habitually uses his right hand more skillfully than his left is considered to have right-hand dominance. Similarly, one who uses his left hand consistently and with greater skill has left-hand dominance. People also show eye preference by favoring one eye over

16. S. Mattis, J. H. French, and I. Rapin, "Dyslexia in Children and Young Adults: Three Independent Neuropsychological Syndromes," *Journal of Developmental Medicine and Child Neurology* 17 (1975): 150–63.

17. A. Harris and E. Sipay, *How to Increase Reading Ability* (New York: David McKay, 1975), p. 269.

the other in such monocular tasks as looking through a telescope, micro-scope, or kaleidoscope and foot dominance by showing preference of one foot over the other in kicking or hopping, although little study has been devoted to the latter. An individual is said to have crossed domi-nance when he is right-handed and left-eyed or vice versa. A person may also have mixed hand or mixed eye dominance when he does not show a distinct preference for using one hand or eye more decidedly than the other. It should be noted that children with mixed dominance are often called ambidextrous. However, they are not ambidextrous in the usual sense of the term. Rather than using both hands skillfully, they use them equally poorly. In this connection, Orton's theories[18] continue to receive considerable attention. He proposed that if an indi-vidual fails to develop consistent dominance of one side in preference to the other, reversal tendencies will result and reading will be seriously affected. He suggested the term *strephosymbolia* (literally, *twisted symbols*) to describe reading disability. More recent research indicates that "absolute dominance of one hemisphere (the left) is by no means always found, and the law of lateralization is only relative in character.[19]

Directionality is the awareness of right and left outside the body and seems to develop after laterality has been established. Harris[20] considers that evidence of directional confusion in reading disability cases is of far greater significance than any pattern of lateral dominance which may appear.

What is the relationship between dominance and directionality? The child first develops awareness of the two sides of his body. As already stated, consistent use of one side of the body indicates that dominance has been established. However, when the child is able to project direc-tional concepts into external space, he has developed adequate direction-ality and orientation. For example, in attempting to grasp an object, a child experiments with movement. He learns that to reach it he must move one way or the other. When concepts of sidedness in the world around him have been established, directionality has become stable. However, many children and even some adults remain uncertain as to directionality. When some people try to open a car door, for instance, after being ordered, "Turn the handle to the right," they automatically move it to the left. They report that they often experience directional confusion in following left-right directions.

---

18. S. Orton, *Reading, Writing and Speech Problems in Children* (New York: W. W. Norton, 1937), ch. 2.
19. A. R. Luria, *The Working Brain* (New York: Basic Books, 1973), p. 78.
20. Harris and Sipay, *How to Increase Reading Ability*, pp. 276 ff.

While the nature of dominance and directionality remains obscure, investigators[21,22] have shown that these factors are related to maturational influences. Immaturity in this area may directly interfere with the recognition of letter or word sequences. Hermann points out the significance of these functions when he states:

> When the individual's orientation in relation to his own body-schema is defective, such that right and left (and also other relations) are not securely fixed in this "scheme," orientation in space will fail at this same time. The function which we have called "directional function" is closely connected with orientation for side in relation to this body-schema. Impairment of directional function disturbs principally the comprehension of symbols, since letters, numbers, notes, and other similar shapes are abstractions which have meaning only by virtue of a very definite position relative to the person's own body, or rather his consciousness of his body—the body-schema.[23]

Children with problems of directionality or spatial orientation may have trouble distinguishing between *on* and *no*, *was* and *saw*. They may also reverse letters and numbers in writing, speaking, or reading. For example, such pupils might write *clam* for *calm*, say *aminal* for *animal*, or read *scared* for *sacred*. These errors are usually due, not to inattention or lack of effort, but to a more basic language disorder. This tendency not only interferes with early learning but often persists for many years. This is evidenced in the poor language usage, spelling, writing, and reading of some bright high school and college students who were found to have experienced earlier developmental difficulties.

Some investigators, such as Doehring[24] view these types of reading errors "in terms of a disorder of visual, verbal, and visual-verbal sequential processing." According to these theories, sequential or serial action is an important component of reading and spelling and frequent transposition of letters and word order in retarded readers suggests that some dysfunction in this process exists. While there have been numerous studies[25,26] dealing with the difficulties poor readers experience in

---

21. Luria, *The Working Brain*.

22. F. Ilg and L. Ames, *School Readiness* (New York: Harper & Row, 1964).

23. K. Hermann, *Reading Disabilities* (Springfield, Ill.: Charles C. Thomas, 1959), p. 139.

24. D. Doehring, *Pattterns of Impairment in Specific Language Disability* (Bloomington, Ind.: Indiana University Press, 1968), pp. 135 ff.

25. I. Liberman, *Speech and Lateralization of Language* (Towson, Md.: Orton Society, 1971).

26. L. Belmont and H. Birch, "Lateral Dominance, Lateral Awareness and Reading Disability," *Child Development* 36 (1965): 57–71.

matching visual and auditory patterns, research is still inconclusive regarding the existence of a specific developmental disorder of sequential ordering.[27]

Intellectual Factors

Obviously, intellect ultimately determines learning ability. As a result, the level of intelligence is used as a criterion for determining the level of reading achievement. Thus, a third grader who is above average in intelligence should be reading above third grade level, while a child of the same age who is below average in ability might be achieving adequately if he reads at second grade level. However, estimates of intelligence or achievement can never be completely valid or reliable; the testing instruments themselves are always subject to a degree of error. Also, such factors as the child's physical, environmental, and emotional condition affect test results. Therefore, any quantitative scores are useful as rough measures only. They merely suggest the level at which a child may be expected to read. Intelligence is a determinant of reading achievement, but intelligence test scores are not yet solid predictors of reading achievement.

Educational Factors

Children show unique learning patterns and differ in their competencies in areas related to learning to read. The latter would include auditory and visual discrimination, auditory blending, visual-motor functioning, understanding of concepts, and ability to give sustained attention. Thus teachers need to be alert to factors underlying the acquisition of reading skills and must also be technically competent in dealing with any aspects likely to impede learning.[28]

27. We are indebted to Joan Raim, Assistant Professor, City College of the City University of New York, for communicating this information from her doctoral dissertation.
28. J. Jansky and K. de Hirsch, *Preventing Reading Failure* (New York: Harper & Row, 1972).

For example, a teacher who lacked the professional background in dealing with a ten-year-old who had a history of slow maturation told his parents that he was "merely a reluctant dragon who had to catch fire" before his schoolwork could improve. In fact, none of his teachers had sufficient insight into the nature of his problem to be able to handle it.

With regard to the disadvantaged child, the extent to which a teacher adapts procedures to sociological factors has an important bearing on the child's initial learning. Frequently much work has to be done in broadening the child's information, fostering verbal skills, and developing abstract ability in relation to verbal concepts. Development of these processes facilitates learning and helps to prevent early failure. Lastly, all children need to acquire a feeling that they *can* learn. The teacher needs to exhibit sufficient confidence in children to communicate that successful achievement is within reach. A constructive attitude on the part of the teacher, along with sound professional training, is indispensable for providing optimal learning.

Cultural Factors

It is well known that the setting in which children live has an important influence on their learning. There are home environments which stimulate children's intellectual curiosity and promote their general knowledge of people and the world around them. Provided there are no interfering factors, these children usually learn to read easily and bring joy and delight to the process.

On the other hand, there are children who come from impoverished homes where they are exposed to a limited range of experiences, where educational materials are scarce, and where language usage is restricted. Such an atmosphere does not prepare a child adequately for school learning. In addition, many such children are bilingual, which increases their difficulty in school.

If teaching methods are not adjusted to the needs of these children, and if instructional materials are unsuitable, they get off to a poor start and are likely to experience difficulty in learning to read from the outset.

Hence, in searching for causal factors, it is well to consider background and environmental elements in order to gain insight and understanding.

Interaction of Causative Factors

Although we have attempted for purposes of discussion to isolate the separate causes of reading disability, the authors believe that these factors rarely act independently. More often one is tangential to the other. The entire focus then shifts, and a whole new constellation arises. Thus the interrelationships are far greater in complexity than are any of the factors taken individually.[29] Furthermore, no matter what the significant causal factors—intellectual, physical, neurological, environmental, or emotional—failure in school will cause negative reactions to appear. These reactions will produce emotional disturbance or heighten any that was already present.

Suppose, for example, that a child is socially immature, "whiny," and helpless. The parents are told not to overprotect or overindulge him. This may create guilt and conflict on their part and may even deprive the child of appropriate warmth and affection. He may then resort to demanding more and more attention. If this is denied, he could conceivably develop strong resistance, which would eventually lead to his not learning in school. The school failure then would create repercussions: upset in the parents, apprehension, disappointment, or dissatisfaction in the teacher, and in the child increased anxiety and agitation due to lack of approval and confidence from those he wishes so much to please. All of these conditions perpetuate the circular constellation of forces.

The same repercussions might occur with a child who is developing slowly and fails to learn because of growth factors. If he has a teacher who is unfamiliar with characteristics of maturational lag and employs inappropriate methods, this can add to his problem. For example, if the teacher requires him to blend sounds together to figure out words, he may be unable to do this because his physiological growth simply has not reached this level of integrative capacity. The frustration on the part of the teacher and the child then becomes serious. The parent, in turn, becomes anxious over the child's failure. The mother may rush out to buy popular books offering various panaceas. She may enthusiastically begin teaching the child herself. But the learning problem by this time has become so intensified by futile, misdirected efforts that the pattern becomes extremely complicated.

Thus we can see the interplay of both obvious and subtle forces in the development of a child's reading ability. The complicated patterns

29. J. Abrams, "An Interdisciplinary Approach to Learning Disabilities," *Journal of Learning Disabilities* 2 (1969): 575–78.

and far-reaching consequences of all the varying possibilities affect the life of the child, the teacher, and the parent. The authors believe that one is never dealing here with a separate school problem or an exclusively emotional, neurological, or developmental one. The continued search for causes of reading disability will throw light on the problem and may help to avoid certain pitfalls. New dimensions will arise, and so the quest for more definitive formulations persists as the pursuit of a broader understanding continues.

Suggestions for Further Reading

Adams, R. "Learning Disabilities: A Developmental Approach." *Journal of Special Education* 9 (1975): 160–65.

Cruickshank, W. "Learning Disabilities: A Charter for Excellence," in S. Kirk and J. McCarthy, eds., *Learning Disabilities: Selected ACLD papers*. New York: Houghton Mifflin, 1975.

de Hirsch, K. "Learning Disabilities, an Overview." *Bulletin of New York Academy of Medicine* (1974).

Feldmann, S. "Diagnosing Perceptual Problems." Speech given at the New York State Reading Conference Mar. 26–28, 1969.

Lerner, J. *Children with Learning Disabilities*. Boston: Houghton Mifflin, 1976.

Lewis, J. et al. *No Single Thread: Psychological Health in Family Systems*. New York: Brunner/Mazel, 1976.

Muller, H. *The Children of Frankenstein*. Bloomington, Ind.: Indiana University Press, 1970.

Sapir, S., and Nitzburg, A. *Children with Learning Problems*. New York: Brunner/Mazel, 1973. Part III.

Selected Research on Emotional Factors

Aaron, R., and Muench, S. "Behaviorally Disordered Adolescents' Perceptions of Adult Authority Figures after Treatment Using a Taxonomy of Comprehension Skills." *Reading Research Quarterly* 10, no. 3 (1974–75): 228–43.

Bishop, D., and Chace, C. "Parental Conceptual Systems, Home Play Environment, and Potential Creativity in Children." *Journal of Experimental Child Psychology* 12, no. 3 (1971): 318–38.

Black, F. "Self-concept as Related to Achievement and Age in Learning-disabled Children." *Child Development* 45 (1974): 1137–40.

Brockman, L. "The Reading Factor in Measuring Security in Children." *The Alberta Journal of Educational Research* 20 (1974): 244–50.

Gardner, R. *Psychotherapeutic Approaches to the Resistant Child*. New York: Jason Aronson, 1975. Chapter 2.

Kohlberg, L. "Implications of Developmental Psychology for Education." *Educational Psychologist*, 1973, pp. 2–15.

McKillop, A. "The Influence of Personal Factors on the Reading Development of Children." In Natchez, ed., *Children with Reading Problems*. New York: Basic Books, 1968. Pages 317–23.

Philage, M. L. et al. "A New Family Approach to Therapy for the Learning Disabled Child." *Journal of Learning Disabilities* 8 (1975): 490–99.

Silver, A., and Hagin, R. "The History of a Language Problem in an 'Organic' Child." In A. Harris, ed., *A Casebook on Reading Disability*. New York: David McKay, 1970.

Singer, E., and Pittman, M. "A Sullivanian Approach to the Problem of Reading Disability: Theoretical Considerations and Empirical Data." In Natchez, ed., *Children with Reading Problems*. New York: Basic Books, 1968. Pages 55–65.

White, W., and Simmon, M. "First Grade Readiness Predicted by Teachers' Perception of Students' Maturity and Students' Perception of Self." *Perceptual and Motor Skills* 39 (1974): 84–89.

Winnicott, D. W. *Therapeutic Consultations in Child Psychiatry*. New York: Basic Books, 1971.

Selected Research on Development and Neurological Factors

Belmont, L., and Birch, H. "The Effect of Supplemental Intervention on Children with Low Reading Readiness Scores." *Journal of Special Education* 8 (1974): 81–89.

Cruickshank, W., and Hallahan, E., eds. *Perceptual and Learning Disabilities in Children*, 2 vols. Syracuse, N.Y.: Syracuse University Press, 1975.

Denckla, M. B. and Rudel, R. "Naming of Object-Drawings by Dyslexic and Other Language Disabled Children." *Brain and Language* 3 (1976): 1–15.

Eisenberg, L. "The Overactive Child." *Hospital Practice* 8 (1974): 151–60.

Freud, S. *On Aphasia*. New York: International Universities Press, 1953.

Geschwind, N. "Language and the Brain." *Scientific American* 226 (1972).

Hinshelwood, J. *Congenital Word-Blindness*. London: Lewis, 1917.

Klasen, E. *The Syndrome of Specific Dyslexia*. Baltimore: University Park Press, 1972.

Luria, A. *Higher Cortical Functions in Man*. New York: Basic Books, 3rd ed. in preparation.

Ross, D., and Ross, S. *Hyperactivity*. New York: Brunner/Mazel, 1976.

Rudel, R., and Denckla, M. B. "Relationship of I.Q. and Reading Score to Visual, Spatial and Temporal Matching Tasks." *Journal of Learning Disability* 9 (1976): 169–78.

Satz, P. et al. "An Evaluation of a Theory of Specific Developmental Dyslexia." *Child Development* 42 (1971): 2009–21.

Silver, L. "A Proposed View on the Etiology of the Neurological Learning Disability Syndrome." *Journal of Learning Disabilities* 4 (1971): 123–33.

Strauss, A., and Kephart, N. *Psychopathology and Education of the Brain-Injured Child*. New York: Grune & Stratton, 1955.

Selected Research on Perceptual Factors

Chomsky, N. *Basic Studies on Reading*. New York: Basic Books, 1970.

Critchley, M. *The Dyslexic Child*. Springfield, Ill.: Charles C. Thomas, 1970.

Flax, N. "The Contribution of Visual Problems to Learning Disability." *Journal of the American Optometric Association* 41 (1970): 841–45.

Gredler, G. "Severe Reading Disability: Some Important Correlates." In J. Reid, ed., *Reading: Problems and Practices*. London: Ward Lock Educational, 1972. Pages 142–60.

Ingram, T. "Symposium on Reading Disability." *British Journal of Educational Psychology* 41 (1971): 6–13.

Keogh, B. "Optometric Vision Training Programs for Children with Learning Disabilities." *Journal of Learning Disabilities* 7 (1974): 219–31.

Laufer, M. "Long-term Management and Some Follow-up Findings on the Use of Drugs with Minimal Cerebral Syndromes." *Journal of Learning Disabilities* 4 (1971): 519–22.

Marwit, S., and Stenner, A. "Hyperkinesis: Delineation of Two Patterns." *Exceptional Children* 38 (1972): 401–6.

Oettinger, L. "Learning Disorders, Hyperkinesis and the Use of Drugs with Children." *Rehabilitation Literature* 32 (1971): 162–67.

Rubino, C. "Psychometric Procedures and the Detection and Exploration of Be-
    havioral Deficits Due to Cerebral Dysfunction in Man: II." *Canadian Psy-
    chologist* 13 (1972): 40–52.
Schain, R. "Neurological Diagnosis in Children with Learning Disabilities." *Aca-
    demic Therapy* 7 (1971–72): 139–47.
Vernon, M. *Reading and Its Difficulties: A Psychological Study*. Cambridge, Mass.:
    Cambridge University Press, 1971.
Wiederholt, J., and Hammill, D. "Use of Frostig-Horne Visual Perception Program in
    the Urban School." *Psychology in the Schools* 8 (1971): 268–74.

3

The Neurological Basis of Reading Disability

by Martha Bridge Denckla*

THE PURPOSE of this chapter is to provide the nonmedical professional with some of the vocabulary and theory which underlie neurological approaches to the problem of reading disability. Since the science of understanding reading disability is, at present, sadly primitive relative to the treatment of reading disability, what follows is in the nature of an invitation to join in seeking common directions for future research, rather than an authoritative presentation. This chapter will attempt to introduce the reader to definitions of *dyslexia* and other important terms, as well as to the relationship of minimal brain dysfunction to dyslexia. There will also be a critique of the concept of maturational lag; a review of research findings on perceptual problems, cerebral dominance, and language disorders; and an assessment of the implications of these findings for therapy (optimistic fatalism).

* Director of the Learning Disability Clinic, Children's Hospital Medical Center, Boston.

Definitions

Dyslexia means faulty reading, that is, reading disability. Until recently, *dyslexia* was used in neurological language to describe the less severe form of *alexia*, which means *loss* of ability to read. (This is a general characteristic of Greek-derived medical terminology; for example, *dysphasia* denotes a less severe impairment of spoken language than does *aphasia*.) In recent years, however, with the growth of interest in childhood learning disabilities, the term *dyslexia* has been set aside from the vocabulary of adult neurology and has been reserved for childhood reading disability—that is, failure to learn to read rather than loss, partial or total, of previously normal reading skill. Nonmedical professionals should free themselves of any sense of being intimidated by *dyslexia*, since it is after all a symptom-descriptive and not a diagnostic term. (Dyslexia is a translation of what the patient tells the doctor, not what the doctor "explains" to the patient.)

When the adjective *developmental* precedes *dyslexia*, it denotes failure to acquire reading skills at the initial time and at the progressive rate expected by the child's society. *Developmental* simply excludes acquired disorders or regressions of skills.

Thus far, having defined *developmental dyslexia*, none of the usual exclusionary clauses have been invoked (see the definition of reading disability as used in this book, in Chapter 1, p. 4). Even narrowing the perspective to a medical person's look at the individual child himself, assuming the adequacy of home, school, and community, the term *developmental dyslexia* might still leave open the possibility that the child might be mentally retarded or have a chronic physical handicap. In common usage, however, the exclusion of sensory, major physical, or mental handicap *is* implied by uttering "developmental dyslexia." The difficulty, as I shall attempt to explain, lies in differing thresholds for what constitutes exclusion of mental or physical handicap. For example, there are children with low I.Q. scores—below the current basal "low average"—whose reading skill acquisition is *still* further below expectation for I.Q. Some would argue that they belong in the category of developmental dyslexia, just as some (myself included) argue that the brilliant child with barely average reading achievement deserves such designation.

This issue brings us to the next adjective, *specific*. Rutter and his co-workers have been the most persistent and sophisticated proponents of defining reading disability by means of a multiple regression equation containing I. Q. variables which generates an expectancy for reading achievement. Thus a child is described as suffering from *specific developmental dyslexia* if he does not read as well as would be predicted from the equation.[1] Similar approaches, such as subtracting "reading age" from "chronological age" or obtaining a "reading quotient" and comparing it to I.Q., have been discussed,[2] and all suffer from the problem of built-in biological circularity or cultural relativism. Nonetheless, since we lack anatomical, biochemical, or any other physical correlate of the problem of reading disability, each of us is forced to admit the limitations of the concept "specific." Yet after all, we utilize the concept in some form in order to narrow our already too-broad group of children. In discussions with others who do research on developmental dyslexia, I invariably find myself arguing against choosing any one I.Q. measure to generate the expectancy for the label *specific* and sadly conclude that we are going to be partially at fault no matter which test we choose. Better, then, to admit the dilemma and choose several measures of "evidence of normal potential," any one of which can be used at least as "light shining through the clouds" for the learning-disabled child. (This is not an act of charity, but rather one of honest heuristic value; indeed, one of the significant fringe benefits of studying dyslexia is the confrontation, daily, like Diogenes with his lantern looking for an honest man, with the haunting question, "What is intelligence?") One significant unavoidable hint as to the neurological nature of dyslexia has come out of the attempt to be "specific": it is very difficult to match reading-disabled children and controls on verbal I.Q. measures, and much easier to match them on performance I.Q. or spatial ability measures.[3,4,5] Please note that the concept of specific developmental dyslexia does not exclude other coexisting disabilities—for example, handwriting, arithmetic, athletic, musical, or social. Whatever else is right or wrong about the child, his "dyslexia" (or reading retardation disability) is still "specific." (For example, I have recently seen a brilliant 26-year-old medical student who came to me with the diagnosis of specific developmental dyslexia.

1. M. Rutter and W. Yule, "The Concept of Reading Retardation," *Journal of Child Psychology and Psychiatry* 16 (1975): 181–97.
2. A. L. Benton, "Developmental Dyslexia: Neurological Aspects," in W. J. Friedlander, ed., *Advances in Neurology*, vol. 7 (New York: Raven Press, 1975).
3. A. Bannatyne, *Language, Reading, and Learning Disabilities* (Springfield, Ill.: Charles C .Thomas, 1971).
4. S. F. Witelson, "Abnormal Right Hemisphere Specialization in Developmental Dyslexia," to be published in *Proceedings of International Conference, The Neuropsychology of Learning Disorders: Theoretical Approaches* (Baltimore: University Park Press, in press).
5. M. B. Denckla and R. G. Rudel, "Naming of Pictured Objects by Dyslexic and Nondyslexic Learning-disabled Children," *Brain and Language* 3 (1976): 1–15.

Her main clinical problem was persistent hyperactivity syndrome, with severe attentional deficit. There was no doubt that she had learned to read quite late and poorly, relative to her obviously superior intellect, yet the diagnosis of specific developmental dyslexia hardly seems to cover the extent of her disability. She had "dyslexia plus _____." The reader should keep this example in mind when reading the section "Minimal Brain Dysfunction" below.

Pure dyslexia is a term which I have used[6] in order to approximate what is meant by some distinguished authorities.[7,8,9,10] All have in common the concept that there are children who are free from any problems other than reading disability, who do not have "dyslexia plus _____," although it is universally allowed that spelling disability is implied as part of developmental dyslexia. Perhaps the most clearly stated modern exposition of pure dyslexia is the paper "Unexpected Reading Failure."[11] As with all such allied views of pure dyslexia, there is a problem about the authors' threshold values for freedom from problems; for example, "no signs of brain damage" or "no oral language disability" are statements which leave the authors open to legitimate quibbles over criteria or cutoff points. Yet certainly there are children who at least approach the limit "pure developmental dyslexia," and it is striking how often such children present us with strong family histories of similar difficulties found in close relatives. (Bannatyne[12] even prefers to call such cases *genetic dyslexia*, although this overreaches the present evidence, which points strongly to *familial*.) Perhaps the most important conceptual clue provided by the "pure dyslexic" cases is that of a nondeficit model, a raising of the important question, "What is the advantage of having a brain for which learning to read is a difficult task? What is different about such a brain, different in a way compatible with survival in the face of the selection pressures of the environment?" The child who seems to be above average in every aspect of life except the academic one

6. M. B. Denckla, "Minimal Brain Dysfunction and Dyslexia: Beyond Diagnosis by Exclusion," to appear in M. Kinsbourne, ed., *Learning Disabilities: Proceedings of Workshop at First International Congress of Child Neurology.*

7. M. Critchley, *The Dyslexic Child* (Springfield, Ill.: Charles C. Thomas, 1970).

8. J. Money, "Developmental Dyslexia," Chapter 19 in P. J. Vinken and G. W. Bruyn, eds., *Handbook of Clinical Neurology,* vol. 4: *Disorders of Speech, Perception, and Symbolic Behavior* (New York: North Holland, 1969).

9. Bannatyne, *Learning Disabilities.*

10. For a discussion of the views of Critchley, Money, and Bannatyne, see Denckla, "Minimal Brain Dysfunction."

11. J. S. Symmes and J. L. Rappaport, "Unexpected Reading Failure," *American Journal of Orthopsychiatry* 42 (1972): 82–91.

12. Bannatyne, *Learning Disabilities.*

presents us with the challenge and excitement of investigating *minimal brain dysfunction.*

That last statement not only brings us to the transition point, on the brink of introducing MBD in all its varied disguises and partisan conflicts, but reveals that all along there was an assumption: namely, that when we use the term *dyslexia* we are intending to implicate the *brain* in the chain or network of causation underlying reading disability.

Minimal Brain Dysfunction and Dyslexia

Since this chapter represents the neurological point of view, it is here that we will explore the various meanings of "MBD": *minimal* (or minor) *brain dysfunction* (or *differences*)—or minimal *neurological* dysfunction. (The recent companion term *learning disabilities* is dealt with in Chapter 1.) For approximately 15 years the adjective "minimal" or "minor," the latter favored by British and other European physicians, has modified preexisting terms such as *brain-damaged, brain-injured, neurologically impaired,* or *neurologically handicapped.* Indeed the older terms remain enshrined in some of our legislation involving categorical funding for special education. The reason for the adjective(s) represented by the M appears to be related to recognition of both more subtle and more complex syndromes (and sometimes even complex mixtures of subtleties) on the part of physicians who deal with children with chronic developmental-onset problems. In this regard, much credit goes to certain pioneering child psychiatrists, for whom the recognition of "organic" factors of a subtle nature—that is, minimal brain dysfunction—represented courageous independent thinking in an era dominated by dogmatically psychodynamic interpretations of behavior. (Elsewhere I have reviewed the history of MBD in terms of "understanding what they were challenging."[13] Separately recognized syndromes such as hyperactivity and dyslexia were thought of as examples of, subtypes of MBD.[14,15]

13. Denckla, "Minimal Brain Dysfunction."
14. S. D. Clements, *Minimal Brain Dysfunction in Children,* NINDB Monograph No. 3, Public Health Service Publication No. 1415 (Washington, D.C.: U.S. Government Printing Office, 1966).
15. J. E. Peters, J. S. Romine, and R. A. Dykman, "A Special Neurological Examination of Children with Learning Disabilities," *Journal of Developmental Medicine and Child Neurology* 17 (1975): 63–78.

Peters explicitly expresses the need for the term "MBD" as a "loose organic line" encompassing not only the relatively pure, but also the complex-mixture cases. Recall the example of the young woman told that her diagnosis was specific developmental dyslexia who had always suffered most from her lack of ability to concentrate upon and complete tasks; it was for such clinical pictures that Peters and his colleagues envisaged the usage "minimal brain dysfunction, manifested by ———."

I wish to emphasize that MBD was intended to include dyslexia, even (but not only) the pure form. In clinical reality, the "pure form" is quite rare, although perhaps the selection factor of being referred to a physician, of *any* specialty, explains this low prevalence. A psychiatrist is likely to see more "pure hyperactive" cases (those whose social-emotional misbehavior is the leading concern), and a reading specialist is likely to see more "pure dyslexic" cases than a neurologist will see. However, in most clinics and schools devoted to children with learning disabilities, *mixed types predominate*. This is in a way fortunate for research into the neurological basis for dyslexia, because comparisons between "specific" but mixed as opposed to "pure" cases allows us to infer *what is necessary* versus *what is sufficient*, neurologically, to allow normal acquisition of reading skill. I have come to feel that the MBD category has rescued the field from years of inconclusive studies of "good readers" versus "poor readers"[16] and allowed us to examine the varieties of "poor readers" in enough detail that the differing varieties no longer cancel each other out. Armed with the "loose organic line" of MBD, clinicians have been freed to examine "poor readers," not only with the exclusionary purpose of earlier purists, but with the inclusionary orientation of investigating as many brain systems as is possible. Findings that there are several different dyslexic syndromes suggest that different brain systems *and* different causes may in combination result in reading disability.[17,18] Although at first glance this might appear to have increased confusion about dyslexia, in fact the comforting aspect of the MBD orientation is that it has clarified the *relevant* brain systems (see the section "Perception, Cerebral Dominance, and Language" below), while other systems now appear less worthy of consideration.

The persisting problem is that many authorities insist that "true" or "pure" or "genetic" dyslexia children have no "soft signs," and

16. Benton, "Developmental Dyslexia."
17. S. Mattis, J. H. French, and I. Rapin, "Dyslexia in Children and Young Adults: Three Independent Neuropsychological Syndromes," *Journal of Developmental Medicine and Child Neurology* 17 (1975): 150–63.
18. Denckla, "Minimal Brain Dysfunction."

therefore should not be thought of as belonging to the MBD category.[19] Here I must undertake to define "soft signs" (defined at greater length elsewhere[20,21]) and to let the reader in on the medical controversy as to the definition. One broad issue is whether such items as attention, language, and perception can yield soft signs. The basic issue is territory; are these items psychology or neurology? My answer, of course, is that they belong to both fields, or to the intersecting field called neuropsychology, and that every neurologist is trained to do a "mental status examination" which checks these items of functioning.

The reader can see the problem: if a dyslexic child has *my* soft signs, consisting of subtle oral language or short-term memory deficits, that same child would be declared free of soft signs by those authorities who insist upon what Benton[22] calls "infrabehavioral evidence." The latter would be derived from the traditional neurological examination minus the mental status! Included would be *cranial nerve functions* (sensory and motor from the neck up), *limb muscle strength, tone, reflexes, coordination,* and *sensation.* Subtle, borderline, equivocal, but still-detectable deviations from normal on the traditional neurological examination, minus the mental status, would meet the most widely accepted definition of soft signs. In other words, something "objective," suggesting chronic, non-progressive, not-very-dramatic imperfections in the brains of the person being examined. Examples would be reflexes which are unequal on the two sides of the body (but neither lateral set of reflexes necessarily outside of the broad range of normal), inability to wink one of the eyes, fixed squint of the eyes, or an "upgoing toe" (Babinski sign) on one side. The reader will note the heavy emphasis on one side being different from the other, because this reflects the neurologist's need—inversely related to the drama of the sign—to use the patient as his own control. Signs such as these are what I have called "pastel classic soft signs."[23]

But what if deviations are equal on both sides? For example, what if both great toes go up when the soles of the feet are stroked? Babinski toe signs bilaterally are normal in an infant up to a certain age (about which some controversy persists). We are confronted with the problem

19. Critchley, *Dyslexic Child*; Money, "Developmental Dyslexia"; Bannatyne, *Learning Disabilities*.
20. Denckla, "Minimal Brain Dysfunction."
21. Denckla, "Dyslexia: A Neurologist's Perspective," in R. Spector, ed., *Developmental Dyslexia* (Springfield, Ill.: Charles C. Thomas, 1976).
22. Benton, "Developmental Dyslexia."
23. Denckla, "Minimal Brain Dysfunction."

of a "statute of limitations" for signs which, when bilateral in a human being below a certain age, are considered normal. If these signs persist for a while (how long?), they are "developmental" (see the section "Maturational Lag" below). Beyond a certain age (when?), the very same signs are pathological, albeit possibly still "soft" because they do not imply severe handicap or progressive illness. (This is yet another medical use of the term "soft"; to indicate that little concern or urgency is implied by the sign).

When dealing with children, and with such traditional neurological items as coordination, the role of development imposes a somewhat different meaning upon "soft signs." As Marcel Kinsbourne has stated it, "If the child were younger, the findings would be regarded as normal."[24] As with Babinski responses, we accept the absence of ability to perform certain acts of coordination, and then accept clumsy performances up to certain age limits. Milestones such as sitting, walking, and talking have broad ranges of normal timing, beyond which there is cause for concern. Descriptively, however, such failures to meet milestones or to perform as elegantly as expected are "developmental soft signs." (What these imply neurologically is to be discussed in the section "Maturational Lag.") With regard to reading disability, the issue again is one of the examination tools and the interpretive threshold of the examiner who declares the dyslexic child free of soft signs. It has been my experience that when "infrabehavioral" items such as coordination are examined against a background of knowledge of developmental expectations, very few dyslexic children are free of developmental soft signs. This is especially the case if the child is ten years old or younger. I have found it useful to designate the infrabehavioral (minus the mental status) neurological status of a child as "developmental only" if the child is "young-for-age" on coordination items but is indeed free of "pastel classic neurological signs." Even if the child's soft signs are developmental only, he legitimately belongs in the very loose general diagnostic category of minimal brain dysfunction.

Why all this fuss? Why not simply agree with Critchley, who states that if such minor signs exist they are not directly relevant to dyslexia? My reasoning is that by investigating the status of many brain systems, most admittedly not directly relevant to reading, and by following the observable changes in development of these brain systems, we have our best chance of understanding the brain-behavior relationships underlying

24. M. Kinsbourne, "Minimal Brain Dysfunction as a Neurodevelopmental Lag," *Annals of the New York Academy of Sciences* 205 (1973): 268–73.

dyslexia. Investigating, developmentally, both functions and dysfunctions, we localize both in time and in space. One might disparage this approach as "research by ambush," but it has the virtue of avoiding premature closure or narrowing of vision.

In closing this section on MBD, in which I have aligned myself firmly with those who view dyslexia as part of the MBD cluster of syndromes, I must point out to the reader the dangers of the term. Like any label, MBD invites reification; we are tempted to use the singular form and speak of "it," rather than zero in on the *particular* syndrome. Because there are medications which are helpful partial treatments for some MBD syndromes, there exists, among the impatient or simplistic, the tendency to react reflexly to MBD by writing a prescription. My contention is that we need more rather than fewer labels (backed up by reproducible observations of course) so that we can communicate economically the particular syndrome description and treatment can be tested for each syndrome. (For example, the reader would be horrified if he were treated for "anemia" without specific knowledge of *which* anemia has been diagnosed; iron will not cure when vitamin B-12 is needed.) Thus we come full circle back to the need for diagnosis by inclusion, rather than exclusion alone, for both MBD and dyslexia. At least let us all be meticulous in describing "about whom we are speaking" before drawing conclusions about treatment.

Maturational Lag

The subject of "developmental only" deviations in MBD provides a natural starting point for a discussion of one of the oldest and most intriguing ideas about the basis for reading disability. Although the term *maturational lag* (or *developmental delay* or *neurodevelopmental lag*) appears in literature going back many years, the operational application of developmental psychology is based upon norms, and has characterized the use of the term in the research of the 1970's (see Usprich[25] for review, Satz and Sparrow,[26] Kinsbourne,[27] Denckla[28]).

25. C. Usprich, "Dyslexiology: Two Nascent Trends and a Neuropsychological Model," *Bulletin of the Orton Society,* in press.
26. P. Satz and S. S. Sparrow, "Specific Developmental Dyslexia: A Theoretical Formulation," in D. J. Bakker and P. Satz, eds., *Specific Reading Disability: Advances in Theory and Method* (Rotterdam: Rotterdam University Press, 1970).
27. Kinsbourne, "Minimal Brain Dysfunction."
28. Denckla, "Neurologist's Perspective."

Both in the older, more anecdotal clinical literature and in this newer, normative-referenced research a basic conceptual issue is hidden: is maturational lag a description (and no more) of the clinical situation or a mechanism? As an explanatory concept, is maturational lag to be visualized in terms of specific parts of the brain or connections between parts? As a description of a state of affairs at a given examination time (again, Kinsbourne's "If the child were younger, the findings would be regarded as normal"[29]), does "maturational lag" imply "'catch-up'"?

Let me begin by addressing the "catch-up" question first, because the answer seems more easily available. Despite a general tendency to expect catch-up implied by the adjectives "merely developmental" or "pending maturation of the defective process,"[30] many experienced researchers, myself included, doubt that catch-up *in the fully optimistic sense* has ever been demonstrated. (I remember my open-mouthed surprise, some six years ago, at an Orton Society meeting, when Katrina de Hirsch arose and declared, "When I say 'maturational lag,' I do not mean that I expect 'catch-up.' " However, older and hopefully wiser, I have come to realize that the catch-up expectation is *not* a necessary part of the usefulness of the "developmental only" descriptive category of which I am a proponent, *nor* is lack of catch-up an impediment to the theory underlying developmental research on a long-time base.)

Let me explain the descriptive use of "maturational lag" for the reader by examining the limiting case—global mental retardation. A child stands before us, chronologically seven years old, but in every respect, across the board, appearing, behaving, and performing on our tests like a four-year-old child. (Note: such truly "global" pictures are rare; most retarded children are unevenly or lopsidedly retarded and overlap significantly with the traditional sense of neurologically impaired or brain-injured, even when their handicaps fall short of "threshold" for the diagnosis of cerebral palsy.) At any rate, what happens when we follow, year by year, this child who at seven appeared to us to be a perfectly developed four-year-old? Does the child catch up? Sadly, the answer is no. The child reaches a plateau (*when*, as for the rest of the human race, is an open question) and is clearly "defective." *It is sad but true that demonstrably deficient brain systems/structures appear during the developmental phase of life (childhood most dramatically) to be "merely delayed."* As a neurologist, drawing upon the knowledge of what is documented for mentally retarded brains, I am forced to be

29. Kinsbourne, "Minimal Brain Dysfunction."
30. Ibid.

fatalistic in extrapolating my expectations to the fragmentary retardations seen in the MBD-learning-disabled clinical population. I do not expect follow-up to demonstrate catch-up.

But now I hasten to return to the optimistic position, both clinically-humanistically and scientifically. My theoretical position is as follows: although the specific fragmentary "developmental only" retardations which we document in MBD-learning-disabled children may reflect permanently deficient brain systems, it is still important to document the rate of development, the level of plateau, and the age at which plateau is reached for those specific-deficient systems. It is equally important to document from early on the normal or superior functions (reflecting normal or superior brain systems) in the context of which the deficient system(s) reach plateau. Implied in my position is the concept that a child who appears selectively "developmentally backward" (even if that reflects permanent deficiency) but who all along the way is otherwise average or superior, cannot be treated as though he were a normal younger child "pending the maturation of the defective process."[31] Focus upon negatives and deficits alone appears to be misleading; "success" does not imply "catch-up" of negatives and deficits, but rather a gradual process of compensation or even a sudden leap to a different way of succeeding. We need follow-up of a very long-term nature, examining both the success in complex real-life tasks (for example, reading) and the status of neurological systems, deficient to superior, at the time of success. (For a profoundly theoretical discussion of this subject, see Usprich.[32]) From a practical point of view, my descriptive orientation toward "maturational lag" raises questions as to the meaningfulness of educational concepts such as "readiness," and the limitations of watchful waiting for the "slow developer." Furthermore, I question the utility of drawing too firm a line between the "developmental only" and the "pastel classic neurologically impaired" in terms of educational needs during the childhood period; lacking a crystal ball, we had best assume that the most rational course is teaching the child with his existing strengths and weaknesses.

Now I must return to the first question posed in this critique on maturational lag. Is there evidence for continued brain maturation of structures and systems which neurologists know to be related to the "developmental" dysfunctions? Satz and Van Nostrand explicitly state that they suspect a "lag in the maturation of the cerebral cortex (primar-

31. Ibid.
32. Usprich, "Dyslexiology."

ily the left hemisphere)."[33] Kinsbourne speaks of "slowed evolution of cerebral control of the relevant activity.."[34] Not only are regions in the cerebral cortex known to be necessary for reading (by negative evidence drawn from the effects of brain damage in adults), but there is evidence that the *connecting* and *associating* areas of the cerebral cortex show the longest period of myelination (the physical process of "insulation" being formed around nerve fibers, important because with such insulation, speed of transmission from nerve cell to nerve cell reaches a critical value). This form of physical maturation continues well past childhood, at least until the thirties, possibly up to senescence.[35] Therefore, any concept of maturational lag that is descriptive or implies physical change must be committed to a very long view of development.

Let me end with one example, echoes of which will come back to the reader in the section "Perception, Cerebral Dominance, and Language." The corpus callosum is a big connecting bundle of nerve fibers linking left and right sides of the brain, at the level of the cerebral cortex. It is myelinated, on the average, at ten years. I assume that by now the intelligent nonmedical professional has been bombarded by many articles in the lay press and knows that for most human beings the left brain-half is essential for linguistic, analytic, and sequential (including motor) processes, and the right brain-half is essential for nonverbal, spatial, simultaneous-holistic processing. Let us put these pieces of information together with two studies of dyslexic children in order to grasp the potential of the maturational lag concept in its modern dress! In 1971, as part of a study of the entire "educationally handicapped" population of Palo Alto, California,[36] such children were asked not only to copy the Bender Gestalt designs, but subsequently to judge whether their reproductions matched those designs. Description of errors was solicited and compared with that of trained psychologists. Results: although the educationally handicapped were once again shown to be significantly impaired in their reproductions of designs relative to control children, the educationally handicapped did perceive and report their

33. P. Satz and G. K. Van Nostrand, "Developmental Dyslexia: An Evaluation of Theory," in P. Satz and J. J. Ross, eds., *The Disabled Learner: Early Detection and Intervention* (Rotterdam: Rotterdam University Press, 1973).
34. Kinsbourne, "Minimal Brain Dysfunction."
35. P. I. Yakovlev and A. R. Lecours, "The Myelogenetic Cycles of Regional Maturation of the Brain," in A. Minkowski, ed., *Regional Development of the Brain in Early Life* (Philadelphia: F. A. Davis, 1967).
36. F. W. Owen, P. A. Adams, T. Forrest, L. M. Stolz, and S. Fisher, "Learning Disorders in Children: Sibling Studies," *Monograph of the Society for Research in Child Development* 36, no. 4 (Chicago: University of Chicago Press, 1971).

errors in reproduction just as accurately as did controls; furthermore, from age 11 years on, the educationally handicapped group was significantly better (that is, closer to trained psychologists' judgments) than the controls.

Similarly, in a study of route-finding (walking in conformity to a map), my colleagues and I have found that although dyslexic children aged 7–10 walk fewer correct moves than do the controls, from 11 years on, the dyslexic group, and most spectacularly the "pure dyslexic" subgroup, outperform the controls.[37] We plan to imitate the brilliant maneuvers of the Palo Alto group and in the future ask dyslexic children to judge the map-walking competence of others rather than to perform the sequence of moves themselves.

The reader should now be asking: Why do children with increasingly good spatial perception (superior after age ten) perform poorly when reproducing patterns with a pencil, and why should dyslexic children's map-walking scores "lag" and then "leap" to superiority after age ten years? My way of putting together the pieces is to suggest that one or both of the following brain systems is physically maturing to a threshold level after the first decade of life: The left brain-half systems underlying sequential processes or the great connecting bundle (corpus callosum) between the left and right brain-half. The right brain-half, mediating spatial processes, may have been normally developed all through that first decade, but if it were "bound and gagged" neurologically it would lack adequate expressive outlets. The reader should store away the adjective "adequate." My whole point about maturational lag is that the connection between right and left brain-halves and/or the left brain-half itself may never be "normal" but if it is "adequate" at some threshold level of development, even permanently deficient systems may support and permit the expression of superior systems. Implications for dyslexia seem clear: in learning a complex skill like reading, the child with a deficiency may be storing up those parts of the skill dependent upon his strengths until such time as, neurologically, his weaknesses are no longer at the handicapping level. At that time the antecedent teaching and learning may "hitch a ride with nature" (critical level of maturation of still-deficient systems) in such a way as to appear suddenly "caught-up." Every experienced teacher of the dyslexic child has humbly reported to me the mysterious "click" or "take-off" point

37. M. B. Denckla, R. G. Rudel, and M. Broman-Petrovics, "Spatial Orientation in Normal, Developmentally Learning Disabled, and Neurologically Impaired Children," in preparation.

after years of struggle. I submit that the years of struggle were not in vain and that waiting for maturation may be neurologically, as well as sociologically, misguided, on the basis of present evidence.

Perception, Cerebral Dominance, and Language

Perception

The example used at the end of the section "Maturational Lag" has already hinted at my main point: there is little or no evidence in favor of the notion that visual-perceptual disability is a significant correlate, much less a cause, of reading disability. Because reading is visual and because "perceptual handicap" is enshrined as a legal category for funding of special education, I will devote time to visual perception. It may well be that auditory perception is a more significant correlate of reading than visual perception, but fewer practical controversies to date have arisen from the "auditory" school, perhaps because the proponents thereof are usually talking about "auditory" in the specific sense of "phonemic," and therefore tend to be overtly concerned with language development.

To return to definitions, I would remind the reader that "perception" means "discrimination" between or among stimuli, whereas "sensation" means "detection" of stimuli. Perception is thus dependent upon, indeed built upon, sensation. The problem is, how do we know whether a person is either detecting (level of sensation) or discriminating (level of perception)? Usually we ask the person to say or do something, which reveals to us what he is detecting or discriminating about the stimuli we present to him. And herein lies the difficulty in many of our so-called sensory (much less intersensory) or perceptual tests: the person being examined may "fail" by virtue of deficient *saying* or *doing* rather than by virtue of deficient sensing or perceiving. We must be smart enough as examiners to circumvent saying or doing, or at the very least to minimize the level of proficiency required of these expressive outlets if we are to find out about sensation or perception. (That is where the trained audiologist excels, auditory detection-sensation-thresholds being his business.) All too often, however, perceptual-motor disability—for example, the poorly *executed* Bender Gestalt—is misinterpreted as showing perceptual disability.[38] Testing perception by means of multiple-choice matching-to-sample or declaration of "same or different" comes much closer to validity in revealing deficient perception. (Even here, the demand for *attention* imposed by matching and discrimination tasks raises a separate but important problem in the interpretation of perceptual tasks. For example, many readers may share my experience of the frequency with which responses of children to the auditory-discrimination tests deteriorate into monotonous "same, same, same . . ." or a singsong alternation "same, different, same . . . .")

In short, perception is hard to test in a valid way. Perception, visual or auditory, is also far from unitary. Recent research has redirected thinking away from the sense organ involved, eyes or ears, and toward the dimension of *sequential* versus *spatial* processes within each sensory system."[39] As described in the previous section of this chapter, the two brain-halves emerge as different in type of process rather than sensory bias. The left brain is no more "auditory" than the right, and the right brain is no more "visual" than the left. Along with this reorientation of recent research have come increasingly cogent challenges to the popular "intersensory integration" form of the "perceptual handicap" theme. This theory is appealing because to common sense the equivalence of "visual" to "auditory" stimuli does seem analogous to what goes on in reading, but it turns out that *within* visual or *within* auditory groups of stimuli the problem can be demonstrated to lie with sequential-spatial equivalence.[40,41] Benton summarized the evidence up to 1975 by pointing out the slender argument for visual-perceptual deficiency as a correlate of dyslexia (where demonstrated, it is found only among the youngest subjects) coupled with considerable evidence in favor of sequential processing deficiencies, auditory or visual, as stable, age-independent correlates. The reader should note that auditory perceptual testing is virtually always sequential, except if the test stimuli are musical chords.

The reader is probably asking, "What about perceptual training?" Having removed part of the rationale for training that which does not appear to be significantly correlated with dyslexia, I searched for good studies of the effects of perceptual training. Bluntly put, I found none.

38. Owen et al., "Learning Disorders."
39. R. G. Rudel and M. B. Denckla, "Relationship of I.Q. and Reading Score to Visual-Spatial and Visual-Temporal Matching Tasks," *Journal of Learning Disabilities* 9 (1976): 169–78.
40. Benton, "Developmental Dyslexia."
41. Rudel and Denckla, "Relationship of I.Q."

Nothing has changed since Hammill's 1972 review.[42] What I found were educational qualms about the validity of perceptual tests[43] and some short-term or anecdotal reports. So I will contribute my own anecdotal report, and to make a general point, will choose to tell of training in oral language skills (heavily correlated with dyslexia, as the reader will find out shortly). Working closely with an excellent language therapist,[44] I have enthusiastically advised and supervised oral language skills training for many children between ages three and six, such that by age six years, entering first grade, these children could pass with flying colors all tests of oral language at age expectation. My language therapist colleague and I sat back contentedly to watch success in reading acquisition follow this success in language training. By March of first grade, it was clear that success was *not* just around the corner; sadder but wiser, we learned that training a child to be "ready" did not change the child's brain such that the next step in language acquisition "came naturally." It was as though we had seen a child swim wearing a buoyant vest; then removed the vest and expected the child to swim. Such children needed continued consistent help at each successive stage of new learning involving the lagging (or deficient) system.

If this is true for "training" the linguistic antecedents or correlates *best* documented to be relevant to dyslexia, then the reader may draw his own conclusions as to the rationale for training the weakly correlated perceptual handicaps.

Another closely related problem is that of oculomotor (eye movement) impairments, perceptual handicaps, and dyslexia. It is well documented[45] that oculomotor impairments and perceptual (spatial) handicaps are correlated, whereas reading is not impaired by these deficits, but in fact may be excellent. That in itself is important, namely that children who cannot move their eyes have no trouble learning to read (except perhaps a sore neck from turning the head as they read). In addition, I will contribute the anecdote of one such child, an excellent reader and speller, followed by me for five years, who despite years of eye-movement exercises never appeared to have improved on neurological examination of the oculomotor system, nor did her spatial disability do anything but grow relatively worse with the years.

42. D. Hammill, "Training Visual Perceptual Processes," *Journal of Learning Disabilities* 5 (1972): 552–59.

43. D. Hammill, "The Validity of Perceptual Tests: The Debate Continues," *Journal of Learning Disabilities* 9 (1976): 332–37.

44. Dorothy Unger.

45. Benton, "Developmental Dyslexia"; Denckla et al., "Spatial Orientation."

In summary, there is no evidence that training of perception, co-ordination, language, or any other "basic" correlate of reading will in any way change the brain or the organization, rate of maturation, or "readiness" of the brain. To put it bluntly, "What you train is what (at most) you get," and there is no evidence for carry-over from one level of skill to another higher skill.

Cerebral Dominance

Much the same conclusion applies to training the peripheral observable manifestations of *cerebral dominance*. My message here is two-fold but not really contradictory: on the one hand, the role of cerebral dominance is extremely interesting and probably important in our understanding of dyslexia; on the other hand, trying to change or reorganize cerebral dominance by means of training hand or eye preference is both futile and harmful (the history of abuse suffered by stutterers is ample testimony to that judgment). First, I want the reader to differentiate cerebral dominance (what we infer about the mutual and interdependent leadership roles of the right and left brain-halves) and preference (what we observe about hand, foot, or eye usage). Lateral preference is not always observably equal to the lateralization of a skill; for example, a right-preferring tool-user is *normally* more skillful with his left hand on tasks involving spatial displacement. (Think of the left hand of the violinist.) The use of "lumped" terms such as "laterally" has tended to obscure such valuable distinctions.

The reader is urged to beware of statements about lateralization which do not tell us the comparative levels of skill, overall and for each side, of the populations described. To push the case to the limit, lateralization of motor function is most clear when one side of the body is paralyzed, but in such a case, well-defined lateralization is not a sign of healthy brain organization. If two populations with the same preference pattern and same overall skill are different with respect to which side is more skillful at a task, then we are onto something interesting about lateralization and cerebral dominance.

There is no question that among dyslexic children the prevalence of anomalies of lateral preference *and* skill have been documented.[46] In my own experience, despite a strong bias against the notion, I have been forced to acknowledge the right-hand, right-foot, left-eye preference

46. Benton, "Developmental Dyslexia"; Witelson, "Right Hemisphere Specialization."

pattern as significantly more frequent among dyslexic children (65 percent). But the reader must note the high frequency of this pattern among controls and conclude, as Zangwill did, as quoted in Benton,[47] that a vulnerability factor in cerebral organization rather than a cause of dyslexia must be revealing itself through this preference pattern. We return to the concept of "minimal brain differences" and resolve to investigate what advantages, as well as what deficits, variations in cerebral dominance may confer upon a person.

Witelson's data[48] on cerebral dominance for tactual discrimination of "nonsense" forms and block letters indicate that right-handed dyslexic boys perform as though spatial ability were mediated by both brain-halves. To put it dramatically, one might restate Witelson's conclusions thus: Dyslexic boys have "one-and-a-half right brains." This of course implies *less* left brain devoted to sequential and linguistic processing, but allows us to focus upon the spatial processing advantage conferred by this type of brain organization.

Witelson's right-handed dyslexic boys were overall just as accurate as controls on tasks of nonsense shape and block-letter matching by touch. On the nonsense shape task, dyslexic boys' right-hand scores were better than controls' right-hand scores. On the letter-palpating task, dyslexic boys' left-hand scores were better than controls' left-hand scores. Conclusion: dyslexic boys were less "lateralized"—that is, more equal right and left—than were controls. On a task involving listening to and reporting digits, dyslexic boys were overall less accurate than controls, but, like controls, were still better reporting from the right than from the left ear.

Would it make any sense to train dyslexic boys to be better with the right hand on block letter recognition? Would it force dyslexic boys to shift to left brain strategies and thus strengthen the left brain for the task of reading? Probably not. With an intact, connected brain, training the right hand to equal or surpass the left on this tactual task would probably be accomplished with the right brain leading or dominating the left brain anyway. For there is evidence from adult neurology that when a left-handed person is forced to write with his right hand, the "chain of command" in the brain is lengthened but not reversed in direction. To give a homely analogy: if a blue-eyed blonde dyes her hair black, her eyes will not turn brown. Changing the outward manifestations of the gene which determines pigmentation will not retro-

47. Benton, "Developmental Dyslexia."
48. Witelson, "Right Hemisphere Specialization."

actively change that gene. So it appears to be with cerebral dominance, about which we are still learning many new and complex mechanisms, including development throughout life. The observable manifestations of cerebral dominance are important clues to the ways in which brains do differ, but changing the manifestations is likely to result only in making things difficult.

Language

Oral language deficiencies are the best and historically longest documented contexts in which dyslexia occurs. This was predicted on the basis of the neurology of acquired alexia.[49,50] Wiig[51] has shown that adolescents with reading disability show persistent oral language deficits (anomia, meaning naming difficulty), and Jansky and de Hirsch[52] find kindergarten children who have difficulty naming objects and pictures are at risk for reading failure.[53] There is mounting evidence that left-brain-dependent functions—sequential, analytic, and linguistic—are impaired to some degree in most dyslexic people of any age. The very fact of the persistence, albeit in subtle and changing manifestations of this cluster of deficiencies, makes it hard to escape the inference that this set of correlates of dyslexia is close to the core of the problem. Elsewhere I have cited literature and given evidence to the effect that the *how*, the causation of left brain dysfunction is not important in the clinical picture, but the level of impairment and the levels of good functions are, taken together, all important.[54] Mattis, French, and Rapin[55] have, like myself, found several kinds of dyslexia, but no evidence that each kind has its own exclusive cause. This is why we find it more honest, more clinically realistic, to keep dyslexia within, rather than set apart from, the MBD category. Whether the child is, by history and neurological pastel classic signs, brain-damaged or is, by familial incidence and neurologically developmental only signs a "pure dyslexic," he will still show one or more of the following problems: naming and

49. M. B. Denckla, "Color-Naming Defects in Dyslexic Boys," *Cortex* 8 (1972): 164–76.

50. M. B. Denckla and R. G. Rudel, "Rapid Automatized Naming: Dyslexia Differentiated from Other Learning Disabilities," *Neuropsychologia*, in press.

51. E. Wiig, "Language Disabilities of Adolescents," *British Journal of Disorders of Communication* 11, no. 1 (1976): 3–17.

52. J. Jansky and K. de Hirsch, *Preventing Reading Failure* (New York: Harper & Row, 1972).

53. Reviewed in Usprich, "Dyslexiology."

54. Denckla, "Minimal Brain Dysfunction."

55. "Dyslexia in Children."

word-finding deficiency; word memorization deficiency; short "digits forward" and sentence memory span; inaccurate articulation of speech sounds, which is most commonly clustered with poor pencil use; and poor perception and/or memory for phonemic details in words and for sequence of phonemes in words.[56] We do not as yet know the life history of these particular deficiencies or combinations thereof. Which are more serious and long-lasting than others? Which may change and look like other deficiencies at a later age? (I harbor a suspicion that verbal memorization deficits are indistinguishable from word-finding deficits during the early years of active vocabulary acquisition, but might appear clearly different in adult life. In terms more familiar to the educator, the difference would be "he takes many repetitions to learn but then retains" as opposed to "he seems to learn something but intermittently doesn't come out with it." The first child has memorization problems, the second has word-finding problems.)

How does oral language deficiency relate to the visual level of reading? I would like to focus upon some very recent research which supports two of my favorite quotations: "Reading is language for the eye"[57] and "Reading is only incidentally visual."[58] I will set out to convince the reader that visual symbols are most highly efficient for everyone, dyslexic and nondyslexic alike, and that even the "visual-verbal" trouble for dyslexic children is not their greatest problem. For example, Supramaniam and Audley[59] have shown that good and poor readers aged 7–8 years were equally good at declaring "same/different name" in response to pairs of letters like "BB" or "bb" or "BD." For good and poor readers alike *this* task, based upon visual characteristics of letters within the same case, was easier than a related task involving mixing of cases, for example, "Bb" and "Dd." For poor readers, the mixed-case, visually-different-but-same-name judgments were markedly more difficult and time-consuming. Liberman[60] (1976) gives evidence that the errors of good and poor readers diverge most sharply on a short-term

56. Denckla, "Minimal Brain Dysfunction" and "Neurologist's Perspective."
57. I. Liberman, "Reading Acquisition and the Language Abilities of the Young Child," paper presented at Boston University Medical Center Symposium on the Neurological and Psychological Problems of the Learning-Disabled Child, April 2, 1976.
58. P. A. Kolers, "Reading Is Only Incidentally Visual," in K. Goodman and J. Fleming, eds., *Psycholinguistics and the Teaching of Reading* (Newark, Del.: International Reading Association, 1969).
59. S. Supramaniam and R. J. Audley, "The Role of Naming Difficulties in Reading Backwardness," paper presented at the British Association for the Advancement of Science, September 1, 1976.
60. Liberman, "Reading Acquisition."

memory task involving phonetic confusion, not visual or word-meaning confusion.

These studies point to an important role of silent, internal word (name) finding and phonetic recoding of symbols in the process of reading.

Attacking the nature of the symbol more directly, our own research group[61] has tried to teach dyslexic and control boys names of Morse code letters (auditory symbols), names of Braille letters (tactual symbols) and names of Braille letters presented visually (*new* symbols, not the familiar visual alphabet). For all children, names for the new *visual* symbols were easiest to learn (although dyslexic boys' scores were always lower than controls' scores of total names learned). The difficulty presented by touching rather than hearing symbols was, however, in opposite directions for dyslexic and control boys. *Most* difficult for dyslexic boys was the learning of names for the auditory sequences of Morse code. Note again that staying completely within auditory conditions, nothing intersensory involved, was the worst situation for the dyslexic children.

We have pursued this matter further in a study of word-finding in which names (nouns) must be given in response to pictures of objects[62] (similar to Denckla and Rudel),[63] objects felt and not seen, spoken descriptions of objects, and sentences constructed so that the last word to complete the sentence is a noun. Dyslexic children differed most sharply from controls on the "auditory tasks" again, particularly the sentence-completion task. Interestingly, the dyslexic children did better than the nondyslexic MBD children on the answering-to-spoken-description task, which is more demanding of categories and associations. I must remind the reader that the dyslexic children were worse than controls on *all* word-finding tasks and that I am pointing out the greatest relative difference occurring in an auditory, spoken-spoken situation. The practical importance of this line of evidence is that visual symbols remain relatively best for dyslexic children, that to reenforce them with touch and movement and any multisensory or meaningful associative procedure is just fine, but there is no justification for allowing symbol substitution to deprive the child of the visual symbol's advantages.

The dyslexic children's special difficulty with sentence completion

61. R. G. Rudel, M. B. Denckla, and E. Spalten, "Paired Associative Learning of Morse Code and Braille Letter Names by Dyslexic and Normal Children," *Cortex* 12 (1976): 61–70.

62. R. G. Rudel and M. B. Denckla, "Effect of Stimulus Context upon Word-finding Performance in Normal and Learning-disabled Children," in preparation.

63. Denckla and Rudel, "Naming of Pictured Objects."

is yet another example of their difficulty with "automatic" levels of language, as suggested in our previous rapid-automatized-naming study[64] and well discussed by Bannatyne.[65] Unless we look at the fine phonetic tuning, sequence-requiring, speed-requiring aspects of language, we are likely to miss the problems of those dyslexic children who are in a general way "highly verbal." In this regard, I cannot resist mentioning my regret at not being able to go into the issue of how "maleness" is another vulnerability factor which, like mixed preference/anomalous dominance, predisposes toward dyslexia, for it is on the fine tuning, fast perceptual-motor aspects of language that girls excel. Our word-finding study, for example, indicates that normal boys have larger vocabularies (know more names) but that girls, when they know a name, get it out more rapidly than do boys. Boys distort names more by errors of sequence and phoneme confusion.[66] Even the left brain weakness of males in general and dyslexic children in particular is not usually a unitary or global weakness; it is simplistic to declare all of them "right-brain people" even if they have good right brains.

Optimistic Fatalism

Dyslexia does exist, as developmental, specific, and pure, in a symptom-describing sense. Even the "pure" cases are not homogeneous in clinical picture or history of how they got that way; however, the clinical pictures are not infinite in their variety, but rather cluster about a few variables which, to a neurologist, strongly imply dysfunction of (or "traffic" into and out of) left brain systems. Both the pure and the far more numerous specific cases of dyslexia share with other learning-disabled children at least some of the characteristics covered by the broad, loose term "minimal brain dysfunction." Observable anomalies of motor preference, skill, and developmental pattern, as well as the vexing, haunting problem of selective attentional deficits, are part of the clinical problems of most dyslexic children. There is no evidence at present that a direct approach to any of the deficits mentioned, even those well-correlated with dyslexia, does anything but waste time.

64. Denckla and Rudel, "Automatized Naming."
65. Bannatyne, "Learning Disabilities."
66. Rudel and Denckla, "Stimulus Context."

Even those described as showing "merely maturational lag" may in fact share with the more classically neurologically impaired (the minimal or "pastel" ones) permanent deficiencies. Such deficiencies, however, may not persist to a degree sufficient to handicap the dyslexic person in his attainment of satisfying real-life achievements. Fatalism, so repugnant to Americans in particular, is of course implicit in my doubt about deficit training and "catch-up" for specific maturational lags. I have found it impossible to reassure parents that their dyslexic children will ever love to read or be good (as opposed to good-enough) spellers. I can reassure parents that good teaching, the nondogmatic trial-and-error kind with large doses of "relationship" as well as reading[67] will enable dyslexic children to read well enough for *their* practical purposes. The opposite side of the coin of my most un-American fatalism is a very American optimism, which cherishes the triumph of the struggling underdog and values the richness of individual differences.

Suggestions for Further Reading

Cruickshank, W. "The Learning Environment." In Cruickshank and Hallahan, eds., *Perceptual and Learning Disabilities in Children*, vol. 1. Syracuse, N.Y.: Syracuse University Press, 1975.

de Hirsch, K. "Language Deficits in Children with Developmental Lags." *The Psychoanalytic Study of the Child* 30 (1975).

Denckla, M. B. "Clinical Syndromes in Learning Disabilities: The Case for 'Splitting' vs 'Lumping.' " *Journal of Learning Disabilities* 5 (1972).

Myers, P., and Hammill, D. *Methods for Learning Disorders*. New York: Wiley, 1976.

Ross, D., and Ross, S. *Hyperactivity*. New York: Brunner/Mazel, 1976.

Rutter, M. "Emotional Disorder and Educational Underachievement." *Archives of Diseases in Childhood* 49 (1974): 240–56.

Touwen, B., and Prechtl, H. *The Neurological Examination of Children with Minor Nervous Dysfunction*. Philadelphia: Lippincott, 1970.

Vellutino, F., Steger, J., and Phillips, F. "Verbal versus Non-Verbal Paired Associate Learning in Poor and Normal Readers." *Neuropsychologica* 11 (1975).

67. Money, "Developmental Dyslexia."

4

The Psychological Basis of
Reading Disability

As DISCUSSED in Chapter 2, there are multiple causes for reading disability including physical, emotional, intellectual, and cultural components. The major contributory factors that influence the course of any learning, however, are the psychological and the neurological patterns. The latter has been delineated at length in Chapter 3. We have made the separation of these two factors because each has its own integrity. Yet both modalities often coexist in children with reading disability, and each one affects the other in a complex aggregation, as we shall discuss.

In describing psychological factors, the first problem we meet is the many different theories on the subject. We will touch on only three of the major ones: Freud's psychoanalytic system,[1] Sullivan's interpersonal formulation,[2] and Maslow's self-actualization concept.[3] Obviously these theories are too complicated to discuss extensively here, but each one concerns understanding human behavior and motivation. Let us look briefly at these theories and relate them to the phenomena of reading and learning.

1. S. Freud, *A General Introduction to Psychoanalysis* (New York: Perma Giants, 1949), Part 2.
2. H. S. Sullivan, *The Interpersonal Theory of Psychiatry* (New York: Norton, 1953), Part 2.
3. A. Maslow, *Toward a Psychology of Being* (New York: Van Nostrand, 1962).

Psychological Theories

Freud suggested that pathology is likely to result when social and cultural forces conflict with the fulfillment of our biological and social needs.[4] To relate this concept to learning, we can substitute the words *reading disability* for *pathology*. Let us see how a child might develop such disability. If all goes smoothly as a child grows, and he receives sufficient loving experiences, he wants to learn simply because he is developing both biologically and socially. Just as he learns to feed and dress himself, he learns to read too when the times comes. All along the way he gets approval and he feels competent.

Many children are not so fortunate. According to Freud, the structure of personality develops through the interaction of what we want, what we can get, and what we come to consider appropriate. Freud, as we know, labeled these personality parts the id, ego, and superego. He reminds us that the child is totally dependent on his mother or a significant person to care for his elemental needs of hunger, protection, warmth, and so on. His dependency period extends for upwards of a dozen years, and the way he is cared for determines his initial outlook on life. He welcomes or shuns people and ideas in direct relation to his early experiences. As his parents care for and "educate" him, he identifies with them and longs for their love and approval. If his experiences are unpleasant, he may wish to rebel against those who care for him, yet he cannot because he is so dependent on them. This situation arouses deep conflict and, if it persists, leaves him with a high degree of intrapsychic disturbance. Learning can become part of this inner conflict. For example, a child may feel his parents' deep resentment (maybe they never wanted a child or they are frightened of the responsibility, and so on). The child cannot understand their lack of affection. He dare not show his anger and terror directly so he withdraws or gets "sick" or disobeys to gain attention. These characteristics can carry over to school. Rogers[5] also has pointed out how this may occur. He indicates that we learn to mistrust our inner promptings because we so desperately wish the approbation of those around us. Love is made conditional by those who take care of the young. The child learns to disregard his own inner experiences whenever they conflict with those on whom he depends. In this way he cuts himself off from his own desires. Consider the possible

4. S. Freud, *Civilization and Its Discontents* (London: Hogarth Press, 1961), p. 77.
5. C. Rogers, *Person to Person* (New York: Pocket Books, 1973), p. 4 ff.

confusion in the child who hears his mother say, "You can't be hungry; you just ate!" Or imagine a child who says that she's afraid to stay alone. If her parents tell her, "Don't be silly; you're not going to be afraid; you're a big girl", she may feel ashamed and bewildered. She is told that her fear is unacceptable, yet she still feels frightened.

If the child disregards his own feelings often enough, he becomes estranged from himself. He loses the chance to harmonize his inner wishes and reactions with demands from those around him. All that he does learn is mistrust—of himself and others.

Freud also pointed out that personality difficulty arises not only when the instinctual needs are frustrated but also when they are over-indulged. For instance, when parents do not wish their child to experience anything painful or disappointing, they may overprotect him so that he will never be "unhappy." "As a consequence, the development of his ego . . . is greatly retarded."[6] He does not put forth the effort to overcome obstacles. He wishes to remain a baby, perhaps, to retain his blissful state. His inability and refusal to cope can include difficulty in learning to read.

Sullivan, like Freud, considers that psychological difficulty occurs when forces are antithetical to human needs, but he views the reactions to this dilemma somewhat uniquely. According to Sullivan, when an individual cannot bear dissonance in his life, he will react with "selective inattention." In other words, he listens only to that which he can tolerate. This even extends to the restriction of his perceptual-cognitive processes and could eventuate in "dissociative security operations."[7] In other words, he may not attend to learning to read because reading represents the unbearable. Again, if the child "really" is not ready to learn for whatever reasons (and we rarely know for certain what factors are interfering unless they involve such extremes as gross brain damage or acute autism), he may blot out reading instruction. These factors can restrict his energy in the learning situation. Furthermore, he may not have the "foggiest" idea what is the matter. (Nor perhaps will his parents or teachers.) Have we not all had such experiences? For instance, if we are unsure of our acceptance by someone important to us and he seems preoccupied in our presence, are we not likely to interpret this as personal rejection? Or if we know that we are fearful of mathematics, are we not likely to draw a blank when we are asked to estimate even the simplest sum?

6. G. Pearson, "Disorders of the Learning Process," in G. Natchez, ed., Children with Reading Problems (New York: Basic Books, 1968), p. 52.
7. Sullivan, *Interpersonal Theory.*

According to Maslow,[8] there is a hierarchy of needs starting with the basics of food, protection from danger and so on, to the more developed ones involving the need to feel loved, to belong, to be accepted, to feel worthy, and finally the need to realize "self-actualization" or the attainment of one's natural proclivities. Thus, if a child in our society fails in learning to read, he loses the self-esteem he needs for his own comfort.

Motivation

A common factor in these theories is motivation. We assume that every child wants to learn about himself and the world. Barring singular, obvious impairment of physical, neurological, or psychological elements, we believe he *can* learn. How is it then that he sometimes does not?

All children are born with certain constitutional components, with certain family constellations, and into a particular culture. This uniqueness allows for endless combinations and permutations in what we are, how we learn, and what paths we follow. To cite just two possibilities: An infant can be born with deficits that are never detected in the learning area because he has come to compensate and master them through high motivation and dogged determination. Yet another child with parallel deficits may suffer years of academic failure. Are we not familiar with this phenomenon? People like Helen Keller or Franklin Roosevelt were able to compensate for their handicaps despite the odds against them. We also know of those who seem limited in their talents but who become stalwart, contributing members of their families, their vocations, and their communities. Perhaps it is not so much what we are born with or into, but how we use what we have.

Curiosity and Anxiety in Learning

We will now discuss briefly two important elements connected with motivation—curiosity and anxiety. Curiosity tends to accelerate learning; anxiety tends to disrupt it. Everyone is born with curiosity. The extent

8. Maslow, *Psychology of Being.*

to which it is fostered or hampered influences the way we pursue learning about the world both informally and academically.[9] We all know how the infant begins exploring. Often his hands first search for a finger to satisfy his sucking pleasure. Then he finds his body, objects, and so on. His search for pleasure and meaning continues. The "whys" begin around two years of age, accompanied by extended exploration—of plugs, cupboards, supermarket shelves, whatever. Although this is wonderful for the child, it is often trying for the adults in charge. We find them saying "No! No! No!" interminably. Too much restriction can kill curiosity; too much protection can make it hard to find meaning and the joy of mastery.[10] These restrictions may or may not be carried over to schoolwork.

A major disruptive force with regard to motivation is anxiety. Freud[11] called anxiety the central problem in neurosis. Horney[12] made basic anxiety a pivotal concern in her theories and suggested that any feared social situation can cause it. Anxiety is uncomfortable; we all try to avoid it. When anxiety is attached to family or school situations in which the child fails every day, he can become a reading problem. Anxiety fosters the need to use defenses such as denial, rationalization, repression, and regression. These defenses tend to intrude upon intellectual functioning and may account for some of the distortions of ideas among individuals with this difficulty.[13]

Anxiety can diverge upon different paths. When acute, it can increase learning by raising motivation to the level of a "challenge," but it usually acts as a deterrent: a disorienting response to a conflicting or frustrating situation.[14] If the child experiences repeated fear—fear of failure, fear of ridicule, or fear of humiliation, it can cause him to have generalized anxiety. If this anxiety is experienced in schoolwork, it can cause a reading disability.

9. D. Elkind, *A Sympathetic Understanding of the Child: Birth to Sixteen* (Boston: Allyn & Bacon, 1974), Part 1.

10. P. Hogan, "Creativity in the Family," in F. Flach, ed., *Creative Psychiatry Series* (New York: Geigy Pharmaceuticals, 1975).

11. Freud, *Civilization*.

12. K. Horney, *Neurosis and Human Growth* (New York: Norton, 1950).

13. C. Rogers, "Learning to be Free," in C. Rogers and B. Stevens, eds., *Person to Person: The Problem of Being Human* (New York: Pocket Books, 1967).

14. J. Grimes and W. Allinsmith, "Compulsivity, Anxiety, and School Achievement," *Merrill-Palmer Quarterly* 7 (1961): 247–61.

Factors Which Contribute to Learning[15]

Most of our theoretical knowledge points to the fact that learning to read depends on total growth factors concerned mainly with (1) the maturing personality in a context of family and society, (2) the integrity of the central nervous system, and (3) the interplay of these and other factors which have their own effect.

Personality Factors

Personality matures through the child's relationship with the significant people in his life. When he enters school, his teachers and classmates assume similar importance. Disturbance occurs or accelerates when the child experiences heavy doses of disregard, ostracism, or other negative attitudes that lower his feelings of worth. When these feelings arouse anxiety and frustration and interfere with his curiosity, he frequently loses motivation to learn. When these feelings also cloud his understanding of his own experience, meaning becomes murky and disorienting. For instance Jimmy listens to his teacher comment, "But, Jimmy, we just finished practicing that word. You *must* know it!! You're in second grade now. You're a big boy." Yet he recognizes that he does *not* know the word. He becomes confused; but it takes courage to challenge powerful grown-ups. Knowing his own feelings and at the same time having others superimpose their notions of how he is supposed to feel reinforces his perplexity. We are reminded of *Dennis the Menace* whose mother has just insisted that he hold her hand while crossing the street because he is so young. He blurts out, "How come I'm such a big boy when you take me to the dentist, and I'm too little to cross the street by myself?" If a child's feelings are repeatedly given little credence, his perceptions become more and more distorted.

Obviously such transactions cause little trouble if they are infrequent. It is the repetitive instances of disrespect, denigration, and discomforting atmosphere that cause varying degrees of emotional upset.

Depending on the circumstances, a wide variety of psychological disturbances can occur ranging from the extreme childhood psychoses, including autism and childhood schizophrenia, to the less severe neu-

15. In this chapter reading is considered one facet of learning. It is not to be confused with the term "learning disability" as defined in Chapter 1.

rotic involvements. The distinct self-referent quality of the acute psychoses makes such children difficult to reach.[16] They usually require special treatment and are *not* the focus of this book.

Constitutional Factors

A second classification of influences on learning is the physical or constitutional factors with which we are born. Although it is difficult to determine pure, innate capacities, they influence our personality development.[17] For instance, some of us are more susceptible to respiratory ailments than others, just as some of us are more musically attuned. This does not mean that these proclivities are stereotyped and inflexible or that there is no chance for change. It *does* mean that our physical makeup facilitates or impairs our psychological reactions in general and those connected with learning itself.

Related to constitutional problems are the neurological components. When they cause delay or difficulty in learning to read, the child develops psychological problems as a result of his failure. For example, long before he enters school, a child may become aware of the superiority of his contemporaries in such things as playing games, handling crayons, paints, blocks, or scissors, or expressive language. Perhaps he is always chosen last for the "team," rejected on the playground, or made to feel like an outsider to the group. As a result, he forms a low opinion of himself. Continued negation from parents, brothers, sisters, playmates, and others will lower his self-esteem and heighten his anxiety still further. If on top of all this he is exposed to reading instruction and does not learn, his feelings of inadequacy increase accordingly.

At the extreme end of constitutional factors are the neurological involvements referred to as severe organic brain damage. Again, these children are not the focus of this book. Instead we will discuss those whose psychological problems contribute to difficulty in reading and the way in which their families and school settings may heighten these problems.

16. A. Bond, "Sadomasochistic Patterns in an 18-Month Old Child," *The International Journal of Psycho-Analysis* 48 (1967), Part 4, pp. 597–603.
17. A. L. Benton, "Developmental Dyslexia: Neurological Aspects," in W. J. Friedlander, ed., *Advances in Neurology*, vol. 7 (New York: Raven Press, 1975).

Similarity of Symptomatology of Children with or without Reading Problems

The dilemma for the educator and specialist is that children can manifest identical symptomatology whatever the primary cause of their reading difficulty. Children with psychological problems are particularly vulnerable to the fear of failure and the competitive atmosphere of peers, school, and community. Their characteristic response to these conditions includes preoccupation, withdrawal, aggression, helplessness, lack of concentration, misbehavior, and cognitive confusion.

It is well known that physical symptoms such as hives, allergies, appetite loss, and so on can appear from emotional conditions such as fear and tension. Even hyperactivity, distractibility, and impulsivity, considered by some the hallmark of neurological symptoms, can be caused just as well by psychological factors.

The child who feels unacceptable may react in any number of ways. At one end of the continuum he shrinks into himself; at the other he lashes out. If he continues to fall below academic expectations, he is in for added disapproval. The vicious interaction of basic and reactive emotional factors has been set in motion.

The same psychological factors can cause reading disability in one instance and promote learning in another. We have all known children and grown-ups with rugged backgrounds, personality disorders, constitutional handicaps—all manner of burdens considered to cause psychological problems—who have become scientists or scholars. Indeed they often tell us that they escaped into learning precisely *because* of their misery. Thus we continue our caution in interpretation.

Effects of Family

To expand the picture let us look at some of the ways that the family affects a child with or without learning disability. The family is the place where most of us receive our emotional support and learn how to be human. At school or work we tend to hide our feelings. We're not supposed to cry, get angry, or even laugh too much; we are supposed to attend to our work; we are supposed to "play" or be "human" outside the workplace. The major responsibility for our humanness falls to the family.[18] If a child's parents are rigid, frightened people and he begins to see the world as a fearful place, he may withdraw. If they try to do everything for him (even in his own "best interests") and try to avoid his finding out for himself, he can lose much of his curiosity—or he may not.[19]

A child can have parents whose relationship to each other is difficult. They may use the child to give meaning and direction to their lives. If he has "problems," they may work in unison to alleviate them in order not to face their own emptiness with each other.[20] A mother who feels demeaned through being "just a housewife" might focus on her child in trouble as a preoccupational measure instead of facing her own discontent.

Notice that in the above examples most of us can recognize children with varying degrees of emotional disorder associated with their reading disability and some who are entirely free from it, even though they share similar family backgrounds.

Effects of School

The school situation can be harsh with children. The pressure for high marks and the shame in not succeeding can contribute to the reading problem.

Even an understanding teacher may become frustrated with a child who doesn't respond. Classmates of a child with reading problems can add discomfort because pupils find it hard to be kind to a laggard; in our competitive society each one is trying too hard to measure up himself. Yet here, too, some children rise above these difficulties and learn despite them.

The cultural milieu also is influential in determining the child's attitudes. Those who live among people where academic standards are high usually feel failure more acutely than those who live under less intellectual pressure. Parents' attitudes toward the school also lend their

18. J. Henry, *Culture against Man* (New York: Vintage Books, 1963), chapter 5.
19. D. Kantor and W. Lehr, *Inside the Family* (San Francisco: Jossey-Bass, 1975), pp. 157–58.
20. D. Bloch and Kitty La Perriere, "Techniques of Family Therapy: A Conceptual Frame," in D. Block, ed., *Techniques of Family Psychotherapy* (New York: Grune & Stratton, 1973).

weight. Often parents who are frustrated, angry, and bewildered by their youngsters' inability to learn blame the schools and the teachers. Sometimes the child basks in this anger. Perhaps he is saying, "It's not my fault; it's the teachers'. So I don't have to do anything." Again, this never holds true in all cases.

Some schools contribute to reading problems by smothering curiosity. Many times we observe kindergarteners and first graders with wide eyes and freshly sharpened pencils waiting eagerly to learn to read and write. They are enthusiastic about school; they bring home notices to their parents with regularity and reliability. Yet by third grade they appear tired and bored. They have lost interest in school and consider it drudgery. Sometimes educational bureaucracy is at fault. Teachers are restricted in what they are allowed to teach and what material they can use. The first three grades are crucial in learning. (The French consider these years so important that they allow only their most skillful and experienced teachers to handle these grades.) Too often the readers introduced in first, second, and third grades contain stale, foolish reading matter. Bettelheim comments on this when he observes that "The pre-primers and primers from which (the child) is taught to read in school are designed to teach the necessary skills. . . . The overwhelming bulk of the . . . so-called 'children's literature' attempts to entertain or to inform, or both. But most of these books are so shallow in substance that little of significance can be gained from them. The acquisition of skills, including the ability to read, becomes devalued when what one has learned to read adds nothing of importance to one's life."[21]

We cannot say that starting children on charming nursery rhymes and folk tales (although that is our wish) will guarantee good readers, but we do consider that such stories will not add the extra burden of dullness. We certainly recommend the search for good material, and we have included suggestions for stories and books in Appendixes B and D.

Interplay among Multiple Factors

The authors believe in the interplay of multiple factors and conclude that there is no one emotional pattern for a child with reading disability. That is, personality disorders can stem from any of the causes delineated

21. B. Bettelheim, *The Uses of Enchantment* (New York: Knopf, 1976), p. 4.

here and in Chapter 2. To summarize, there can be constitutional components which comprise intellectual and neurological deficits, or family environments which contribute to distorting the child's emotional development, or educational situations which cause or exacerbate the child's poor self-concept. Any one or more of these aspects can touch off psychological upset as seen in the many examples we have just described. For purposes of clarity, we discussed these examples as if they occurred mainly in separate situations or from individual characteristics and experience. Now consider how any one entity can intensify another *ad infinitum*. For instance, a child with low intelligence finds it more difficult to compensate for any neurological deficits he has; or a child with high anxiety may find it difficult to get along with teachers or attend to school learning. These hindrances raise doubts in parents and teachers about the child's ability to handle schoolwork. These reactions have their own emotional impact and the multicausal process is set in motion. The permutations and combinations are endless. For children with reading disability, it is the school failure itself which heightens any emotional problem they bring to the learning situation and initiates upset where none was present at the start. So no matter what the cause or causes, *every poor reader is at psychological risk, although not each to the same degree or kind.*[22]

How do we distinguish and handle these intertwined emotional problems? The issue is to try to determine the full nature and degree of the emotional problems in the context of any additional contributing elements.

To elaborate, a diagnostician might discover that a child with reading disorder has personality disturbances and needs psychotherapy. If this choice alone is instituted and the child still does not learn within a reasonable length of time, he falls farther and farther behind. Even worse, whatever emotional problems were present will be exacerbated through daily academic failure. This does *not* discredit the psychodynamic stance. It simply states that when other factors continue undetected or ignored, the child can try, even try *hard*, only to flounder, fumble, and finally despair.

Or a specialist might decide that emotional problems are minor and that neurological factors are the cause of his reading failure. He considers that the child brings "faulty equipment" to the learning task. He might suggest appropriate teaching procedures to compensate for the

22. L. Eisenberg, in D. Duane and M. Rawson, *Reading Perception and Language* (Baltimore: York Press, 1975), pp. 221–22.

child's poor memory, inadequate integrative capacity or whatever. Perhaps this will alleviate the problem if the child learns to read fairly quickly. If not, he will develop reactive emotional disturbance that needs specific attention too.

Thus there never need be an either/or decision for choice of treatment. Neither psychotherapy nor remedial work alone is always sufficient to clear up the reading problem. Where psychotherapy is secured (and the high cost of treatment and limited facilities often make it unobtainable), every effort needs to be made to improve school functioning too. Few therapists treating neurotic adults would suggest that a patient forego working and wait until major changes in his attitudes occurred. Yet one hears again and again, "There's no point in trying to teach him until his emotional problems are cured."

We do not mean that teaching is a substitute for intensive psychotherapy. Such therapy is indicated for any child whose problems warrant it. But when the child is experiencing difficulty in school, his problem is likely to increase both academically and emotionally. Then he will need help with his schoolwork as well as his attitudes.

Building Self-Esteem in the Classroom

Although psychological problems may take many forms, we need to be particularly attuned to building self-esteem.[23,24] A knowledgeable and understanding teacher who incorporates basic psychotherapeutic principles with reading instruction is crucial. When the teacher can help the children sense their own competence in class they can appreciate encouragement and praise. Then there is every chance of raising their self-worth. If they do not experience success, however, no amount of praise or encouragement assuages them. It is similar for us when we lose confidence in our work and failure stares us in the face. For instance, if someone wishes to learn to type 60 words a minute to attain a particular job, he is not comforted by praise and encouragement for his achievement of 50 words a minute. He is likely to rage at such praise and feel worse that he is so inept.

23. E. Sylvester and M. Kunst, "Psychodynamic Aspects of the Reading Problem," American Journal of Orthopsychiatry 13 (1943).

24. H. Myklebust, Progress in Learning Disabilities, vol. 2 (New York: Grune & Stratton, 1971), Chapter 6.

Once innovative approaches to education are combined with efforts to improve communication between students, teachers, parents, school administrators, and community leaders, there is an optimum chance to enhance the school's impact.[25] When parents and teachers, in particular, try to understand the child, they can add strength and support. Sometimes family treatment is needed in addition, to relieve the child of a trying situation such as being "scapegoated" or exploited.[26] Sometimes counseling may be necessary to consider alternative possibilities such as individual tutoring, a shift in classroom, or a change to a different type of school, better equipped to handle the problem; sometimes individual, family, or group therapy is indicated.

In dealing with children who have failed, the reading teacher and the regular classroom teacher who see them most have a chance to use sound therapeutic practices in developing a caring relationship with the child. This has a substantial influence on his inner being. When they help him to replace his sense of failure and doubt with visible progress and increased confidence, they emphasize the most forceful aspect of remedial treatment. This may account for its reaching down to the deepest levels of the child's personality. For very disturbed children, teachers can be a vital auxiliary; for those who are less disturbed or whose maladjustment is directly caused by poor school performance, teachers can effect positive personality changes that are fully restorative. Chapter 5, "Psychotherapeutic Principles in Remedial Reading Instruction," contains elaboration on the specific principles that teachers can use as suggestions for dealing with children who have difficulty learning to read.

Suggestions for Further Reading

Bloch, D., ed. *Techniques of Family Psychotherapy*. New York: Grune & Stratton, 1973.
Colm, H. *The Existentialist Approach to Psychotherapy*. New York: Grune & Stratton, 1966.
Connolly, C. "Social and Emotional Factors in Learning Disabilities." in H. Myklebust, ed., *Progress In Learning Disabilities* II. New York: Grune & Stratton, 1971.

25. I. Zieman, "Improving Communication in Schools," in G. Gottsegen, ed., *The Relevance of School Psychology to Today's World*. (New York: Division of School Psychology, New York State Psychological Association, 1970).
26. P. Watzlawick, J. Weakland, and R. Fisch, *Change* (New York: Norton, 1974).

Gardner, R. *Psychotherapeutic Approaches to the Resistant Child.* New York: Jason Aronson, 1975.

Illich, J. *Deschooling Society.* New York: Harper & Row, 1971.

Jackson, D., ed. *Therapy, Communication, and Change.* New York: Science and Behavior Books, 1973.

Moustakas, C. *Existential Child Therapy.* New York: Basic Books, 1966.

Natchez, G. *Gideon.* New York: Basic Books, 1975.

Sapir, S., and Wilson, B. "The Education of the Handicapped Child." In Joseph, ed., *Pediatrics*, 16th edition. New York: Appleton-Century-Crofts, publication date 1977.

Singer, E. *Key Concepts in Psychotherapy.* New York: Basic Books, 1970.

5

Psychotherapeutic Principles
in Remedial Reading
Instruction

GOOD TEACHING has far-reaching therapeutic results. Throughout
the ages, teachers such as Plato, Rousseau, Moses, Confucius, and
Dewey have had immeasureable influence on their students. As Henry
Adams said, "A teacher affects eternity; he can never tell where his influence stops."[1] Teachers who work with children with reading disability
also have effected remarkable changes in the lives of their pupils. Their
influence is crucial and can make the difference between the success and
failure of an entire life. It is not the techniques of instruction which are
of such lasting influence. It is the attention, inspiration, and understanding that the children receive which help them overcome the massive
frustration, despair, and resentment that they have stored for so long.
Then positive feelings come to the fore, and they are finally able to use
capacities which were formerly misdirected or lying dormant.

We realize that those who work with children with reading disability
apply many of the basic principles of psychotherapy, perhaps without

1. *The Education of Henry Adams* (New York: The Modern Library, 1931),
p. 300.

being aware of them. In order to make the process more conscious and thereby perhaps more effective, we shall elaborate some of the fundamental principles that are inherent in any good teaching situation.

Establishing Relationship

One of the cardinal principles of psychotherapy is developing a good relationship. This is achieved through the total acceptance of the child as a human being worthy of respect, regardless of his failure in reading. It also encompasses a collaborative spirit within a planned structure, compassion without overinvolvement, understanding without indulgence, and, above all, a genuine concern for the child's development.

Teachers are troubled by pupils who do not learn satisfactorily. Not only do they consider it a burden to deal with the "slow" ones in their classes, but they feel that lack of progress is somehow their fault and a reflection on their teaching ability. It is understandable that teachers frown on problem cases because they require extra attention and their low test scores bring down the class average. Remedial teachers also share some of these feelings. Although they do not have to worry about lowered class averages, they are under pressure to have their pupils improve because they often need to justify their very existence to administrators by showing overall gains. Hence, concern over pupils' improvement can undermine a teacher's confidence.

When a teacher's confidence in her own ability is impaired, it is difficult for her to show approval toward the poor achiever. As a result, the child feels uncomfortable and fearful of the teacher. This can cause an even greater drop in his performance.

Anna Freud[2] has commented on children who equate receiving good grades in school with being loved and failure with being unloved and worthless. Even if such drastic comparisons are not made, certainly children who get poor report cards again and again lose status with all those on whom they depend for affection and approval. They may develop a kind of free-floating anxiety toward schoolwork—always dreading it, always anticipating failure.

Since children with reading disability live in an atmosphere of rejec-

2. A. Freud, "Psychoanalysis and the Training of the Young Child," *Psychiatric Quarterly* 4 (1935): 15–24.

tion and disapproval, they often conclude that they have no ability or talent, that they are good for nothing, and that they rate no recognition whatsoever.

If children with reading disability feel so defeated and teachers feel so burdened by them, what can be done? A teacher needs to have confidence that she can help, but she needs to realize also that she is not personally responsible for lack of progress. She must understand that a child's weakness in reading is simply a reality that must be remedied. When a teacher realizes that her own status is not threatened, she is in a better position to accept her pupils. She can then recognize the child's ultimate potentialities, not his present achievement. To paraphrase Goethe, the child is treated not as he is, but as he can become.

Collaboration

Although the teacher knows the best methods and materials, she may not know which ones would be most suitable in planning a reading program for the child. Thus, she tries out many approaches, and as they work together, she can determine by the child's responses which work well and which do not.

For example, the teacher chooses the grade level of the materials, but the choice of subject matter may often be left to the child; for example, would he prefer to read sport stories, science fiction, or folk tales? Where the child is reading at a low level, perhaps he may be permitted to make a selection from two or three readers at a suitable level. When this is not advisable (because the teacher wishes to use certain books for specific reasons), then the choice is up to her. But the pupil continues to participate actively even when the teacher assumes full leadership. Thus she does not foist her preconceived plans on him, and the child can feel the nature of the collaborative experience.

Treating his poor performance in a matter of fact way, as something that will eventually respond to one alternative or another, often relieves the pupil's anxiety considerably. His problems, which heretofore have been vague and mysterious, become evident and tangible. He may then be able to view his problem more objectively and accept a reasonable responsibility for it. The tone of the sessions, however, remains cooperative throughout, with both pupil and teacher entering into a give–and–take relationship.

Structure

Besides knowing what is expected of him, the child becomes aware of what is acceptable behavior and what is not. Although his reactions during the sessions are welcomed, he is not allowed to be destructive or totally unrestrained.

Structure as well as limits is even more important in teaching disturbed children, since it introduces order into their chaotic lives. Children who come from very unstable, inconsistent environments, where they do not know what to expect from one minute to the next, can be transformed from perverse, boisterous pupils to orderly, manageable ones as soon as they get accustomed to a routine that they understand and appreciate. When they finally become used to a routine, any change must be introduced carefully. If they are not adequately prepared for a shift in plan, they may revert to their former agitated behavior.

A planned program also eliminates discussion and disagreements over which activities should be performed and in what order. Children soon lose respect or become confused by being asked what they want to do next or which story they wish to read.[3] A child's natural reaction is, "If you don't know which book I should read, how am I expected to know?" Lack of direction and continued floundering of the teacher must be very disappointing to a child who comes for remedial instruction hoping that at last he will be helped. Moreover, where the child is given considerable leeway, too much time may be spent on unimportant activities. It also places unwarranted responsibility on the child. Furthermore, in an unstructured setting, the child's aggression might easily get out of hand, or he might decide to sit passively and do nothing.

The atmosphere should be neither too permissive nor too rigid. As a criterion, the teacher uses rational authority which has competence as its source.[4] The child is given freedom within reasonable limits.

After the sessions have been planned by the teacher in the best interests of the child, the question arises, "What happens if he does not abide by the plan?" In a good teaching program, where methods and materials are suited to the child and a collaborative spirit prevails, this difficulty rarely occurs. When it does, the teacher can shift to one of the child's favored activities. If this is insufficient, a frank discussion that

---

3. C. Dahlberg, F. Roswell, and J. Chall, "Psychotherapeutic Principles as Applied to Remedial Reading," *The Elementary School Journal* 53 (1952): 213.
4. E. Hall, "The Paradox of Culture," in B. Landis and E. Tauber, *In the Name of Life* (New York: Holt, Rinehart and Winston, 1971), pp. 219–35.

reveals the teacher's acceptance of the child's occasional deviant behavior not only relieves his guilt, but enhances the human element in their relationship. Continued lack of cooperation, however, needs further investigation as to cause and treatment.

Sincerity

Children detect immediately whether a teacher has sincere and honest attitudes. In discussing this subject, one of our graduate students exclaimed that she knew one "must never display annoyance or disapproval." However, if such attitudes are present, the children soon catch the insincere undertones, no matter how much the teacher tries to conceal them.

Thus honest appraisal is necessary. If the child's work is poor, the teacher does not tell him that he is reading well. Instead, she tries to minimize his anxiety about errors and inconsistencies by telling him that many children have had similar difficulties and that they are unavoidable at his present stage. She might add that it is not his errors that are so important, but what matters is to find out how to overcome them. She assures him that ultimately he will improve as many others have.

Children often appear incredulous when they are treated this way, because they are so used to being conscientiously corrected, reprimanded, or given poor grades because they do not respond to instruction.

The teacher is also able to be more genuine if she encourages the child to work mainly for himself, not for anyone else. It is his life that will be affected if he does not learn. Particularly in reading disability cases, where motivation is so important, the child must be led to recognize the importance of work. He benefits from the support of a friendly, sincere ally with whom he shares his efforts and his difficulties. But in the long run, it is he who must become totally involved in the task.

Success

Obviously, achieving success in reading is paramount for the child in remedial treatment. But can a teacher provide experiences which engender these feelings merely by preparing a suitable program and proper materials? With reading disability, it is not that simple. Although all competent teachers know that materials must be within the range of the child's ability, they know too that they dare not risk permitting him to fail. Does that mean that the books he is given must be so easy that he will never miss a word? Does it mean that the child should never be permitted to falter? Many teachers reflect commonly accepted pedagogy when they answer, "A child with reading difficulty should be given a book at least one year below his reading level or even two; he must succeed!" A feeling of success is not always achieved through giving the child easy materials which he can read without error. Building up feelings of success in these defeated children is a very complex problem, which has long been over-simplified by reading specialists and educators. Teddy, for instance, is ten years old, in the fifth grade, of average intelligence, and is reading at third grade level. A book one year below his reading level means we must give him a second grade book. Will this make Teddy feel successful? It will be hard enough to find a book at third grade level which will be sufficiently mature without going lower. More important than finding books which he can read without error is to show Teddy that reading words incorrectly is not fatal, that a certain amount of unevenness is to be expected, and that he will not be reprimanded for his mistakes. As long as the teacher supplies unknown words while he reads aloud, Teddy could use third or possibly fourth grade books. (This does not apply to independent reading. In this instance, it would be advisable to suggest books at third grade level, which he can read with little or no assistance.)

Children need stimulation. Their curiosity and interest must be constantly aroused and furthered. Reading very easy material perfectly is less rewarding than making errors in more stimulating stories, provided, of course, that the child is receiving instruction in developing the necessary reading skills.

Are there cases where offering more difficult material may be harmful? Yes, very definitely. As in all remedial work, nothing is ever absolutely right or wrong. Everything depends on the needs and the vulnerability of the child. One must assess the child's capacity for making mistakes without his becoming extremely upset over them. There are some children who have suffered so drastically because of their failure that misreading words arouses the dread of failing again. Nonreaders, let us say, who are 14, 15, or older cannot possibly be given materials sufficiently challenging for them. In these cases, the teacher explains that the simple books will be discarded as soon as possible.

Interests

The chances of success are increased through providing reading materials based on the child's interests. However, determining true interests is not as easy as it seems. Actually, many children with reading disability have only transitory interests or no interests at all. Sometimes the teacher uses an interest inventory or asks the child what activities he especially enjoys—sports, tropical fish, snakes, stamp collecting, and so on. In order to please her, he may name one at random. Unsuspecting teachers may attempt to find materials based on this false response. They try hard to find articles about the topic that are exciting. But to get information within the desired reading level is almost impossible. Probably these children's knowledge, based on television and other visual media, so far surpasses what they can read that they are utterly bored with the selections finally presented. We have observed teachers, in their attempts to coordinate material with interests, exhaust all available resources, only to end up exhausting themselves and, no doubt, the child.

Even when appealing selections on a specific interest are discovered, they are useful only for a short while or as an introduction. If pursued, they become too narrow and confining. Reading competency cannot be built up merely on sports, mystery stories, or any other single category. Gradually, the child must be weaned away from a restricted field.

To discover true interests, the teacher cannot depend on what the child may originally report. She provides a variety of stimulating material and evaluates his responsiveness to it. Careful observation of the child's reactions offers the best and safest clues as to his true interests.

Bibliotherapy

For many years, the authors have been closely observing children's reactions to the themes of stories. They have noted their sheer delight and excitement with particular material. They have been impressed, too, with the opportunity for personality development and pupil-teacher relationship which these stories afford.

Certain themes seem to have universal appeal for children as well as grown-ups. For instance, the Cinderella story has been woven into adult and children's plays, novels, and movies throughout the years. It has maintained its appeal because so many of us can identify with ill treatment, and our wishes are fulfilled in the happy ending.

In children's books, there are various versions of the mistreated, pathetic figure who is victorious in the end. One story especially satisfying to boys is "Boots and His Brothers," in which Boots is always the underdog—the child rejected by his brothers as well as his parents. The king is faced with an impossible situation. He becomes so desperate that he offers half his kingdom and the princess in marriage to the one who solves his problem. Boots inevitably performs the difficult tasks and conquers all obstacles in the end. The boys are very intrigued with this story. Frequently they ask to read more like it. Then their resistance to books begins to lessen.

Humorous stories tend to cause children to relax. When the teacher and pupil share genuine laughter, it encourages a free and easy situation conducive to learning. Biographical sketches are apt to stimulate dramatic reactions, particulary those that show the hero who rises above disaster. These and other moving themes have a profound effect on children with reading disability because they identify so strongly with those who suffer misfortune.

The term *bibliotherapy* is sometimes used in this connection, referring to reading as a means for promoting personality development. Shrodes[5] has described the "shock of recognition" that comes when the reader beholds himself or those close to him in a piece of literature. At times, the shock is so great that dramatic changes take place. The following cases of Claude and Barry illustrate this process.

Claude—A Change in Attitude through Compelling Stories

Claude, aged 12, with average intelligence, was in seventh grade. He was the youngest of four children. All the others did well in school. Claude had difficulty with spelling as well as reading. His mother reported, "Everybody feels sorry for him. He tries hard but he gets nowhere. He has no friends and spends his time alone. During the past three years he has been annoying his classmates and teachers by acting like a clown in class."

5. C. Shrodes, "Bibliotherapy," *The Reading Teacher* 9 (1955): 24–29.

Basic Considerations

Claude was most resistive during the diagnostic examination and presented a façade of not caring about his poor achievement in most of his school subjects. In fact, it seemed that establishing a good relationship in this case would be a long and arduous task. Test results were as follows:

Gray Oral Reading Test	4.7
Metropolitan Intermediate Achievement Test	
Reading	5.8
Vocabulary	6.1
Spelling	5.6

It seemed advisable to use materials no higher than fourth grade level at the beginning because of his intense fear of failure. He came to the first remedial session under strong protest. During this session he was given *Greek and Roman Myths* in the hope that the mythical characters might appeal to him, but he remained unmoved. Because of Claude's marked rebelliousness, it was impossible to get even an inkling of any interest he might have. The author who worked with him could not reach him at all at this point. During the second session, she tried another type of story, Hans Christian Andersen's life in a reader on fourth grade level. Claude became so enamoured of this story that he suddenly became cooperative and willingly engaged in spelling and the other activities that had been planned.

In trying to analyze why Claude's attitude changed, it seemed likely that he was relating to the serious problems in Hans Christian Andersen's life that were similar to his own. He seemed to share Andersen's anxieties, his quality of oddness, and his feelings of rejection. Claude was probably able to develop hope about himself as he read of Andersen's final triumphs. He was astounded when he heard that the story "The Ugly Duckling" was about Andersen's own life.

In succeeding sessions, we continued in the same book reading the stories of Stephen Foster and William Tell. These did not have too much personal significance for Claude, but he enjoyed them and continued to be cooperative. Soon humorous stories were introduced, and these definitely made Claude more relaxed. As he and the author shared their enjoyment, the first sign of a closer relationship became apparent.

The next story which seemed to have special meaning for Claude was that of Thomas Edison in *Teen-Age Tales*, Book I, about high fifth grade level. He identified with the "Edison boy" who was looked upon as "queer" by his neighbors. As a child, he didn't play much with other children; he was always asking questions, and he was thought to be dull and stupid. He lasted only three months in first grade; the teacher saw no hope for him. These three months were all he ever had of formal schooling. After that his mother took him out of school and taught him herself. The story described Edison's struggles, working many hours alone in the basement, revising his experiments and laboring assiduously. His attempts at selling his gadgets frequently ended in failure. He was often penniless and hungry and had many ups and downs before his eventual success.

Claude seemed to identify closely with Tom Edison. Not that he for a moment thought he was another great inventor, but he could see the similarity between himself and Edison, who was given up by his teacher, had no friends, and was considered stupid and queer.

Much later Claude read about Dr. Fleming and Madame Curie in a seventh grade book. Claude, like many adolescent boys, was very intrigued with the account of how Dr. Fleming happened to discover penicillin. According to the story, Dr. Fleming worked for ten years trying to find something that would kill diseased bacteria in a person's bloodstream. He accidentally discovered a green mold which later became the base for penicillin. He wrote two papers which were published in a scientific journal in Great Britain in 1929. Apparently he received little if any recognition from them. Yet he kept on with his research. It was not until World War II that penicillin was produced on a large scale, and Dr. Fleming was at last given a measure of recognition. Claude was astonished that Fleming "didn't give up even though it took all those years before he finally made it."

The story of Madame Curie is similarly vivid, appealing, and absorbing. In addition, it offers a fascinating discussion about the discovery of radium and the nature of radiation.

Besides identifying with these characters, Claude was fascinated by the factual content. It happened that related topics were being covered in class, and he took great pride in contributing his share to the discussion. The author seized upon this sudden spurt of interest and through judicious choice of exercises from study-type materials, it was possible to open new vistas that were coordinated with school topics. As he became familiar with different fields, he continued to contribute to class discussions. His parents reported that he also had lively dinner conversations with them on diverse topics.

Claude's growing fund of information enabled him not only to do

71

better in school, but to relate more easily to people as well. Instead of feeling sorry for him, his parents and teachers were suddenly aware that he really knew his subject matter and, even more important, was genuinely interested in it. As people around him began to pay attention to what he had to say, Claude was slowly able to develop positive feelings about himself. Gradually his self-image changed from a person who felt worthless to one who at last had something to offer. His need to act as a clown in order to gain his classmates' attention disappeared entirely.

Claude had a total of 39 weekly 45-minute sessions in one year. Besides training in comprehension of stories and subject matter, he received help in spelling and in advanced word recognition techniques. Scores on comparable tests at the beginning and end of remedial instruction were as follows:

	Metropolitan Achievement Test	
	Grade Scores	Grade Scores
	(Intermediate)	(Advanced)
Reading	5.8	9.4
Vocabulary	6.1	8.5
Spelling	5.6	8.3

Claude's responsiveness to the stories had engendered positive attitudes toward the other aspects of the reading instruction. It also motivated him to improve in his school subjects. Learning about the trials of people who had surmounted their troubles seemed to strike home. This inspiration spurred him forward, while the author's guidance sustained him along the way. After he had reached this stage, remedial treatment was discontinued. Claude was able to keep up with his class and function on his own. At the last follow-up, he was in the tenth grade in high school and still functioning well.

What are the therapeutic effects of such articles and stories? There is ability to identify on an emotional level. The child finds he is not alone in having failed. He finds that others were able to surmount their shortcomings. He finds out that factual material can be interesting and useful. He learns that school can be worthwhile and rewarding rather than senseless and painful. Since he has been continually admonished and prodded with such commands as "Do your homework," "Work harder," "Apply yourself," "You can do it if you want to," he is astonished to discover that intellectual endeavor can be rewarding.

Claude, like most children who have failed, divided his classmates into two distinct categories: "the brains" and "the stupid ones." He believed that only those people who manifest superiority in their early years ever succeed. To achieve success after failure he did not consider possible.

The stories of Edison, Fleming, and Madame Curie pointed to the need for perseverance in the face of failure. He saw that even people who had been ridiculed and rejected and who had failed in school had eventually become loved, respected, and even famous.

These insights seemed to be the impetus for improvement in every area. He became ambitious even in subjects in which he was still doing poorly. He wished so earnestly to succeed that he began to develop stronger inner resources. From a resistive, indifferent youngster, he grew resolute, determined, and enterprising.

Barry—Inspired through Identification with Stories of the Jungle and Primitive Life

The next case is more complex. Barry, the son of a well-known writer, was a bright 11-year-old in sixth grade. He was an extremely disturbed child. After a long period of intensive psychotherapy, his psychiatrist felt that Barry's progress was being impeded by his failure in school and recommended remedial instruction. Shortly after this, therapy was discontinued. The following account of remedial treatment covers a period of two years.

Barry had considerable difficulty in interpersonal relationships. He had no friends and barely spoke to adults. He daydreamed a great deal and enjoyed a world of fantasy. Rapport was difficult to establish and was developed only gradually. Because of Barry's very unfavorable attitude toward school, the usual remedial program was greatly modified. There was almost exclusive reading aloud, with the author reading one page, Barry the next.

Barry showed a strong leaning toward tales of the jungle and primitive modes of living. He sought them out wherever he could find them. They all revolved around the son of a tribal chief who never was as brave as his father. The son in each story worried about how he would eventually take his father's place as head of the tribe. Barry loved the descrip-

73

tions of primitive dwellings made of mud and straw or baked clay. There was never any furniture, so everyone usually sat on the dirt floor. The children played with birds and animals. Their toys were of the simplest kinds, which they made themselves. The children learned how to climb a tree as fast as a monkey. The stories to which Barry returned over and over again were "Kintu" in *Roads to Everywhere,* fourth year level; "Simba" in *Days and Deeds,* fifth year level; "Child of the Jungle," in *Let's Travel On,* fifth year level; and "Mafatu" in *Doorways to Discovery,* seventh year level.

A summary of one of the stories is offered as an example. Mafatu had been christened "Stout Heart" by his proud father, but he was afraid of the sea. How could Mafatu provide the fish that were a part of every family's food? Kana, the one boy who had been friendly to Mafatu, called him a coward and so voiced the feeling of the whole tribe. Mafatu found the skeleton of a whale. He wanted to make tools from it, but his "hands were all thumbs." Mafatu's feelings as he reflects on life were described; he felt cowardly, inferior, frightened, and worried about his status in his family. At last, with a knife made from the skeleton he had found, Mafatu stabs a shark. The struggle with the shark and his eventual victory were extremely meaningful to Barry. He understood his icy fear, his trembling, his torment. Other reading material was covered, but he never seemed to tire of these selections and went back to them periodically. Barry's singular identification with Mafatu was apparent from his facial expression and his bodily movements.

It might be interpreted that Barry was reacting against his over-civilized world, where everything was handed to him ready-made. Perhaps his life seemed exceedingly complex. There was no recognized role in which he could find his own strength. He rarely had the opportunity to explore or contribute to his family's affairs. In Mafatu's primitive world, he seemed vicariously to get to the element of living. Primitiveness might have meant freedom to move and to create. If he could start out at this simple level, perhaps he too could accomplish something worthwhile and finally find himself.

But even more important consequences seemed to result from Barry's fascination with the stories. Slowly he was able to express his astonishment that anyone else could feel so helpless, terrified, and isolated. From this beginning he talked more and more readily and formed a closer relationship with the author. His parents reported that he now played with children more easily, too, and got along better in the family. As time went on, these changes became more and more marked.

It may be conjectured that when Barry read about others who had the same problems as he, he felt less alone. They had conquered their terror; he might overcome his, too. From Mafatu's struggle, Barry derived hope. Perhaps this lent him the courage to change as he did, to reach out to others, and to move forward slowly toward the world.

Thus reading can foster vital changes in a child's life. Shrodes[6] has presented a rationale in this connection, which is paraphrased here. Bibliotherapy, drawing upon the novelist's and playwright's ability to plumb the depths of man's nature, is founded on the relationship between personality dynamics and vicarious experience. It is a process of inter-action between imaginative literature and the perceptions of the reader which stirs his emotions and frees them for more conscious use. The reader, of course, perceives according to his own wishes, desires, needs, and background experiences. Thus a character may become particularly arresting to him. The identification may be positive and enhance the individual. Or it may be negative, and then he may project his feelings onto the character. In this way bibliotherapy resembles psychotherapy—promoting insight, identification, and release.

From this point of view, stories can be extremely vital in a child's life. Adults are moved, influenced, and enriched through literature because it represents the world. Inspiration from stories has compelled many of us to an unaccustomed course of action and startled us into seeing our problems from a new perspective. With children who have reading difficulty, themes in stories can serve several additional purposes. Relating to a story can lead the way for enjoyment in reading, never before possible. Reading can fill in background, extend knowledge, and widen horizons that have been closed for so long. Finally, learning about the experiences of others, particularly people who failed, can foster release and insight as well as personal hope and encouragement. When children identify with others who are downtrodden, estranged, ridiculed, or unloved, or in contrast, noble, brave, and courageous, they get a glimpse into the lives of other people and other families. They can vicariously share some of their inspirations and some of their regrets. Relating in this way to characters and themes often diminishes the heavy sense of loneliness and isolation so common, not only to these children, but to all individuals.

Thus the psychotherapeutic principles in remedial reading are not something diffuse and intangible. Developing contact with others, achieving academic success, and inducing constructive attitudes toward

6. Ibid., p. 24.

work for its own sake causes feelings of failure, discomfort, and misery to diminish. It is then that dormant attitudes such as perseverance, hope, and application can come to the surface. This type of remedial treatment can be one of the most provocative, stirring experiences in the child's life.

We do not focus so much on "success" in reading *per se*. In our society there is enough pressure for that. We try to mitigate such pressures by emphasizing the way the child reacts to his predicament. Perhaps he can accept the fact that he is not near the "top" of his class. He may even come to understand that being on top is precarious too—one can so easily be toppled. We encourage him to make his own contribution in his own way and to accept himself as much as possible. If we as adults condone our own strengths and limitations and gain some peace thereby, perhaps the child may catch our attitude and learn to deal with his own life in a way that satisfies and fortifies him.

Suggestions for Further Reading

Colm, H. *The Existentialist Approach to Psychotherapy.* New York: Grune & Stratton, 1966.

Eisenberg, L. "The Human Nature of Human Nature." *Science* 176 (1972), 123–28.

Gardner, R. *Psychotherapeutic Approaches to the Resistant Child.* New York: Jason Aronson, 1975.

Henry, J. *Culture Against Man.* New York: Vintage, 1963.

Landis, B., and Tauber, E. *In the Name of Life.* New York: Holt, Rinehart and Winston, 1971, Part I.

Levenson, E. *The Fallacy of Understanding.* New York: Basic Books, 1972.

Moustakas, C. *Existential Child Therapy.* New York: Basic Books, 1966.

Natchez, G. *Gideon.* New York: Basic Books, 1975.

Resnick, L. "Motivational Aspects of the Literacy Problem." In *Toward a Literate Society*, edited by J. Carroll and J. Chall, pp. 257–77. New York: McGraw-Hill, 1975.

Singer, E. "Hypocrisy and Learning Disability." In *Interpersonal Explorations in Psychoanalysis*, edited by E. Witenberg, pp. 262–74. New York: Basic Books, 1970.

Weigert, E. *The Courage to Love,* New Haven, Conn.: Yale University Press, 1970.

Witenberg, E. *Interpersonal Exploration in Psychoanalysis.* New York: Basic Books, 1970. Parts 1–3.

Part II

Diagnosis

6

Evaluation
of Reading Disability
by the Classroom or
Reading Teacher

MOST of the cases of reading disability are of necessity handled by teachers. Therefore this chapter deals with the approaches which a classroom teacher, remedial reading teacher, or reading specialist might use in evaluating the disability. There is only a very small proportion of cases with problems so severe that they require referral to a psychologist or reading consultant for diagnosis. Chapter 7 describes the type of examination which is indicated in such cases.

Investigation of Reading Disability

When a teacher suspects that a child has a reading problem, she tries to identify the contributing factors, find out if he is doing as well as he is able, and discover his specific reading deficiencies. On the basis of her findings, she plans a program for remedial instruction.

Diagnosis

Exploring Background Information

The teacher confers with any individuals who might be familiar with the child's background, such as former teachers, guidance counselors, or the school nurse. She consults available records for information regarding intelligence and achievement test results, the child's absences, number of schools attended, the school physician's notations, and other relevant matter.

In many instances such exploration might suggest the need for referral for further diagnosis and treatment. For example, if there are indications of a defect in vision, the teacher might confer with the school physician or nurse so that suitable arrangements can be made for an eye examination.[1] Other available specialists, such as a psychologist or guidance counselor, might be consulted on the advisability of referral for other forms of treatment, including those that deal specifically with emotional and neurophysiological problems.

Whether or not the causative factors are alleviated, the problem of helping the child overcome his reading difficulty nevertheless remains. Thus the teacher analyzes whatever data she has and administers the necessary tests in order to understand the ways in which the reading difficulty is manifested.

Estimating Intelligence

If I.Q. scores are listed on the child's record card, these scores are generally based on group tests which may or may not require reading. Those administered above third grade level usually require the ability to read. Obviously the results of such tests cannot be relied upon when given to children with reading deficiencies. Furthermore, the teacher must bear in mind that even those group intelligence tests which do not require reading yield at best an approximate estimate of intelligence. Therefore, in addition to using such ratings, the teacher can form some idea of the child's intellectual ability from his general responsiveness in class.

1. Most schools use an instrument such as the Snellen Chart for detecting difficulty in visual acuity. However, this does not identify other visual factors of causal significance, such as eye muscle imbalance, astigmatism, and so on. A screening instrument for school use, which is comprehensive in scope is *The Keystone Visual Survey or Telebinocular Test*, Keystone View Co., Davenport, Iowa, 52803. For further discussion on screening devices see G. Spache, *Diagnosing and Correcting Reading Disabilities* (Boston: Allyn & Bacon, 1976), pp. 20–3, and A. Harris and E. Sipay, *How to Increase Reading Ability* (New York: David McKay, 1975), pp. 286–87, 582–88.

She notes his understanding of current events and the kind of general information he has acquired from outside sources. She observes the level of insight he displays during class discussions pertaining to subject matter presented orally or visually. His ability in arithmetic computation (not arithmetic problems, which require reading) provides another indication of intellectual functioning.

Determining the Extent of the Reading Disability

By definition, a reading disability exists where there is a discrepancy of one or more years between the child's current reading level and his intellectual level. Thus the teacher compares the pupil's intelligence with his reading level. Reading ability is more easily estimated if the teacher is familiar with a child's reading performance. From observing his classroom work, she knows which books he can read easily for pleasure and at what level he can read to obtain information. If she is uncertain about his abilities she might do well to undertake a more extensive investigation. Tests and techniques for such investigation can be chosen from those described in this chapter.

In determining the extent of the reading disability, the teacher uses her best judgment to arrive at representative scores for both intellectual capacity and reading ability, recognizing that, at best, given scores can only approximate a pupil's capabilities.

In order to ascertain the extent of the discrepancy between the child's capacity and his achievement, a simple procedure to follow is the one developed by Harris.[2] He subtracts five years from the mental age; this is the reading expectancy. The teacher then compares this "expected" grade-level score with the child's current achievement. If the mental age level is not available, the teacher multiplies the child's chronological age by his I.Q. to obtain it. For example, if a child is aged 10 years 6 months, and his I.Q. score is estimated at 100 multiply 10.5 (10½ years) by 1.00. (I.Q. scores are always computed in hundredths.) The result is his present mental age (M.A.). In this example, the M.A. is 10.5 (10 years 6 months). In order to determine the child's reading expectancy in terms of grade level, subtract five years from the M.A. The result—in this case 5.5—is the grade level (middle fifth grade) at which a child of the given age and intellectual capacity can be expected to read. This estimate is compared with his actual reading achievement to determine the extent of retarda-

2. A. Harris, *How to Increase Reading Ability* (New York: Longman, 1971), pp. 299 ff.

tion. We still consider this formula the simplest to follow although Harris has since revised it.[3] Other authorities recommend several alternate formulas for determining reading expectancy [4,5]

It cannot be overemphasized that the quantitative scores and formulas for determining reading disability, although they can be useful, should not be relied on exclusively. They must always be interpreted in the light of the teacher's judgment and as much background information as can be gathered about the child so as not to neglect any child who may profit from individual reading instruction. This is given particular emphasis in the cases of Tod and Ralph in Chapter 13.

Analysis of Reading Achievement

Not all pupils will need the extensive reading analysis to be described in the rest of this chapter. The choice of techniques depends upon the severity of the problem that the child presents and the amount of time the teacher has available. Thus the teacher can make as simple or as detailed an investigation as is warranted. Suggestions are offered for using informal procedures when, for various reasons, standardized tests cannot be administered.

In order to obtain a comprehensive evaluation of a child's reading ability, the teacher appraises mastery of oral reading, word-analysis techniques, and silent reading. From these tests she decides at what level he can profitably handle different types of reading material. This is discussed further under "Interpreting Oral Reading Test Results" and under "Interpreting Silent Reading Test Results" in this chapter.

Oral Reading Tests

Oral reading tests are designed to provide an indication of the level at which the child can read, his competence in word-analysis techniques, his attitudes toward his difficulty, and his fluency, articulation, and ex-

3. A. Harris, *How to Increase Reading Ability*, 6th ed. (New York: David McKay, 1975), pp. 152 ff.
4. L. Rodenborn, "Determining, Using Expectancy Formulas," *The Reading Teacher* (1947), pp. 286–90.
5. K. Dore-Boyce et al., "Comparing Reading Expectancy Formulas," *The Reading Teacher*, October 1975, pp. 8–14.

pressiveness in reading aloud. They also suggest the level of the silent reading test that should be administered. This is especially important, for the teacher or psychologist frequently has no other clue to an appropriate silent reading test. Obviously the child's chronological age and the grade in which he is enrolled are of no use as criteria, for a child of any given age may be reading at virtually any level.

Both standardized and informal instruments are available to test the pupil's ability to read aloud. Whereas standardized oral reading tests yield a grade-level score, results of the informal tests provide an approximation of the grade level at which the child can actually handle a book. However, they do not provide information about comprehension.

Standardized and informal tests also facilitate detailed analysis of the types of errors a child makes in oral reading. Analysis of errors can, of course, suggest his needs in remedial work. For example, examination of errors can reveal whether the child used any systematic method for figuring out unfamiliar words, what word recognition skills he has mastered, and which still need to be developed.

Standardized Oral Reading Tests

Standardized tests are convenient to use because they contain a number of paragraphs of increasing difficulty, from first grade up as high as 12th grade level, in some tests.[6] The more familiar the teacher is with a test, the more useful it is to her. It is therefore recommended that she use the same battery regularly, particularly when retesting a group of pupils. Increasing familiarity will enable her to compare a given child's responses, not only with the standardized norms, but also with the responses of other pupils whom she has examined. This procedure helps to develop insight into the strengths and weaknesses of the instrument.

Informal Oral Reading Tests

If standardized tests are not available, the teacher might devise her own instrument, choosing appropriate paragraphs from a series of graded readers or from informal reading inventories.[7] If the teacher thinks that the child is reading at about second grade level, for example, she might

6. These tests are listed and described in Appendix A, as are tests of reading readiness, spelling proficiency, silent reading, word-analysis skills, and intelligence.
7. N. Smith, *Graded Selections for Informal Reading Diagnosis* (New York: New York University Press). Grades 1–3, 1959; Grades 4–6, 1963, or appropriate selections from any standard Basal Reader series.

choose three selections—one at high first, one at low second, and one at high second grade level. (If the teacher finds that she has misjudged the pupil's ability, she can of course add lower or higher level books.) The child reads aloud until he finds a book he can read with relative ease. How to judge ease of readability on informal tests is discussed in the following section.

Administering the Informal Test

It is helpful to approach the oral reading inventory (or any other testing situation) as a collaborative venture in which teacher and pupil together attempt to assess the child's strengths and weaknesses in reading in order to bolster the former and remedy the latter. The teacher begins by explaining the test and the reasons for giving it. She might say something like, "You know you seem to be having some trouble with reading. By listening to you read, I will be able to tell which books are best for you. After you finish reading, I can show you where your greatest difficulties lie, and I'll know the kind of help you'll need. This test has nothing to do with any marks for classwork or for your report card."

The teacher might describe briefly the general content of each selection to be read. Then the child begins to read aloud at sight. If he makes more than five significant errors per 100 words,[8] he is given an easier book. Ultimately the examiner should know which book or books (if any) the child can read with ease, which with assistance, and which with difficulty, or not at all.

Although many examiners ask content questions after the pupil has read aloud, the authors do not advance this practice. Many children, particularly those with reading disability, find the mechanics of reading aloud so absorbing or trying that they are unable to attend to content, just as most adults, asked to read aloud during an eye examination, would be unable to answer detailed questions concerning the meaning of the reading matter. Some children experience such anxiety in struggling to pronounce words that they cannot possibly pay attention to their meaning, regardless of their ability to understand them. Their inability to answer questions on content is therefore not necessarily an indication of a lack of comprehension.

8. Significant errors are renderings which are highly inaccurate and distort the meaning—i.e., *wagon* for *capon*, *family* for *father*, and so on. Mispronouncing the names of people and places is considered insignificant, as is saying *wouldn't* for *would not*, *a* for *the*, and the like.

Recording Errors

It is important to establish a systematic method of recording errors so that the examiner can analyze the child's performance and compare it with his performance on tests administered previously or subsequently.

When a standardized oral reading tests is used, a duplicate copy is usually available on which the teacher can record errors. This convenience is lacking when an informal test is used, but the teacher might request permission from the publishers to reproduce the selected passages so that she can mark her copy as the child is reading the material. The symbols that the authors find most convenient are presented below.[9]

> If a word or portion of a word is mispronounced or read incorrectly, it is underlined, and the word the child said is written above it.
> A wavy line indicates repetitions. Although not counted as errors, they contribute to qualitative analysis of the child's reading.
> A capital P is written over words that the child has failed to recognize. (After a lapse of five seconds, the teacher pronounces the word in order to minimize the child's frustration.)
> Omissions are encircled.
> Parentheses are placed around self-corrected mistakes, with the mispronunciation written above the word. These do not count as errors in scoring.
> A caret indicates insertions made in error.

The paragraph below illustrates the use of these symbols.

Mother said, "Now we can go to work. The house is quiet." Tom did not want to work. He wanted to go outside and play.

The way to evaluate these errors is described in the section "Interpreting Oral Reading Test Results" which follows next.

If the teacher cannot reproduce passages from the readers as we have suggested, she can record the child's errors on a separate sheet of paper, as follows:

Word said for	Word in Book	Nonrecog- nitions	Repetitions	Insertions
how	now	not	he wanted	to go
home	house	outside		

9. These symbols have been adapted from those used in the *Gray Oral Reading Test* (see Appendix A).

Diagnosis

In addition to his errors, it is sometimes useful to record any unusual aspects of the child's behavior as he reads aloud, so that the teacher can assess the degree of discouragement that the child has experienced and his resultant attitude toward reading. If the teacher is to reduce the child's negative behavior, she must be aware not only of the mechanical aspects of his reading but also of how he feels, how he tries to cope with the subject, and what interactions are taking place. The teacher should understand the meaning of these reactions so that she can handle the child in the most effective way possible.

Interpreting Oral Reading Test Results

As we have implied, some mistakes on oral reading tests indicate relatively severe reading difficulty, while others need not be considered important. Merely counting the errors overlooks the most valuable part of the examination. For example, such mistakes as reading *a* for *the* or *Annie* for *Anne* and repeating a word or phrase usually do not alter meaning. Children with reading disability tend to make a large number of errors of all varieties. It is therefore wise to exercise wide latitude in interpreting mistakes as indications of proficiency level. Weighting all errors equally, regardless of their nature, yields a distorted picture of a book that the child can handle. Naturally, inaccurate reading is not desirable, but if mistakes are interpreted too rigidly, the pupil might be assigned reading material on a much lower level than is desirable in light of his maturity, interests, and need for information.

From the specific types of error that the child makes while he is reading aloud, the teacher can ascertain which techniques of word recognition the child has already mastered and which he lacks. Does the child know the basic sight words, such as *want, anyone, same,* for example? Does he have difficulty with consonants, consonant combinations, or vowel sounds? Does he understand the rule for the silent *e* and the rule for double vowels? Is he able to make use of context clues, or is he just guessing wildly? With a little experience, the teacher will begin to perceive a definite pattern. She might prepare a list of the major skills, make copies, and use it as a check list to indicate each pupil's deficiencies and progress.

The teacher can also gain valuable information about the child by observing his approach to the reading material. Is it markedly different from his approach to other tests and other situations? Does the child overestimate or underestimate his ability? Is he reluctant to expose what he considers poor achievement? Many children attempt to cover up for inadequate skills. For example, a child might read accurately but repeat words or groups of words frequently. This tendency might be due to insecurity in reading, or he might be stalling for time because he cannot easily recognize some of the words that follow. Perhaps he often loses his place and has difficulty focusing his attention on the line. Natchez[10] investigated children's approaches to oral reading and found that hesitations, interruptions such as the child's asking, "Is that right?," long pauses with no attempt to figure out the word, and angry outbursts were related to the pupil's characteristic reactions to frustrating situations in general. Kaplan's[11] study also examined the interaction between individuals' characteristics and their oral reading performance. Her study suggests that readers' anxiety significantly influences their responses. Thus, observing a child during oral reading sessions can yield clues to his personality pattern. In this sense, oral reading tests can be useful projectively.

Fluency of reading is also taken into consideration. However, the rate at which a child "should" read aloud cannot be determined. In an informal test, the teacher simply uses her judgment as to the degree of fluency. (It is true that paragraphs in standardized oral reading tests are generally timed. However, the timing factor is usually provided to yield a bonus for fluent reading rather than impose a penalty for slowness.)

Tests of Word-Recognition Skills

The ability to figure out unfamiliar words is basic to all reading. Children with reading disability at all levels, even through high school, are commonly deficient in this ability. Obviously inaccurate word recognition techniques interfere seriously with reading comprehension, for misreading words changes the meaning of the material. Although some evidence of the pupil's word recognition difficulties can be gathered from oral reading tests, word-analysis tests specify the skills he lacks more precisely.

Widely used oral tests of word-analysis skills include the *Durrell Analysis of Reading Difficulty*, the *Gates-McKillop Reading Diagnostic Test*, the *Roswell-Chall Diagnostic Reading Test*, and the *Roswell-Chall Auditory Blending Test*.

---

10. G. Natchez, *Personality Patterns and Oral Reading* (New York: New York University Press, 1959).
11. E. Kaplan, "An Analysis of the Oral Reading Miscues of Selected Fourth Grade Boys Identified as Having High or Low Manifest Anxiety" (doctoral dissertation, Hofstra University, 1973).

Diagnosis

When many children have to be tested and the teacher does not have the time to administer a test of word-analysis skills to each child individually, she can use either a group diagnostic test or she can gain some impression of the children's basic knowledge of phonics through a group test which she can make up containing an inventory of initial consonants, consonant blends, and short vowel sounds.

The teacher can prepare a master sheet with key words to be used in associating the letter sounds to be tested. Each pupil would need a duplicate sheet, subdivided into spaces and numbered according to the way the master sheet is planned.

In presenting initial consonants, for example, the teacher might use key words such as *hill, match, table, lamp*, and so on. As she pronounces each word, she asks the pupils to write in the designated space the letter corresponding to the very first sound they hear. She proceeds in a similar way with words that begin with consonant blends such as *spill, tree, blue, stop*, and so on. In presenting these words, she asks the children to write the first two letters that represent the sounds they hear. To judge the pupils' knowledge of short vowels, the teacher dictates words such as *bag, top, mud, sip*, and *pet*. The children are instructed to write the whole words.

The results of this informal test will give the teacher a general idea of her pupils' needs. For example, errors on the test records will reveal which pupils should be grouped for help with particular initial consonants or consonant combinations and which ones need training with certain vowel sounds. She can plan a word-analysis skills program accordingly.

Silent Reading Tests

Silent reading tests are used to determine the level at which the child can read silently with comprehension. Among the most widely used are those listed in Appendix A. Selected subtests are administered to determine the extent and nature of reading disability in the areas of paragraph meaning, vocabulary, and sometimes spelling. As we have pointed out, the results of an oral reading test suggest the level of the silent reading test to be administered subsequently. For example, if the pupil can read aloud only first grade material, a silent reading test designed for primary levels should be used, regardless of the pupil's age or grade. If his score puts him at fifth grade level in reading ability, a test designed for children reading at fifth grade level should be administered, and so on. This method of selecting silent reading tests produces a more accurate assessment of the silent reading skills of children with reading disability than does the routine administration of standardized tests chosen on the basis of the child's grade.

Interpreting Silent Reading Test Results

Some test results frequently seem to underestimate or overestimate the child's ability. Pupils whose reading ability is poor may mark items indiscriminately. The results in such cases may be more indicative of their good fortune in guessing correctly than of their proficiency in reading. Conversely, when a pupil misses many of the relatively easy items at the beginning of a test, because of initial anxiety in the test situation, but gets the harder ones right, or when he becomes so frustrated that he gives up, the score may underestimate his reading ability. Grade scores alone, therefore, do not provide sufficient information about a pupil's silent reading skills. The test results must be analyzed qualitatively for additional information that may shed light on the nature of the reading problem.

Analysis of test patterns at primary levels is somewhat different from analysis at advanced levels. At primary levels, the tests for the most part measure the degree to which the pupil uses word-recognition skills and his accuracy in using them. The teacher looks for consistent errors. For example, some tests contain illustrations, each followed by a list of words of which one is the correct designation. Children may use a variety of skills in selecting the word that represents the picture. Let us suppose that a picture of a book is followed by the choices, *look, bat, farm,* and *book.* If the child selects *look,* he may be using similar configuration; if he chooses *bat,* he may be relying on initial consonants; a choice of *farm* would probably indicate pure guesswork. Similar errors on sentence and paragraph reading subtests indicate which skills the child has mastered and which he still lacks. Consistency in errors suggests the area in need of instruction.

At higher levels, word recognition is still important, but comprehension plays a greater role. Thus the pupil's ability to use context influences his test results, as does the extent of his background information. Previous knowledge of the subject and adept use of context enable him to supply a particular word (or one close in meaning) even if he were unable to recognize it in isolation. For example, a pupil who uses context skillfully could probably answer questions on the following paragraph even if he were not able to recognize the italicized words.

It's over an hour until the *scheduled* takeoff, but there is plenty for us to do. We don't have any *particular* worries about the plane. After every 900 hours of flying time each engine is *completely* rebuilt.

General background information also influences the ability to use context even when every word is known. For example, each word in the following title is probably familiar to the reader: "Experimental Study of the Quenched-In Vacancies and Dislocations in Metals"; yet without an engineering background, few can decipher its meaning. Thus the way in which a pupil answers questions may reveal deficiencies in word recognition, comprehension, use of context clues, or background. If the teacher is uncertain as to the nature of the reading problem, it might be advisable to allow the student to go beyond the time limits of the standardized test and answer as many questions as he can. (The results in this case can be used for qualitative evaluation only, not as actual test results.) If he sustains a high accuracy score, his problem is probably related to slow rate. Or the teacher might have the pupil read some of the paragraphs aloud. Discussion can help in locating where the difficulties lie.

In analyzing vocabulary subtests, it is important to try to determine whether low scores are due to poor word recognition skills, difficulty in word meaning, or slowness in handling the test. For example, if a child misreads words (e.g., *profession* for *possession*), he cannot possibly find the required synonyms. The examiner can determine whether or not this is the case by checking some of the incorrect responses orally, after the test has been completed. Pupils who appear to be deficient in vocabulary are frequently found to know the words very well when they are presented orally; the pupils simply cannot read them accurately. This, then, is evidence of word recognition difficulties—not meager vocabulary. Also, the errors might be analyzed to see whether or not they tend to occur in highly technical words related to specific subjects rather than in more general words. Even pupils who have no reading difficulties tend to miss words in areas in which their background is weak. Since many pupils with reading disability have done little or no reading in the content areas, they are likely to miss such words as *resource, ingredient,* and *metallic* with greater frequency than words of a more general character.

Spelling

Most standardized achievement batteries have separate spelling subtests from which the teacher can assess the level of spelling proficiency and the types of error the pupil makes. Some of the most widely used include the *Metropolitan Achievement Tests*, the *Stanford Achievement Tests*, and the *California Reading Tests*. However, at upper levels the spelling tests of many batteries consist of multiple choice items which involve choosing the correctly spelled word from clusters of four or five. This requires mainly *recognition* of correct spelling and is an entirely different skill from that of writing words. The latter entails revisualization of word patterns, including proper sequencing of letters and recalling the correct number of syllables—abilities with which pupils who have spelling problems are often deficient. Therefore, we prefer to use the tests which require writing words from dictation, such as the *Wide Range Achievement Test*, the spelling subtest from the *Gates-McKillop Reading Diagnostic Test*, or others noted in Appendix A. In this way the types of errors can be analyzed and implications for remedial work ascertained. For example, if the pupil writes *jast* for *just*, the examiner infers that he needs practice with vowel sounds and perhaps more extensive phonic training. Whereas if he attempts to spell words phonically where phoneme-grapheme correspondence is irregular such as *frendly* for *friendly*, other methods are tried such as the visual-motor or kinesthetic, described later in this chapter. Still another approach which is frequently helpful is pointing out special features in words. Thus when *familiar* is spelled *furmilyer*, the student is shown that the word derives from *family*. Colloquial mispronunciation of words often results in misspellings, such as *Febuary* and *reconize*. Noting the correct pronunciation can facilitate accuracy.

Trial Lessons as a Diagnostic Technique

When formal testing has been completed and the results analyzed, a fairly clear picture of the child's achievement pattern should emerge. Essential as it is to administer these standardized tests, the teacher or examiner still does not know, at their conclusion, which methods and materials to recommend for remedial instruction. Also, the child himself has little understanding of what is actually wrong with his reading and in all probability remains apprehensive about his difficulty. The teacher tries to relieve the pupil's anxiety in any way she deems appropriate. It is also vital that the teacher and pupil discover ways in which he can cope with his problem. Enlisting the pupil's participation not only is therapeutic in and of itself, but it serves as powerful motivation for future learning in remedial sessions and in school. Therefore, trial lessons are recommended as an integral part of the diagnostic examination to give the teacher a definite guide as to which procedures will be most effective and to demonstrate to the pupil those methods most suited to his learning.[12]

In contrast to the controlled standardized test situation, trial lessons are conducted in an informal, spontaneous atmosphere. The teacher tells the pupil that there are several methods and many kinds of reading matter especially designed to teach those who have difficulty similar to his. Several appropriate readers or stories are made available to the pupil.[13] The teacher and pupil try them out to decide which ones are most suitable. In presenting reading materials, the teacher encourages the pupil to react as freely as possible and designate which stories he likes and dislikes. When the pupil realizes that he can really say that a selection is dull or uninteresting, he often experiences immense relief at finding someone who understands how he feels. No longer does he have to resist, suffer, or pretend that he likes meaningless exercises.

The teacher observes whether the pupil is slow or quick to grasp salient points, whether he needs a great deal of repetition, support, and encouragement, how well he recalls what he has read, how much effort he puts forth, and so on. However, the whole session is a collaborative one. The teacher explains which techniques seem suitable and helps the pupil understand his problem. The more insight a pupil gains, the more likely it is that he will summon the strength he needs to improve. Trial lessons contribute to such insight in a way that the regular test situation cannot. They may be used with pupils at all levels, from beginning read-

12. Trial lessons geared to children reading at primary levels were developed by Albert J. Harris and Florence G. Roswell and published in Harris and Roswell, "Clinical Diagnosis of Reading Disability," *Journal of Psychology* 3 (1953): 323–40. The present authors have revised and extended these lessons upward for older pupils.

13. The teacher can choose selections from the list of books in Appendixes B and D.

ing through high school. The areas to be investigated at the different stages can be divided roughly into reading levels 1 through 3, 4 through 6, 7 through 9, and 10 through 12.

Reading Levels 1 through 3

For a nonreader or one who has mastered a minimum of word-analysis techniques, the three major word recognition approaches—visual, phonic, and visual-motor[14]—should be tried. If none of these methods is successful, the kinesthetic approach might be used. (If it is found that the child can learn by only one of these methods, it is used in treatment merely as a starting point to ensure a successful experience. Before long it must be supplemented by other procedures because a successful reader needs a variety of techniques at his command.) In addition to finding suitable methods for word recognition, the teacher offers several readers or short stories to find the type of reading material that is most acceptable to the child.

Visual Method

The simple visual approach to word recognition involves learning words by means of picture clues. *If the child reads at a second grade level or above, this procedure is omitted, for it has already been established that he is able to use this method.*

Several cards are needed, each with a picture illustrating a well-known object, like a book, man, coat, and so on. The identifying noun is printed under the picture. On another set of cards the words are printed without pictures. The child is first tested on the cards with the word alone to make sure that he does not already know them. After the unknown words are selected, the teacher presents a picture card, pointing to the word and pronouncing it. The child is asked to say the word several times while looking at it. He then finds the corresponding nonillustrated card containing the same word. After five words have been studied in this manner, the child is tested with the non–illustrated cards. (If time allows, he is retested after a short interval.)

14. All of these methods are fully described in Chapter 8. The teacher should be familiar with the way in which each method is taught. However, for use as a diagnostic technique, they are summarized succinctly in this chapter.

If the child can grasp a visual procedure readily and shows some knowledge of letter sounds, the teacher immediately proceeds with step one of the phonic approach.

Phonic Approach

Step One: Word-Family Method. A rudimentary blending technique, sometimes called the word-family method, is especially useful with children who are not yet able to cope with a letter-by-letter blending procedure. It affords a limited degree of independence in word analysis. For example, a known word such as *book* may be changed into *took*, *look*, or *hook* by substituting different initial consonants. Several initial consonants are taught, studied, and combined with the appropriate word ending. Other words learned in the visual lesson may be developed in the same way: *boat*, *goat*. If the child cannot learn initial sounds readily, he needs practice in auditory discrimination of letter sounds.

Step Two: Combining Separate Sounds. In order for a pupil to master the phonic method, he must be able to combine separate sounds to form whole words. To determine this, the teacher first tries an informal auditory blending test without written words. She pronounces one syllable words slowly and distinctly, emphasizing each sound as *t-a-p*, and so on. The child tries to distinguish the word from the separate sounds. She tries several other words in this way. If the child can figure them out, he has the ability to combine sounds, and it is safe to try the phonic approach.

The teacher reviews the sounds taught under step one and then introduces a short vowel sound. For example, she prints the letter *a*, telling the pupil its name and short sound—"ă" as in *apple*. She then prints a suitable word, like *fat*, to demonstrate how the vowel can be blended with known consonant sounds to form words. Several different consonants are then substituted at the beginning of the word as in step one. After the child practices them sufficiently, the teacher changes the final consonants—that is, *fat* to *fan*, *mat* to *man*, *sat* to *sad*, and so on—and asks the child to sound them out. If the pupil has difficulty, he is assisted in blending the sounds together. The teacher then proceeds to a more difficult step: interchanging initial and final consonants alternately. Finally, the teacher presents the most difficult step of all—reading words in mixed order: *mat*, *fan*, *sad*, *bat*, and so on. The degree to which the pupil is able to recognize the words in these progressive steps indicates the kind and amount of phonics work that he will need in remedial sessions.

Visual-Motor Method

To determine whether a child is able to recall words with irregular letter-sound relationships, the visual-motor method should be tried. The teacher chooses about three words with which the child is unfamiliar (about five to seven letters in length), such as *fruit*, *night*, and *again*. She presents each word separately as follows:

She prints the word *fruit* on a card and tells the child what the word is. She suggests that the pupil look at it carefully and then shut his eyes and try to see the word distinctly with his eyes closed because he will be asked to write it from memory. He opens his eyes and takes another look if necessary. The teacher asks him to name the word so as to remember it. Sometimes it is necessary to show the card several times before he sees the word clearly enough to write it. The card is then removed and the child writes the word from memory. If he has much difficulty with one particular word, another should be tried. If he reproduces the word correctly, he writes it several times, covering up the words he has previously written so as to be sure he is recalling the word from memory rather than merely copying it. Other words are taught in a similar manner. After a period of time has elapsed, the words should be reviewed.

Kinesthetic Method

For pupils who have difficulty visualizing words as is required in the visual-motor approach, the kinesthetic method may be tried. The child is told that there is still another way of learning words which cannot be sounded out, namely through the aid of his fingers. Words are written in large letters with a felt-tipped pen in either manuscript or cursive writing depending on which the child is accustomed to using. The child traces one word with his index finger over and over until he believes he knows it. He then writes it without reference to the model and, if correct, covers it and writes it several times (always covering the word so that he reproduces it each time from memory). If incorrect, he retraces the word. In some cases it helps the child to write the word in sand or with finger paints and such; some teachers prefer having the child rub his finger over sandpaper letters or any rough material. Many variations can be used to aid him in feeling the configuration through his fingers. This helps to imprint the word. Kinesthetic procedures are more fully explained in Chapter 8.

Diagnosis

At the conclusion of the session, both pupil and teacher have a fairly clear picture of the methods which may be used successfully in teaching word recognition and which book or books he prefers to use for reading. The cases of Randy and Neil in Chapter 8 illustrate how trial lessons served not only to evaluate their instructional needs but also as a powerful motivating force for future remediation.

Reading Levels 4 through 6

For pupils reading at fourth through sixth grade levels regardless of their ages, trial lessons include investigation of advanced word-analysis techniques, comprehension skills, and reading material best suited to the pupil's reading level and interest. As already stated, it is especially important to have appealing reading material so that the pupil will become more involved in helping to improve his reading ability. If the results of standardized tests indicate deficiencies in phonics he is shown how he will be taught any sounds and combinations that he does not know. If the pupil has difficulty with spelling, several approaches are tried such as the visual-motor, kinesthetic, or calling attention to distinctive spelling patterns. In addition, the teacher evaluates the pupil's knowledge of specialized vocabulary (the technical words connected with the separate subject areas). She selects about ten words from the pupil's texts. Words from a social studies text might include *hemisphere, glacier, laser, primitive*. If the pupil is unfamiliar with them, the teacher shows him how they can be learned through various methods. The meaning is explained, if necessary, through graphic illustrations or vivid explanation. The pupil finds out how learning the specialized words connected with his different subjects can be a big boost in understanding his studies. He realizes that to some extent at least it was not the text he had so much difficulty with, but simply that the special vocabulary was unfamiliar to him.

The teacher has available a number of workbooks containing interesting articles to be used for developing comprehension skills. The level of the material is determined by the pupil's performance on standardized tests. The pupil is told that such selections will help him understand his textbooks better, since they incorporate factual reading. As soon as he learns how to get information from the articles, he will be shown in future lessons how to transfer these skills to his textbooks. It is important to discover which workbooks a pupil likes, which ones he may have already used in school, and if so, whether he has grown tired of them. Since there is a wide choice of appropriate materials, the pupil is encouraged to find those which he can readily accept.

In the same way the pupil samples recreational reading that has been carefully chosen. Stories can be selected from those listed at intermediate levels in Appendix D. The experienced teacher usually has a few excellent ones which she knows from past experience are apt to arouse the pupil's interest.

However, at times the pupil may not like any selections too well. He may have developed such intense distaste for reading that everything seems tiresome and uninteresting. In these cases, it is well that he receive some immediate reassurance so that future remedial sessions have a better chance of succeeding. The teacher might state that she has known other pupils who felt this way. To help him overcome his dislike, certain procedures will be tried. For example, very short passages will be used as a start. Secondly, many different topics will be chosen; sooner or later something will appeal to him.

In the end, the pupil should have a clear idea of any word-analysis or comprehension skills that he needs and the kinds of material that he will be using for remedial instruction. When he completes the session, he should have become fairly confident that, with such help, he can improve his reading and progress with less difficulty in school.

Reading Levels 7 through 9

Pupils with reading disability whose scores on reading tests range from seventh through ninth grade levels vary in age, intelligence, maturity, and interests.

A brief period might profitably be spent answering the questions that must be uppermost in the student's mind. Even more than younger pupils, he wants to know the outcome of the evaluation, the meaning of his test scores, and above all by what manner and means he can be helped.

The structure of the session and the procedures used are essentially the same as those described for pupils reading between fourth and sixth grade levels. However, the presentation is on a more mature level, and the materials selected are those designed for the pupil's level of functioning.

Reading Levels 10 through 12

As described above, this student is also very much interested in receiving an interpretation of his test results and finding out how he might be helped.

His major problems are likely to center on a slow rate of reading and lack of flexibility in handling different kinds of material. The teacher then describes what methods and materials might be used to good advantage. As the student looks over the workbooks, he finds that they contain articles which have been condensed from high school and college texts. He sees how practice with factual articles followed by pertinent questions will prove valuable in handling his own texts, as it will enable him to learn how to extract information quickly and efficiently.

The student is usually struck by the abundance of material available for high school and college students, specially designed to help university students in the many reading centers throughout the country. The effect is usually electric. He wants to know what has helped them and how he can proceed. Perhaps it has never before occurred to him that so many others have similar problems.

The teacher explains that articles with different formats, varying lengths, and many types of questions will help him shift his pace from one kind of reading matter to another. His rate of reading will be guided according to purpose, and he will thus develop flexibility.

If he reveals anxiety about working within time limits, he is assured that this is a fairly common concern. Even though most students are bothered at first by the use of a stopwatch, after a while they get so accustomed to it they do not notice it. Finally, the teacher gives the student some idea of the methods he may adopt in order to speed up his reading. (These are discussed in Chapter 13.)

At the conclusion of the session, the teacher as well as the student has an overview of the program that will be devised on the basis of his particular needs. The student knows where to begin and how to go ahead. He is more aware of how much depends on his own efforts even though he will be given all the assistance possible. Having his problem interpreted and described in concrete fashion often offers him added incentive and encouragement.

In this way, trial lessons at all levels are extremely helpful in preparing the pupil for remedial instruction. Instead of leaving the examination with a vague feeling of "something's wrong with my reading," he knows *what* is wrong. He has been shown in which areas he needs help. It has been demonstrated that he can alleviate his difficulties, and he has seen the specific methods and materials which are available. Gradually, as the pupil recognizes his problem and understands what he can do about it, he becomes more hopeful. His anxiety is lessened, and the foundation is laid for effective remedial treatment.

Suggestions for Further Reading

Bauman, E., and St. John, J. "The Clinical Usefulness of Some Tests of Visual Perception." *Psychology in the Schools* 8 (1971): 247–49.

Bersoff, D. "Current Functioning Myth: An Overlooked Fallacy in Psychological Assessment." *Journal of Consulting and Clinical Psychology* 37 (1971): 391–93.

Boder, E. "Developmental Dyslexia: Prevailing Diagnostic Concepts and a New Diagnostic Approach." In H. Myklebust, ed., *Progress in Learning Disabilities*, pp. 293–319. New York: Grune & Stratton, 1971.

Chomsky, C. "Reading, Writing and Phonology."*Harvard Educational Review* 40 (1970): 287–309.

Cicirelli, V. et al. "Performance of Disadvantaged Primary-Grade Children on the Revised Illinois Test of Psycholinguistic Abilities." *Psychology in the Schools* 8 (1971): 240–46.

Early, G., Early, Frances, and Heath, E. "Classroom Evaluation of Learning Disabilities." *Educational Technology* 11 (1971): 40–43.

Gensemer, I. et al. "Using the Peabody Picture Vocabulary Test with Children Having Difficulty Learning." *Journal of Learning Disabilities* 9 (1976): 179–81.

Larsen, S. et al. "The Use of Selected Perceptual Tests in Differentiating between Normal and Learning Disabled Children." *Journal of Learning Disabilities* 9 (1976): 85–90.

Levine, M. "The Academic Achievement Test: Its Historical Context and Social Functions." *American Psychologist* 31 (1976): 228–39.

Oliver, R., and Kronenberger, E. "Testing the Applicability of Koppitz's Bender-Gestalt Scores to Brain-Damaged, Emotionally Disturbed and Normal Adolescents." *Psychology in the Schools* 8 (1971): 250–53.

Rudel, R., and Denckla, M. B. "Relationship of I.Q. and Reading Score to Visual, Spatial, and Temporal Matching Tasks." *Journal of Learning Disabilities* 9 (1976): 169–78.

7

The Psychologist's and Learning Specialist's Approach to Diagnosis and Treatment

THE learning disability cases which come to the attention of the specialist are usually children who have not responded sufficiently to educational procedures or who show deviant behavior. Specialists are particularly useful when they assess the qualitative aspects of the problem, since quantitative test scores can be misleading. For example, Karl,[1] age 12½ and of normal intelligence, scored 2.2 on the *Metropolitan Achievement Test* in comprehension. However, when the consultant worked with him, she found that she could use material at the third and fourth grade levels. Thus, his score grossly underestimated his capability. Had she stayed with the lower level material Karl might have taken much longer to apply himself to the kind of schoolwork consonant with his grade placement.

Tod[2] is another example where test scores alone could confuse the examiner. His achievement scores happened to be congruent with his intelligence and taken literally meant that Tod had no reading problem. Nevertheless, Tod himself was dissatisfied with his reading. The con-

1. Full discussion of Karl is included in Chapter 12.
2. See Chapter 13 for description of Tod.

sultant encouraged his desire to improve so he could keep up with the high academic standards set by his family and the school. She trusted his dedication to his goal and recognized that he had hidden abilities that could not possibly be revealed in scores alone. Two additional children, Charles and Hank, are discussed at length later in this chapter. Both students' problems were interwoven with their family situations, Charles to a lesser extent than Hank. The specialist was able to identify the nature of each child's problems and suggest appropriate intervention.

Thus, specialists need to undertake qualitative as well as quantitative investigation of those factors for which they are professionally trained,[3] such as personality disturbance, individual intelligence, and perceptual and academic achievement measures. Since the examination presumably will be carried out by an experienced consultant, only those aspects of psychological testing which are especially pertinent to reading disability cases will be discussed. As recommendations for treatment add considerably to the usefulness of the findings, they are included in this chapter.

Background Information

The specialist gathers the pertinent background information required for a complete case history. To determine the possibility of neurological impairment, maturational lag, basic emotional disturbance, or poor educational training, he obtains as complete a developmental history as possible, paying special attention to (a) birth and early infancy, with special reference to the possibility of central nervous system dysfunction; (b) speech development; (c) early school experiences and attitudes; (d) present school experiences and attitudes; (e) attitude toward reading; (f) possibility of converted handedness; (g) attitude of the family toward the disability; (h) amount and kind of help that has been provided by the family and the school; and (i) presence of similar or related difficulties in other members of the family.[4] It is important to ascertain whether there

3. L. Silver, "The Playroom Diagnostic Evaluation of Children with Neurologically Based Learning Disabilities," paper presented October 1974 at the American Academy of Child Psychiatry, reprints from the author—Department of Psychiatry, Rutgers Medical School, University Heights, Piscataway, N.J. 08854.

P. Vorhaus, "Rorschach Configurations Associated with Reading Disability, in Natchez, *Children with Reading Problems* (New York: Basic Books, 1968), pp. 251–70.

4. A. J. Harris and F. Roswell, "Clinical Diagnosis of Reading Disability," *Journal of Psychology* 36 (1953): 323–40.

was any illness during pregnancy, whether the child was full term or premature, whether labor was prolonged or especially difficult, whether high or low forceps were used, and whether or not there was any injury at birth or any illness during pregnancy.[5] In addition, inquiry is made as to possible difficulty in establishing respiration at birth because even short periods of oxygen deprivation can cause damage to brain cells.[6]

The diagnostician also inquires as to the possibility of difficulty in sucking and swallowing or of convulsive seizures and also asks when the child cut his first tooth, sat up, stood, walked, said his first word, and put two or more words together. Was there any evidence of delayed speech or of any difficulty in articulation or enunciation? What childhood diseases, accidents, or unusually high temperatures did the child suffer? Was there evidence of awkwardness, clumsiness, or poor coordination? Which hand did and does the child prefer?

School attitudes are important too, beginning with the child's reaction toward nursery school, kindergarten, first grade, and so forth, as well as his teacher's impressions and the child's attitudes toward his teachers. It is also useful to know the parents' attitude toward the child's disability, his teachers, and current educational methodology. Many parents are extremely critical of modern methods of teaching reading and of teachers, too. This information is frequently important, not only because it offers insight into parental attitudes, but also because it may reveal the ways in which the child was handled at school and at home. Even the distortions and misconceptions of parents may shed light on the problem.

Of course, evidence of severe emotional disturbance is investigated, particularly disturbance which developed before the child entered school. Such symptoms as enuresis, feeding problems, recurrent nightmares, stuttering, excessive fearfulness, and phobic reactions offer important diagnostic clues as to the possible origin and degree of the emotional disturbance.

5. A. Kawi and B. Pasamanick, "'The Association of Factors of Pregnancy with the Development of Reading Disorders in Childhood," *Journal of the American Medical Association* 166 (1958): 1420–23.
6. M. B. Denckla, "Clinical Syndromes in Learning Disabilities," *Journal of Learning Disabilities* 5 (1972): 401–6.

Intelligence

It is important, first, to establish as valid a measure of intelligence as possible. Verbal and performance tests are usually selected at appropriate levels from the well-known *Wechsler Intelligence Scale for Children*,[7] the *Stanford-Binet Intelligence Scale*, the *Wechsler Adult Intelligence Scale*, the *Peabody Picture Vocabulary Test*, and other tests. In order to arrive at a rough approximation of the extent of the disability, a comparison must be made between the child's reading achievement and his potential, which indicates a measure known as his "reading expectancy" (see Chapter 6). Reading expectancy scores must always be interpreted broadly since they are influenced by the amount of schooling and the degree of experience of the child as well as the probable errors of measurements on the tests involved. For example, a seven-year-old child with a mental age of ten years can only in theory be expected to read as well as the average ten-year-old, because he has not had the same amount of academic exposure or comparable years of experience. He would, however, be expected to read considerably better than the average seven-year-old pupil.

Physical Factors

Physical problems may directly or indirectly influence a child's ability to focus his attention on learning. Therefore, a medical examination is frequently indicated to determine whether any physical condition may be causing or contributing to the learning problem.

The responsibility of the specialist in these connections varies with the parent's ability to arrange for medical diagnosis and carry through on recommendations. The specialist must decide the type of referral indicated, whether to a private physician or a medical clinic. It is important in any case that relevant findings be reported to the specialist so that he can integrate all the diagnostic information.

7. All tests mentioned in this chapter are listed in Appendix A.

Neurological Factors

The psychologist or other qualified specialist undertakes the evaluation of neurological development according to his professional training and expertise. The areas to be assessed are clearly designated in Chapter 3. They generally include language development, perceptual functioning, visual-motor coordination, integrative capacity, sequencing, orientation, visual and auditory memory, abstract thinking, information processing, and attention span. If according to the examiner's judgment further investigation is indicated, the child is referred for neurological examination.

A precise differential diagnosis between neurological and psychological problems is frequently difficult to ascertain because symptomatology is often similar. The case of Paul may highlight this dilemma.

Paul—Difficulty in Making a Differential Diagnosis between Neurological and Psychological Factors

It was eventually discovered that Paul's difficulty was neurological in nature. However, because of the unmistakable presence of psychogenic factors, Paul's reading disability was at first treated primarily as an emotional problem.

Paul was 9 years old when he was first referred for diagnosis to one of the authors. He was repeating second grade because of his extreme difficulty in learning to read. (Reading was at high first grade level.) His birth and developmental history were within the normal range. His speech had been somewhat immature until the age of seven. There was no indication of neurological impairment on any of the psychological tests. The reading tests revealed that he had marked difficulty in synthesizing sounds to form words, a strong tendency to reverse letters, such as *b* for *d*, and a tendency to confuse left and right. Tests of laterality showed consistent right-hand and right-eye dominance. Projective tests revealed Paul to be very dependent and immature, with a great deal of anxiety and an extremely weak ego. In addition, it was learned that Paul's mother was overprotective and very controlling. Because the problem seemed to be primarily due to emotional factors, psychotherapy was instituted.

After one year, no appreciable improvement had taken place in his schoolwork. Paul still read at a high first grade level, although he was scheduled to enter third grade the following fall and was close to ten years of age. Diagnostic instruments that had not previously been used were administered to search further for possible causes. His poor performance on some of these tests strongly pointed to the possibility of neurologic impairment. Most revealing of all was Paul's continued inability to blend sounds, his faulty memory, and his tendency to confuse and reverse letters in reading and writing. He repeatedly transposed sequences in writing, such as *rnu* for *run*, *hwo* for *who*, and even *Plau* for *Paul*. Therefore, a complete neurological examination was undertaken. The findings of this examination, which included an electroencephalogram, were positive. The results of this investigation further suggested that Paul's emotional problems—his insecurity, immaturity, weak ego, and anxiety—were probably reactions to a neurologic disorder. This is one example of many cases which are treated as primary emotional disturbances where the neurological examination shows unequivocal evidence of central nervous system abnormalities. Paul was subsequently placed in a class for severe learning disabilities where special educational techniques were employed. This example is but one of many which shows the advantage in using all the means at the psychologist's disposal to ensure an accurate estimate of emotional factors and their possible causes.

Educational Factors

School has a major influence on the youngster's development, because he spends so great a portion of his life there. Such experiences as frequent moves from school to school, absences, or shifts in teachers have an obvious effect. In considering other school influences, it is advisable in some cases to observe the child while he is engaged in academic and free-time school activities with particular focus on his interpersonal relationships in the classroom.

For example, if a child shows poor concentration, restlessness, and difficulty in recalling information that he has recently heard, does the teacher recognize that such characteristics are often displayed by children with reading difficulties? Does the teacher perhaps label the child "dyslexic" and believe that she does not have sufficient background to cope with his problem? Does she show concern for the child or does her frustration impede constructive efforts? Has she made attempts to ascertain methods with which the child is likely to succeed, and has she used materials that are suitable to his maturity and reading level? Is the teacher hampered in her efforts by her supervisor or is she free to devise an individualized program for the child? Is the classroom atmosphere so permissive that the entire class lacks appropriate structure or is it so inflexible that the pupils exhibit tension under the stress?

In school observations, the skilled specialist is aware of the role played by covert attitudes. Here his understanding of dynamic human relationships can prove invaluable. Observation also aids him in gaining perspective as to the weight that each contributing factor may have. Here he may see the child's characteristics as he is influenced by and interacts with his classmates, the teacher, and the required schoolwork. From the teacher, he may also acquire information regarding the parents' attitudes toward the child's poor schoolwork and toward the child himself.

What part do parents play in all the interactions related to school? Are they resentful of what they regard as the school's role in their youngster's failure? As one mother complained, "It's a sad commentary on the schools today that they cannot teach my child how to read." Are they indignant about the fact that "none of the other children have this trouble"?

If the specialist discovers that the parents are very authoritative and that their attitudes distress the child, is the distress intensified by the school situation? Or if the child is repressed, is this condition sufficient to make all attempts to teach him futile?

In assessing school adjustment, the specialist must also take into account any additional help the child may be obtaining. If he is receiving remedial instruction, for example, what kind of help is it? Are sound procedures being used? What is the child's attitude toward the remedial teacher? Is he profiting from the assistance? If not, does the problem lie in the child, the teaching techniques, or the teacher? Is the teacher qualified for remedial work? Has she been given adequate materials, or is the remedial program a makeshift arrangement to satisfy a directive from the administration? How are the teacher's attitudes affecting the child? How does the family influence the child's learning? What is their attitude toward the problem? The answers to these questions can explain why remedial treatment is or is not helpful.

Thus the specialist observes the child in a variety of situations and acquaints himself with as many aspects of the child's school life as possible. Insights gained from such knowledge can aid him in collaboration with the teacher to help the child in class, to provide additional treatment, or whatever else is needed.

Charles—A Seventh Grader Reading at Fifth Grade Level

Even where drastic change of procedure cannot be instituted, the specialist can be of enormous help by explaining to the teacher, parents, and wherever appropriate to the child himself what is aggravating the problem and what might be done about it. Consider, for example, the case of Charles, a 12-year-old boy in the seventh grade. With average intelligence, Charles barely read at fifth grade level and was failing all his subjects. He was referred to a child guidance clinic for diagnosis. No gross physical defects were found, but there was some indication of immaturity, dependence, and fear of the father. Charles' parents were extremely concerned about the boy, who was an only child, and were willing to do everything possible to help him. However, the father became very anxious when he saw the child's failing reports and threatened to beat Charles if he did not improve. Investigation of his school behavior showed that Charles had been guilty of some 40 minor infractions that year, such as sharpening pencils when he was not supposed to do so and not bringing in homework on time. He was the lowest achiever in the class. The only other seventh grade class to which he could be transferred consisted of boys with severe behavior problems, and it was felt that he might be influenced adversely by them. The author who handled Charles' case considered that circumstances did not permit the institution of major changes, but the situation was relieved to the extent that the child had a chance to make some progress in school. The result was better marks and fewer violations of the rules. The teacher was helped to find alternate ways of handling Charles in class. At a conference, the writer suggested that the reason for Charles' neglect of homework was that he just could not do it. He sharpened pencils because the work was so far above him that he became restless. Simpler books and materials were therefore supplied so that the teacher could give more realistic assignments to him.

In addition, the author explained to Charles that he had probably had difficulty learning in the beginning because he had not been able to distinguish letters and sounds as well as many children of his age could.

This caused him to fall farther and farther behind until he had become "lost." However, he could now profit from the kind of work the teacher would give him. This would help him to "catch up" in reading. Such explanations helped to lessen Charles' tendency to blame himself, made him grasp the problem better, decreased some of his apprehension, and made him more amenable to cooperation with the teacher.

Interpreting the boy's problems to his parents relieved some of their anxiety also. As Charles' marks improved, his parents became less and less apprehensive. Had the school and family situation not been investigated, few practical recommendations could have been offered and little could have been accomplished.

In assessing emotional factors in children with reading disability, it has often been assumed that such children suffer from an emotional disturbance which must be cleared up through some form of psychotherapy before they can benefit optimally from reading instruction. This assumption is highly questionable not only because our theoretical framework is as yet on shaky foundations,[8] but because a great number of children with reading disability may be displaying emotional disturbance as a direct reaction to their poor schoolwork.[9] In addition, poor performance in school reinforces and intensifies any emotional disturbance that was already present. Illustrations of such developments have been implied throughout this and other chapters. Yet psychologists who have been trained in personality diagnosis, with little or no emphasis on educational problems, continue to investigate the behavior patterns, unconscious conflicts, and defenses of the child with reading disability in the same fashion as they do emotionally disturbed children who are free from academic problems. This sometimes has led to incomplete and distorted results because (1) a child who is not able to succeed in an area as crucial to his well-being as school is under a constant threat to his ego. The results of such threat can cause as great a constellation of personality disturbances as any other anxiety-provoking situation. (2) If poor schoolwork is the seat of the anxiety, psychotherapy or family treatment alone, useful though they are, may not be able to reach the crux of the problem.[10] Perhaps tutoring in conjunction with therapy is an alternative because the longer the poor reading persists, the worse the personality disturb-

8. L. Silver, "Emotional and Social Problems of Children with Developmental Disabilities," in *Handbook on Learning Disabilites*, R. Weber, ed. (Englewood Cliffs, N.J.: Prentice-Hall, 1974), pp. 97–120.

9. J. Abrams, "The Role of Personality Defenses in Reading," in *Children with Reading Problems*, G. Natchez, ed. (New York: Basic Books, 1968), pp. 77–79.

10. J. Kagan, "Reflection-Impulsivity and Reading Ability," *Child Development* 36 (1965): 609–28.

ance is likely to become. (3) It is entirely possible that one set of factors in a child may cause the emotional disturbance, while quite another set may cause the reading disability.[11] Thus the most faithfully executed personality descriptions, accurate though they may be, may have little or no relationship to the cause of the reading disability and be of no help in diagnosing or treating it. This can result in years of mismanagement of the problem. (4) Doing nothing about the reading problem because psychotherapy is being inaugurated, or awaiting psychotherapy which is difficult to implement because of the well-known factors of lack of facilities, inability to pay, resistance on the part of the child or his parents, and the like, can waste years of valuable time. In the interim, schoolwork can become worse and worse.

Therefore, the specialist's main concern is not merely to find out whether there is or is not evidence of emotional disturbance in the child with a reading disability; signs of emotional disturbance will be his most likely discovery. What has to be assessed is (1) the nature, degree, and complexity of the emotional problem itself; (2) the ways in which the emotional maladjustment is related to the reading disability or is reinforcing it; (3) how it may have arisen; whether it antedates the reading problem or is reactive to it; (4) whether it has arisen as a reaction to other causal factors such as physical immaturity, neurological impairment, or unfavorable environmental, familial, or educational circumstances; and (5) how it may affect future school achievement. Results from such assessment can help to decide which mode of treatment is indicated.

The case of Hank illustrates the way in which one of the authors assessed his problem and determined an avenue of treatment. Whereas the school saw him as needing only educational management, his attitudes and the way they were intertwined with the famliy proved to be crucial and indicated involvement for the whole family.

Hank—A Boy of 14 Failing in School

Extensive diagnosis revealed that Hank had sufficient intelligence (bright normal was the category) and he consistently earned over the 77th percentile in reading achievement on silent and oral reading tests. School

11. L. Eisenberg, "Psychiatric Aspects of Language Disability," in D. Duane and M. Rawson, *Reading, Perception and Language* (Baltimore: York Press, 1975), pp. 215–30.

personnel agreed that Hank had mastered some of the basic skills, but claimed that he failed his daily work and final exams anyway. Comprehension seemed to be a problem and his vocabulary was meager. He refused to complete assignments and rarely responded to daily class work.

His mother contacted an educational therapist. On the phone she explained that they had a lovely family of four children and that if it only weren't for Hank, "everything would be beautiful." There followed a harangue of his failings—he was flunking at school; he was inconsiderate; he stole money; he fought "all the time"; and he frequently played truant from school.

Since this information seemed to indicate that Hank's attitude was the factor that most seriously interfered with his schoolwork, the reading specialist, who was also trained as a psychotherapist, decided to ask the whole family (mother, father, three sons, and a daughter) to attend a session together. Her philosophy followed family system theory that considers one member's problem to be part of the family pattern—each one contributing to, as well as being affected by, the other's behavior and attitudes.

On the appointed day, Mother and three of her four children arrived on time. They explained to the therapist that father was in the lobby waiting for Hank. In talking together, the therapist learned that most of the children grumbled that they had to see a "shrink" when it was Hank who was always in trouble.

A few moments later Father arrived alone. He said that he'd called home only to find out that Hank was being detained at the police station. He had talked back to an officer and called him an unacceptable name. Mother and Father were furious and claimed that this was typical of how he caused trouble. The therapist told them how frustrated she was too, but admitted that she couldn't help admiring his ingenuity in dodging the session so effectively.

The therapist went on to say that since they were in the office anyway, they might as well proceed. This would give all of them a chance to see what happens in such sessions. No one objected, so the therapist started by asking how any member of the family might like something at home changed. There was a moment of silence and then Sam, the ten-year-old, started by saying that he would like to sleep on the upper bunk bed in the room that he shared with his younger brother. His mother said that as soon as he could be trusted not to wet his bed he could sleep there. Sam answered, "But I've been good for six months!"

Mother answered, "Haven't you had a couple of accidents in that time? Tell the truth."

Sam, ashamed and frustrated, said in a subdued voice, "Well . . . once or twice."

The therapist mentioned that it seemed whatever Sam did was never enough. The mother remained adamant and said that they could talk about this at home. They wanted to talk about Hank.

The therapist understood the mother's concern, but said she also needed to hear how each one reacted to what was happening in the family and how they felt about Hank also. Bob, Sam's younger brother, then started to talk about Hank and said that he was a real friend to him—that he helped him with his homework and that he liked him. He was a "good guy." Most members stated that Hank was both likable and frustrating. But Father was angry and said that he had lost all trust and respect for him and that it would have to be earned back. By this time the therapist asked permission to tape the session so Hank could hear it if he wished. All agreed. At the end of the session the therapist said to Hank, on the tape, that she was sorry he wasn't there to hear the discussion in person and that if everyone agreed, including him, she would see them all tomorrow.

The whole family appeared the next day. Hank was the first to speak saying that he was angry that he was the one most talked about on the tape, but that he was also glad to hear how much everyone cared for him. The therapist asked how he felt being in this family. After much hesitation, he said that he "felt in the middle." The therapist asked him to place people in the family to show physically in tableau form how it was for him to be in the middle. He then placed two of his brothers on one side of him and his sister on the other, and said, "I'm in the middle." There was a pause and Bob said, "But I feel in the middle too." When asked to elaborate he said, "Well, it's very crowded for me." They then proceeded to play out a pantomime. Hank placed Father at "work all the time at this desk"; Mom was in the kitchen cooking; Kathy was "out driving the car"; Bob and Sam were playing separately. It turned out that each member felt isolated and ignored.

"Where does that leave all of you?" the therapist asked.

"With my friends." Hank answered. In reply to how that felt for him, he continued, "I steal in order to show them I can *be* somebody. I make trouble in school too, to be a big shot."

Father threw his wallet at him and said, "There, take it; you don't have to steal it. What do you want? Should I just give it to you?"

Mother said to Hank, "You're killing me. I want to run away; I want to kill myself; I'm afraid to answer a phone; I'm afraid it will be the police or the school. I can't stand it anymore. Why can't you think of me?"

Hank froze. The therapist went over to him and said, "When I did something bad as a kid and my mother made me feel guilty, I felt hopeless and misunderstood."

He answered in a low voice. "I don't want to be this way. I don't want to steal or do bad at school."

Father repeated, "You'll have to earn back my trust." One brother said something preachy; Mother continued to cry.

The therapist asked if anyone had heard Hank say that he didn't want to be the way he was. There was a long silence and some sighs. The session came to an end.

In this family, many sessions were held over a period of months. It was soon evident that most of the children felt that they were not getting the attention and understanding that they wished. The parents were willing to look into themselves and realized some of the unspoken messages they were giving Hank and his brothers and sister, namely that they should do what they were supposed to do and leave the parents in peace. As they became more understanding, the children responded also.

The specialist concluded that Hank did not need special tutoring. Instead, the family met for a series of therapy sessions. As of now he is passing in school. Although there are still many problems, the family members can talk about them and work them out without using Hank as the scapegoat and the only one who doesn't do things "right." This has helped Hank to feel better about himself and his capabilities. Hank has been freed to use the reading skills he always had and implement them in his schoolwork, too.

Reading Evaluation as an Integral Part of Psychological Diagnosis

To complete the investigation of a child with reading disability, a reading diagnosis is conducted as described in Chapter 6. It consists of oral, silent, and diagnostic reading tests together with their quantitative and qualitative interpretation, as well as trial lessons. These are administered to find out in what way the child best learns, where his strengths lie, and how he can be helped to overcome his difficulties. From this information, recommendations can be formulated as to which methods are most suitable for the child. Such suggestions are particularly meaningful to the teacher, since they are directly connected with helping to overcome the reading disability.

Making Recommendations in Relation to the Diagnosis

Recommendations need to be as inclusive as possible, consider all the causes of the reading disability, and emphasize the strengths that the child possesses.

Whether or not the diagnosis is definitively established, suggestions as to how to handle the child's difficulty in learning to read remain the responsibility of the diagnostician.

If the school is cooperative, a conference should be held with the parent, the teacher, the principal, and other school personnel concerned with the child in order to explain findings and discuss measures which might help to alleviate the child's problems.

A well-defined program for remedial work is of vital importance. If the psychologist is not professionally trained to make suggestions with regard to remedial work, the services of a reading specialist or remedial teacher should be sought. Ideally, the specialist maintains contact with the school.

If educational planning is needed, is it better for the child to be in a less competitive class or a more structured one? Is it more advantageous for him to be with a particular teacher regardless of the class composition or vice versa? Is there any other school the child might attend?

If remedial work is to be undertaken, is there an experienced teacher available or perhaps an appropriate group in the school for the child? Is the remedial work suited to the needs of the pupil?

If psychotherapy or family treatment is advisable, is there a mental health clinic or family agency with facilities available? These agencies may have long waiting lists, whereas the schedules of private therapists are also crowded and their fees are beyond the reach of most people. Sometimes arrangements can be made for a child to attend a clinic once a week. If the child is deeply disturbed, however, being seen so infrequently may be insufficient for him. In these instances too much reliance cannot be placed solely on such treatment.

However, where therapeutic treatment *is* available, it is usually most advantageous when the efforts of the therapist are coordinated with those of the school in planning for a more favorable learning environment. This would include trying to keep anxiety-arousing situations in the classroom at a minimum and improving the child's functioning through effective remedial instruction. In addition, if counseling or therapy can be obtained for the parents, this might also add to the effectiveness of treatment.

Thus recommendations are made with regard to reality. Rarely are ideal solutions found. The specialist tries to alleviate the difficulties to the extent possible.

When a plan is decided upon, all those involved—the parents, the teachers, and the specialist who is going to treat the child—share the responsibility for carrying out treatment. The treatment plan is interpreted to the parents, the child, and the teacher so that they all understand the problem, the ways in which it will be handled, and each one's part in the plan.

Many diagnoses must of necessity remain tentative. Children continue to grow and develop, and the present difficulty may gradually disappear due to a number of intervening factors. It has been found, for example, that many disturbed children who are given remedial instruction, but no psychotherapeutic treatment, make substantial progress in emotional adjustment as well as reading. Some children who show extreme difficulty in learning are eventually able to learn to read adequately despite their handicaps.

It is extremely rare to find a child so impaired that he cannot learn. There is little evidence in the literature to show, for example, that children with neurological or personality dysfunction will never be able to perform the tasks in reading that are needed.[12] Also, where repression of intellectual drive exists, all avenues to learning need not be closed. Thus we cannot give up hope. We must find ways to teach the child, choosing the best possible alternatives from the resources available. Sometimes a change of educational milieu is the best solution; sometimes intensive remedial work with a skilled tutor is the best answer; sometimes a change to another teacher is reasonable; sometimes extensive therapy must be inaugurated; sometimes both remedial instruction and psychotherapy are advisable; but at all times, recommendations are made with a view to their practicability and feasibility.

12. A. Strauss and N. Kephart, *Psychopathology and Education of the Brain-injured Child* (New York: Grune & Stratton, 1955), 2, p. 177.

Suggestions for Further Reading

Carroll, J., and Chall, J., eds. *Toward a Literate Society: A Report from the National Academy of Education.* New York: McGraw-Hill, 1975.

Guthrie, J., ed. *Aspects of Reading Acquisition.* Baltimore: Johns Hopkins University Press, 1976. Pages 205 ff.

Harris, A. and Sipay, E. *How to Increase Reading Ability.* New York: David McKay, 1975. Chapter 8.

Koppitz, E. *Children with Learning Disabilities: A Five Year Follow-up Study.* New York: Grune & Stratton, 1971.

Myklebust, H. *Progress in Learning Disabilities.* New York: Grune & Stratton, 1971. Chapter 11.

Natchez, G. *Children with Learning Problems.* New York: Basic Books, 1968. Part II.

Neisworth, J., Kurtz, D., Ross, A., and Madle, R. "Naturalistic Assessment of Neurological Diagnoses and Pharmacological Intervention." *Journal of Learning Disabilities* 9 (1976): 149–52.

Sapir, S., and Wilson, B. "The Education of the Handicapped Child." In A. Rudolph, ed., *Pediatrics,* 16th ed. New York: Appleton-Century-Crofts, 1977.

Silver, L. "The Playroom Diagnostic Evaluation of Children with Neurologically Based Learning Disabilities." Paper presented October 1974 at the American Academy of Child Psychiatry. (Reprints from the author—Department of Psychiatry, Rutgers Medical School, University Heights, Piscataway, N.J., 08854.)

Wepman, J. *The Auditory Discrimination Test.* Chicago: Language Research Associates, 1973.

Part III

Treatment

8

Methods of Teaching
Word Recognition to Children
with Reading Disability

COMPETENCE in word-recognition skills is basic in learning to read. There is no one method that is more effective than others. Furthermore, overreliance on any one approach impedes ability to develop fluency in reading. Therefore, the child needs to learn gradually a variety of strategies: whole-word recognition, sound-blending techniques, identification of larger units within words, and how to figure out words through the use of context clues.

Innumerable cases of children have come to our attention who were so firmly attached to one particular method that they were completely at a loss to handle words that did not conform to the only approach they knew. This was particularly apparent in those instances where teachers or parents stressed the learning of letter sounds as the key to mastery of reading. Despite their good grasp of basic phonic skills, many of these children could not even handle a pre-primer; because as soon as they met phonically irregular words, their single strategy led to confusion and frustration. Furthermore, in the course of remedial instruction, it was extremely difficult to help them overcome this firmly entrenched approach. Therefore, from the outset, flexibility in word-recognition skills needs to be emphasized.

Treatment

The ultimate objective in teaching word–analysis techniques is to help the child learn to read and derive meaning from what he reads. This chapter describes the basic word-analysis skills necessary for pupils of any age and grade in order to develop competence in reading. Chapter 9 shows how these skills may be adapted for pupils of varying ages, both individually and in a classroom. Although word recognition is never separated from understanding, for purposes of clarification comprehension techniques are elaborated in Chapter 10.

Sequence of Word-Recognition Instruction in Remedial Reading

Although many of the word–recognition skills that are taught in remedial reading are the same as those in a regular program, there are certain major differences. In the usual program, sometimes known as the developmental reading program, there are a large number of skills that are presented according to a systematic plan. In remedial reading, however, instruction is simplified. The number of skills are cut to a bare minimum to make it easier for children with reading disability who have already been exposed to them unsuccessfully for one or more years.

Reading authorities differ as to which skills in remedial reading are most important and which sequence is most effective. The authors favor the sequence of skills that is listed below. Of this sequence only those skills are taught that the pupils do not already know. Thus the authors first identify the gaps in the pupils' word-recognition skills and adapt the program accordingly. This streamlined procedure serves to keep the pupils' discouragement at a minimum at the same time that it promotes rapid and effective progress in reading. Instead of spending an undue number of lessons on numerous rules and techniques, the additional time is spent in reading as many stories and books as possible. The pride of continued accomplishment—even though the reading may remain somewhat uneven—often spurs children's acceptance of the reading process until they are able to develop more proficiency.

The word-analysis skills for remedial reading listed below form a basis for figuring out many unknown words.

Poor readers who do not know 50 to 100 sight words, such as *were*, *always*, *same*, learn those that are introduced in the easy materials they are using. More advanced readers learn any of the basic sight words that they do not already know—perhaps five to ten at a time. In addition, the teacher introduces letter sounds that need practice. She presents one vowel sound simultaneously with the sounds of four or five consonants. This allows practice with the phonic approach as soon as possible. Once the children learn the additional skills listed and apply them in their reading, they seem to learn more rapidly any other word-reconition skills that they may need.

WORD-ANALYSIS SKILLS FOR REMEDIAL READING
(In Suggested Sequence for Teaching)
  1. *Sight words*
     (a) The 95 most common nouns (see Appendix E)
     (b) The basic sight vocabulary of 220 words (see Appendix E)
  2. *Initial consonants*— *s, d, m, t, h, p, f, c, r, b, l, n, g, w, j, k, v, y, z*
     (Four or five initial consonant sounds are taught at a time, along with one vowel sound.)
  3. *Short vowel sounds*—*a, i, o, u, e*
  4. *Consonant digraphs*—*sh, ch, th*
  5. *Consonent blends*—*sm, sp, st, sk, tr, gr, br, cl, fl*
  6. *Long vowel sounds*, taught in conjunction with the two vowel rules:
     (a) *The silent e:* When *e* is added at the end of a one syllable word, it usually is silent and makes the first vowel long, e.g., *at, ate; bit, bite.*
     (b) *Vowel digraphs:* When two vowels come together, the first is usually long and the second silent, e.g., *paid, seat.*
  7. *Syllabication:* The two major rules are:
     (a) In case of two adjacent consonants, the syllables are divided between them.
     (b) When two consonants are not found together, the word is divided after the first vowel.

Teaching Word Recognition

In introducing word-analysis skills, sight words are usually taught first. These words make up a large part of the material that children meet in their books—for example, *this, their, what, whose, come, many.* They are called "sight words" because the pupil must learn to recognize them at a glance. They occur so frequently that inability to recognize them prevents fluency. Many of them cannot be figured out phonically; many are similar in configuration; many are abstract and elusive in meaning. Often they are difficult to learn. Pupils are encouraged to recognize such words in their entirety rather than sound them out. The teacher can refer to any one of the several published lists of sight words to decide which words warrant special study. Dolch's list of the 220 words that comprise the basic sight vocabulary and his list of most common nouns are reproduced in Appendix E. Other word lists, such as those of Otto, Carroll, and Johnson, all compare favorably with the Dolch list.[1]

There are several ways of teaching sight words: the visual, the visual-motor, and the kinesthetic methods.

The Visual Method

The visual method consists of exposing words again and again until the pupil learns to identify them by their general configuration. Children with reading disability tend to have difficulty perceiving accurately and are likely to confuse words of similar shape. Such pupils frequently can learn words in isolation and yet be unable to recognize them in context. They may know the words one day and forget them the next; they may recognize them in one sentence and mispronounce them a few lines later in a different context. Adults often show similar difficulty in associating faces and names. For example, one may know the face and name of one's mailman, yet be unable to recall his name or to identify him if we see him at the movies. Pupils need to see sight words in a variety of contexts until the word is firmly fixed in their minds. For this reason, sight words are presented in as many different ways as possible—in picture cards, stories, games, workbooks, and worksheets.

Learning Sight Words through Picture Cards. In presenting sight words, the teacher might use commercially prepared or homemade picture-word cards.[2] She chooses nouns unfamiliar to the children but representing well-known objects. Each word is printed under a picture. (If the teacher makes her own cards, she might mount pictures cut from magazines.) Identical cards contain the word alone. The children look at the picture cards first, pronouncing the appropriate words. Then they match the non-illustrated card to its illustrated counterpart. The picture card is then removed and the children try to say the printed word. This is repeated several times.

1. A. Lowe and J. Follman, "Comparison of the Dolch List with other Word Lists," *The Reading Teacher*, October 1974, pp. 40–44.
2. E. W. Dolch, *Picture-Word Cards* (Champaign, Ill.: Garrard Press), presents the "Ninety-five Commonest Nouns." Cf. Appendix E.

Each child can keep his own pack of picture-word cards and practice them by himself until they are learned. The illustration thus serves as a self-checking device. He can also compile an individual picture dictionary, drawing or cutting out pictures corresponding to the words.

Learning Sight Words in Stories. To improve carry-over from isolated word practice to recognition of the same words in context, emphasis is placed on sentences and stories that use these words. The children are given the most interesting books that can be found at their level and asked to read aloud. The teacher should supply unknown words as quickly and as unobtrusively as possible so that the reading proceeds smoothly. Often the child can remember these words if they appear again. If not, the teacher supplies them as often as necessary until they are recognized. Appropriate support during reading plus constant repetition of the same words apparently helps the children to learn as they read. The joy of completing story after story adds immeasurably to the child's positive feelings toward reading as well as reinforcing recognition of sight words.

The Visual-Motor Method

Words that the children have not been able to learn by the simple visual approach or sight method can sometimes be mastered by the visual-motor method. This method is particularly useful in learning irregular words. Some children have considerable difficulty in visualizing words either because of poor visual discrimination or poor memory. In such cases, the use of the method should be discontinued.

The teacher chooses three words, each about five to eight letters long, that are unfamiliar to the pupils. The words are clearly printed on cards or chalk board and presented one at a time. The teacher says, "This is the word *fruit*. Look at it carefully. What is the word? Now close your eyes. Can you see it with your eyes closed? Look again. What is the word?" The word is covered and the children write it. They then compare their written word with the model. If the written word is incorrect, the procedure is repeated. No erasures are permitted. If a child makes a mistake, he starts over again. Sometimes it is necessary to show the word several times before the children are able to write it correctly. When the word is reproduced accurately, the children write it several more times, covering up each previous sample to make sure that they are recalling the word from memory rather than merely copying it. The teacher checks carefully to see that it is written correctly each time. Another word is then introduced, and the procedure is repeated. After a period of time has elapsed, the words are reviewed.

The Kinesthetic Method

The kinesthetic approach, developed by Fernald[3] is relatively laborious and time-consuming and is most effective for individual cases under careful supervision. It is recommended when all other methods have failed. In this method, the teacher writes or prints unfamiliar words on unlined paper in letters approximately two inches high. The child is told that he will be taught by an entirely new method—through his fingers.

The child then looks at one word, is told what it is, and traces it with his index finger, simultaneously pronouncing each sound of the word. If he makes an error or is uncertain of the word, he retraces it, again saying each part of the word aloud. Then he tries to reproduce the word without reference to the model. Erasure is not permitted. He continues to trace and say it over and over until he can write the word easily without consulting the original sample.

As soon as the child can write these words adequately, he begins to make up his own stories, asking for the words he does not know. Each of these words is written for him and taught as just described. Whatever he writes is typed out for him quickly so that he can read it while it is still fresh in his mind. Each pupil keeps an alphabetical file of the words he has requested so that he can practice them at his leisure and refer to them if necessary in writing additional stories.

Games and Devices

After the teacher introduces sight words, systematic practice is afforded by games and devices based on reliable word lists and by workbooks or made-up materials which use these words in different contexts. The teacher can make up her own games, use those that can be obtained commercially, or refer to compilations of classroom games such as are found in pamphlets published by Basal Reader Companies and special "game" books. These and recommended games are listed in Appendix C under "Devices for Teaching Sight Vocabulary."

For quick recognition of words, the teacher can make a hand tachistoscope or use a commercial one such as the one put out by the Reading

3. G. Fernald, *Remedial Techniques in Basic School Subjects* (New York: McGraw-Hill, 1943), Part 2.

Institute of Boston.[4] This tachistoscope, called Pocket-Tac, consists of a small case with a mechanically operated shutter that flashes sight words or numbers. Several sets of material are available for practice at elementary through high school levels.

Workbooks

Workbooks must be used with caution since they often do not fulfill the pupils needs. Few workbooks are designed just for teaching sight words. Therefore the teacher selects exercises carefully. The most useful ones for teaching sight words include such features as picture dictionaries for ready reference, simple riddles, or sentences using the words to be practiced. They may be selected from any of the standard workbooks that are used in connection with primary reading.

Although the separate skills for teaching sight words have just been described in sequence we always experiment until we find the approach most suitable for helping a child learn to read. Remember we are dealing with children who already have been exposed to these skills at least once. Until we investigate, we do not know which skills they may have retained and which we need to stress. José, for example, had had a surfeit of phonics instruction with no success. He could not distinguish letter sounds despite his classroom teacher's conscientious persistence. When he was exposed to sounding out words once again by his reading teacher he became so frustrated that she considered suspending reading sessions for a while in favor of nonreading activities with special emphasis on language development. Let's see what she did with José.

José—A Total Nonreader in Third Grade

At 8 years, 6 months, José was in third grade and could not read at all when he was referred to a reading clinic for help. His intelligence was in the borderline range and his marked tendency to fantasize interfered with his ability to sustain attention. Very often he went off on a tangent in the middle of instruction, which frequently upset and distracted his tutor. He came from a non-English-speaking family of very low income and poor educational background. His parents were separated and he had siblings

4. This and other tachistoscopes are listed in Appendix C.

who showed signs of serious emotional disturbance. His problems were exacerbated by recent severe traumatic experiences.

José was handsome, well-coordinated, and physically well-developed but pale, obviously fatigued, and poorly nourished. His expressive language was meager; his vocabulary was limited and his naming of objects was often inaccurate. He could barely retell a narrative in a coherent manner. His receptive language was equally limited. One had to speak slowly and with a restricted vocabulary. Any book read to him had to be paraphrased into short, declarative sentences in the present tense. Most illustrations were hard for him to understand. He could not grasp any material that he himself had not experienced, no matter how simply an explanation was presented. Here is the tutor's account:[5]

"Because of José's massive language deficit, I thought it important for him to use language directly, to communicate feelings verbally and to tell stories, in order to achieve some notion of the power of language. Before attempting to introduce reading instruction, I felt that José needed to understand the connection between letter and sound, print and speech, reading and speaking, and speaking and feeling. So, for about one month José drew pictures, told stories, dictated stories to me, chose pictures from magazines, and made up stories about them.

"When José was first seen, he could not identify the name or give the sound of any letter, nor could he point to the appropriate letter if given its name or sound. He seemed unable to hear initial consonant sounds or to rhyme words. He could match letters, words, and shapes (while unable to read or identify them), and he could write his name and copy letters. His visual perception seemed adequate as did his fine motor control; however, his insecurity and imagination made it very difficult for him to concentrate on any task.

"Since José had sung the alphabet song with great pride, energy, and gusto, I decided to teach him the names of the letters. I used a felt board and felt letters, traced the letters on his back or hand, tried visual clues for reinforcement, and asked him to write the letter while saying its name. However, José could not remember the name of a letter for even two minutes. A phonic approach was tried next, using Catherine Stern's *We Discover Reading*.[6] We used the accepted method of associating letters with familiar objects. This was discontinued after a month because it proved ineffective for José. Since he could not retrieve the names of objects, he could never associate or find the proper initial consonant.

5. Catherine Lipkin, reading specialist.
6. C. Stern, ed., *We Discover Reading* (New York: Random House, 1976).

When I tried to teach *f* he called *finger* thumb, and *fork* spoon. When I tried to teach *c* he called *cup* glass. I even chose items where the name of the letter was identical with the name of the item, such as TV for *t*. However José's learning style was so chaotic that he forgot the items almost immediately. For whatever reasons, he could not learn to read using these materials.

"I should mention that José was never angry or belligerent. He could work, and he tried very hard. And he knew that something was desperately wrong.

"Because of José's extreme difficulty in grasping reading instructions, I thought that it might be advisable to discontinue instruction temporarily, and instead give José a sense of mastery, perhaps by having him construct things with wood and glue.

"When I discussed this possibility with one of the authors, she told me that it was imperative for José to feel a sense of mastery in the reading itself. If he could learn to read despite his previous failures, he could gain confidence and satisfaction. We thought of several alternatives: Perhaps he could learn street signs such as *Walk, Don't Walk, Danger*, and *Columbus Avenue*. Or he might be able to read simplified preprimers in which a minimum number of words were introduced gradually. This would emphasize the visual approach and would give José a chance to understand what he read in contrast to sounding out words from which he derived no meaning. (Phonics could be reintroduced much later, after he had a solid beginning.)

"If I had had more time, José might have profited from ancillary measures such as cutting, pasting, and woodworking and at the same time have expanded his language acquisition. But important as this is, it would not have directly touched his sense of learning to read.

"Accordingly, I introduced the Detroit Reading Series, and José did begin to read. This series uses a sight approach. It is simple visually and conceptually. There is little printed material on a page, and the pictures are extremely simple. The vocabulary is controlled and limited and introduced very slowly. There is a reassuring aspect to this series, due to its pace, consistency, and vocabulary repetitions.

"Because José learns so slowly, all words had to be reinforced with many techniques. For example, I found pictures from magazines which illustrated the words (such as *cat, read, run*). He matched the words on index cards with the illustrations or wrote the appropriate word under the illustration. I made little books for him; he wrote little books himself. He wrote a great deal and he dictated to me. We used the words in many ways. I tried to introduce varied activities which would reinforce the words in visual, auditory, and kinesthetic ways.

"In retrospect, it seems to me that the first advance occurred when José could communicate feelings orally (we talked to each other). Second came his understanding that print carries meaning (I wrote down his ideas and stories). Finally came his ability to recognize and read and write words himself. With this last step came a tremendous sense of pride and desire to improve further.

"The sessions then essentially followed this pattern: (1) José read aloud from the series; (2) I wrote new words on cards for him to learn; (3) I dictated some words and sentences which he wrote; (4) he made up sentences and wrote them; and (5) we drew or wrote stories or I read to him.

"After we finished the Detroit series, he was unable to go to a higher level. I had to find books on the same level. He read *Who Can, Get Set,* and *Outdoors and In.*[7] He was able to read (with me) some fiction: *Go, Dog, Go,*[8] *Are You My Mother?,*[9] and *Who Took the Farmer's Hat?*[10]

"Our work did not consist of stressing phonics or drilling names of letters. It dealt with the communication of experience and expression of feelings. Once José had talked to me about things in his life which mattered to him, he began to read; once he began to read his concentration increased. Previously his responses were automatic; any answer was better than none. Now he can read for as long as 30 minutes. His physical manner has changed. He seems more confident, more energetic, more in control of himself. He has gained self-esteem.

"Of course, his deficits are still glaring. His sight vocabulary is limited and it is difficult for him to learn new words. His language problems are still significant and profound. He is often difficult to understand. He still doesn't have basic information like the names of the days of the week. He cannot even give the names of most letters. But he can read, and of that achievement he is very proud. He enjoys reading to people and will take his pile of word cards and read to whoever will listen. He is attentive and cooperative and eager to achieve. He loves to be read to.

7. K. Choi, ed., *Who Can* (New York: Macmillan, 1975); O'Donnell, *Outdoors and In* (New York: Harper & Row, 1967); C. Fries et al., *Get Set,* book 4, of New Merrill Linguistic Reading Program (Columbus, Ohio: Charles E. Merrill, 1974).

8. P. D. Eastman, *Go, Dog, Go* (Westminster, Md.: Beginner Books, Division of Random House, 1961).

9. P. D. Eastman, *Are You My Mother?* (Westminster, Md.: Beginner Books, Division of Random House, 1960).

10. J. L. Nodset, *Who Took the Farmer's Hat?* (New York: Harper & Row, 1963).

He is beginning to hear initial consonant sounds and said two weeks ago, looking at 'run' and 'read': 'They start the same.' He is now developing auditory skills and it seems to me that he is ready for a systematic approach to reading.

"In spite of his hyperactivity and his massive emotional and environmental disadvantages, José has been reached and he has begun to read."

Randy—Reading at Preprimer Level in Second Grade

Randy's problem was different from José's but almost as severe. He did not seem able to remember most sight words despite his being well into second grade. He got the idea that he had "no memory." Randy was examined by one of the authors, who also served as consultant. Treatment was carried out by a reading specialist in collaboration with his classroom teacher.

Randy's problem was not as severe as that of José. Randy could read a simple preprimer, but his ability to learn was markedly impeded by his conviction that he had a severe memory problem. His recurrent comments during the testing session were, "I don't know; I can't remember." In a very amiable way he conveyed a feeling of helplessness, almost as if by engaging the examiner's sympathy she might not expect too much of him, nor push him too hard. Yet, his intelligence was about average with his highest scores on tests involving memory for digits and memorization of new symbols. On the other hand, his fund of information was very low. He did not know how many pennies there were in a nickel or the number of days in the week, and he could not even name the day of the week on which he was tested.

There was no doubt that this child's learning problem needed a many-sided approach. It seemed important first for Randy to find out that he could learn and retain what he had been taught. This was accomplished during trial learning periods at each of the testing sessions where there was careful control of the level and amount of material introduced.

For example, he was given a simple preprimer containing only 11 words, in addition to names of characters. These words were presented gradually emphasizing the special features of each word. Whenever proper names proved troublesome, they were supplied. Soon Randy began to recognize that he could read and remember the words taught. Even though there were only a few words on a page, Randy reacted with a sense of achievement as he read page after page successfully. He was encouraged to apply any meaningful clues, such as letter sounds, visual impressions, or tactile-kinesthetic senses that could facilitate recall. By the third session he was able to handle a second preprimer which included those words in the first preprimer plus a limited number of new ones. As the trial lessons proceeded, explanations were given to Randy regarding how the various methods used could help him retain what he learned. Much to Randy's satisfaction, he found that he could remember.

At the conclusion of the examination, a conference was held with both his classroom and special reading teachers. It was apparent that even though they were using suitable materials at an appropriate level, they were bombarding this child with too many workbooks and too large a vocabulary load. Therefore, they were advised to introduce new words and materials very gradually and wait until previous work had been mastered so that Randy could develop a sense of having grasped what he had been taught. Both teachers were asked to coordinate their programs and to ensure that expectations were being kept within their proper scope.

The last recommendation was made to the parents. Because of Randy's striking deficiency in his fund of knowledge and lack of awareness of what was going on around him, it was suggested that his parents keep bringing everyday events into sharp focus and call his attention to aspects of time and space such as the days of the week, the months of the year, and special features of places they visit. In other words, they should attempt to fill the gaps in his experiences and information in order to bring them more in line with those of children his age.

Follow-up after several months disclosed that Randy had made decided progress and never mentioned his faulty memory. In a short period of time he had mastered the Dolch Basic Sight Vocabulary and was handling a high first grade reader. His teachers reported that they have worked together to carry out the suggested program. For example, to help Randy build up a sight vocabulary, they presented only a few words at a time in easy-paced steps as follows: (1) child matched words so as to sharpen his perception of similarities and differences in word forms; (2) teacher named words and child identified them; (3) child read words; (4) child wrote selected words and simple sentences from dictation; and (5) teacher presented words in different sizes, colors, and types because of the difficulty some children have in shifting from one format to another. Thus, the gradual stages of teaching word recognition apparently helped Randy grasp and recall what was taught.

In addition, his teachers emphasized the learning of such information as Randy's address, telephone number, and birth date; also the names of the days of the week and concepts such as *before* and *after*. For connected reading, both storybooks and linguistic readers proved suitable. Games were used mostly for reinforcement of sight vocabulary.

Because of the satisfactory progress that Randy made, his parents and teachers asked about the poor memory with which everyone had been so concerned. Apparently Randy initially had somewhat of a problem learning to read because of some lag in maturational development. When instruction was offered at a pace too fast for him, he stated that he could not remember. His parents and teachers attributed his difficulties to a severe memory deficit.[11] This led Randy to retreat into a state where he felt justified in not learning.

This case illustrates one of the many negative adaptations that failing children can unconsciously develop, as well as the risks inherent in teachers' and parents' accepting a particular label without further investigation of its solidity. Fortunately, Randy's problem was recognized early and appropriate remedial measures rectified his rationalizations for not learning.

The Phonic Method

The learning of sight words must be taught concurrently or supplemented as soon as possible with phonics so that the child gains greater independence in word analysis. This knowledge is then used immediately in sentences and reading matter. Many children with reading disability, however, have difficulty in blending sounds together to form whole words. In most cases, this difficulty is overcome at about nine years of age, at which time a systematic phonic approach may be used. In rare cases the child is 10 or 11 or older before he can synthesize sounds together. If, despite all the teacher's ingenuity, the child is still unsuccessful with the phonic method, it must be discontinued and the alternate methods discussed in this chapter used until such time as the child is able to profit from phonic instruction. However, the teacher does not merely wait without trying to demonstrate from time to time how sounds can be combined to form words. Sometimes a little assistance in this direction can help the child use the procedure. For instance, the teacher might

11. For further discussion of memory factors see R. Klatsky, *Human Memory* (San Francisco: W. H. Freeman, 1975).

encourage him to fit sounds together the way links of a chain are combined. Also, she can pronounce the separate sounds simultaneously with him to help capture the sensation. This procedure is known as choral blending.

In the phonics procedure the pupil first learns the sounds of the letters, then how to substitute initial consonants in known words in order to figure out new ones, and finally how to blend separate sounds together in words. When using the phonic method with reading disability cases, the teacher must remember that most of these children have been exposed to similar procedures many times before. Therefore, she seeks to minimize embarrassment by choosing material and techniques suitable for older pupils.

Teaching Sounds of Consonants and Consonant Blends. The teacher introduces the selected sounds by presenting them in upper and lower case with pictures whose content is mature in format. Some children can learn as many as four or five sounds in a single lesson. The consonants listed below have suggestions for illustrations that the writers have found appropriate.

s—sun	b—button
d—door	l—ladder
m—matches	n—nest
t—television	w—window
h—house	j—jacks
p—pencil	k—key
f—fish	v—violin
c—cake	y—yellow
g—gate	z—zebra
r—radio	

The teacher should have the children name each object pictured to avoid possible confusion—for example, "fence" for "gate," or "boat" for "ship."

When teaching several sounds in succession, the teacher is careful to use those which differ markedly in appearance and sound. (For example, *b* and *d* are easily reversed and hence confusing.) The order in which the letters are listed on page 120 follows this principle, but the teacher always chooses the order most suitable to her pupils' needs.[12]

12. For the letters *g* and *c*, the hard sounds are introduced first (*g* as in *good, c* as in *cup*.) The soft sounds (*g* as in *gem, c* as in *circle*) are best delayed until later as they occur less frequently. The letters *q* and *x* have not been listed because they do not have single sounds (*q* in words is always followed by *u*, sounding as *kw*; *x* usually sounds like *ks*). Pupils are less confused if they are taught these sounds when they meet them during their reading.

Auditory Discrimination

The children are told the name and sound of one letter at a time. Vivid associations are given wherever possible. In teaching *h*, for example, the teacher might say, "You can make steam on a window pane or mirror when you go 'hhhhh.' "[13] The children listen to words beginning with *h* and then are asked to distinguish a word that begins with a different letter sound. The teacher shows them a picture of a house with *h* printed in upper and lower case alongside it. At the same time the children pronounce the name of the letter and its sound. The teacher then pronounces other words that begin with *h*, such as *hat, hit, hose*, asking the children to listen carefully to the beginning sound. She then asks them to volunteer additional words beginning with the same sound. (They often have difficulty thinking of examples.) The teacher might then ask riddles:

Here are some riddles that give you hints of the words that I am thinking of that begin with *hhhh*.

1. You have two of them. You use one to write with. (hand)
2. You climb it. (hill)
3. In the summer it is sometimes very (hot).
4. You do it when you go up and down on one foot. (hop)

The teacher might develop the children's auditory discrimination further by pronouncing groups of four words, three of which begin with *h*

1.	hat	hit	miss	hope
2.	fake	hose	here	him
3.	have	card	help	hero
4.	hot	hall	head	bear

The children are asked to listen carefully as she says the words and to indicate the one that does not begin with the sound being taught by clapping or raising their hands. The teacher does not go on to a new group of four words until the children have identified the word that begins differently. This is continued until sufficient auditory discrimination has been attained. Other letters are then taught in the same way. Where children learn letter sounds easily, the teacher can dispense with training in auditory discrimination.

13. The authors have found it effective with reading disability cases to isolate the sound at the beginning. Of course, extraneous vowel sounds at the end of a consonant, such as *huh* for *h*, should be avoided.

Treatment

When the children have learned several consonants and one short vowel sound, they are shown how to blend them together into words. The picture clues for the separate sounds are left in evidence for ready reference as long as necessary.

Consonant blends are taught in the same way as single consonants. The teacher points out how two consonants already learned are combined to form blends. There is no need to dwell on teaching a large number of blends because many of them tend to fall into similar patterns such as *tr, gr, br*. However, the consonant digraphs which represent a single sound do have to be taught as entirely new sounds, such as *sh* and *ch*. *Th* has two sounds: *th* (as in *thimble*) and *th* (as in *those*). Many games for learning consonants and consonant blends are listed in Appendix C.

Rudimentary Blending of Sounds

If the child can grasp a visual procedure readily and shows some knowledge of letter sounds, a rudimentary phonics, or "word-family," method may be tried. This technique of word analysis is especially useful for children who are not yet able to blend sounds letter by letter. However, it affords only limited independence in word analysis. This approach consists of changing a known word into many new words by substituting for the first letter other letters whose sounds are being taught or reviewed. Thus the known word *cold* is changed to *gold, hold, sold*, and so forth.

A variation of this method is to substitute the same initial consonant in several words that the pupils already recognize, thus changing them to entirely different words. For example, if the pupil knows the words *sat, fill, Sam, like*, and *day*, the teacher tells him to read the list aloud substituting the letter *h* for the initial consonant in each word and to pronounce the new word that has been formed. (The words in which the substitution is made must be chosen carefully, so that the pupil has only the new sound to deal with and need not struggle with anything additional.)

Practice in word families is presented to children in context instead of isolated lists wherever possible. For instance, the child is shown how he can extend his sight vocabulary as he reads by noting similarities in words and applying his knowledge of sounds accordingly. That is, if the pupil comes across the word *hike* in his reading he is encouraged to figure it out from those elements which he knows—the sight word *like* and the sound of *h*.

Teaching Vowel Sounds

Vowel sounds are taught in the same way as consonant sounds, but they are much more difficult to distinguish and hence usually take longer for the pupils to master. Although there are many different sounds for each vowel (dictionaries may list six or more separate sounds for *a*), only the short and long sounds are taught at the outset to children with reading disability. The authors recommend that the short vowel sound be taught first because words of one syllable, as *tag, mat,* and so on, are readily sounded out and written from dictation. As the pupils' mastery of reading and writing increases, diphthongs and other vowel combinations are taught. The pupils can begin to draw their own generalizations as they go along, from their growing familiarity with the construction of words.

In learning the vowel sounds, many children have considerable difficulty distinguishing between the short sounds of *a* and *e*. Therefore, it is advisable to postpone teaching the short *e* until the other vowels are learned. Whatever sequence is followed, however, vowel sounds are presented one at a time, interspersed among the teaching of consonants. All the while the sounds are used in words, sentences, and stories. As for *y*, the children learn that sometimes it is a vowel, sometimes a consonant. Its use as a vowel is given little emphasis; instead, the children discover its function in connection with words that they encounter in reading.

The vowels might be illustrated by the following words:

Aa	Ii	Oo	Uu	Ee
Apple	Indian	Octopus	Umbrella	Elephant

Auditory Discrimination of Short Vowel Sounds. In introducing vowels for the first time, the teacher shows the children the five vowels and explains that every word in the English language has at least one vowel in it. They might next be challenged to suggest a word without a vowel. The teacher then presents the vowel sound. The procedure is similar to that of consonants except that only one vowel is taught at a time. (As already stated, it may be taught simultaneously with four or five consonants in one lesson.)

For example, the teacher presents the letter *a* and says, "This is *a*, and the sound is ă as in *apple*." The use of an accompanying picture may serve as a cue for remembering the sound. The children learn to hear it at the beginning of other words (*absent, answer, after*). Then they listen to groups of words, one of which has a different sound at the beginning (*act, ill, am, add*) and try to distinguish the one word in the group that begins differently. After the pupils have distinguished the sounds satisfactorily, one-syllable words are presented with the short *a* in the middle (*fat, can, lap, pat*). Then one word in each group is changed to a different medial sound, and the pupils indicate the word that does not have the ă sound in the middle (*fan, but, tag, had*).

After the pupil has learned the short vowel sounds and has shown ability to apply them in figuring out consonant-vowel-consonant words, the long vowel sounds are taught. This is discussed on pages 136–137

Blending Separate Sounds. To determine whether blending sounds can be used successfully with children who have reading disability, an informal test of auditory blending is given. The teacher pronounces a word—*set*, for example—first quickly, then slowly, *s-e-t*. Similarly, the word *fat* is pronounced naturally and then slowly as *f-a-t*. The pupils are then asked to identify other words that are said only slowly (*s-i-t, p-e-t, t-o-p*). If they can learn to recognize words from hearing the separate sounds, the phonic approach can be introduced. It should be remembered, however, that these children often need encouragement and help in understanding what they are expected to do.

In introducing blending, the pupils are shown several letters that they have learned. For example, the consonant sounds of *s, d, m, t, h,* and *p* are reviewed along with the short vowel sound of *a*. The letters might be printed on the chalkboard, or on a sheet of paper, or selected from a set of lowercase letter cards.

A word such as *hat* is printed for the child. The teacher illustrates how the separate sounds *h-a-t* may be blended together to form the word *hat*. She gives as much assistance as necessary in helping the child synthesize the individual sounds into a whole word. She then illustrates how *hat* may be changed to *mat, sat, pat* in word families as described in rudimentary blending. This makes the introduction to synthesizing separate sounds fairly easy. The next step, which involves substituting final consonants, is much more difficult for children to learn, such as changing *hat* to *had*, *mat* to *map*. The hardest step of all is reading words in mixed order, as *sap, pan, had, mat*. Frequently much practice is needed before children master the last two steps. To reinforce learning of letters and their associated sounds, the teacher may dictate words which the children sound out and write simultaneously.

Dictation. The dictation of simple phonically regular words can help the pupils connect letters with the corresponding sounds. This usually helps their reading as well as their spelling ability. The teacher dictates word families first since they are easier. If the pupils know the consonants *h, t, n, f, l, d,* and *s* and vowels *i* and *a,* for example, the teacher dictates *fit, hit, lit, and sit;* then *sin, tin, fin;* and finally *fat, hat, sat, tan,* and *fan.* During the next stage, she dictates the words in mixed order: *lit, tin, sit,* and *fin.* Later still, she might try more difficult dictation such as *fin, fan, sat, had, lit,* and so on, interchanging initial and final consonants and middle vowels. The pace, of course, depends on the pupils' progress.

Further Practice with Blending. The teacher presents additional vowel sounds as soon as she considers the pupils ready. The children read words containing the added vowel. Sufficient practice is given throughout so that when all the consonants and vowels are learned, the children can write or sound out accurately any phonically regular words in whatever order they appear as: *pet, map, hid, rug,* and *job.*

In presenting phonics exercises, the teacher avoids using nonsense syllables and words which children rarely meet. Exercises are not used merely as isolated drills, but are applied immediately in sentences, poems, limericks, or stories. A collection of poems and limericks may be gradually developed as the teacher comes across them in books and anthologies of children's literature. Words of some folk songs and certain stories which have rhyming in them, such as those by Dr. Seuss, may provide additional sources for practice. Phonics exercises are presented systematically at each session, but the presentation remains brief lest the children become resistant or satiated.

Teaching Long Vowel Sounds. Once short vowels have been mastered, the sounds of the long vowels are introduced. These are simple to learn since the long sounds just make the vowels "say their names." Nevertheless, the rules governing their usage are more complex and depend to a large extent on knowledge of the short vowel sounds. It is unnecessary to go through auditory discrimination training as described with regard to short vowels. Long vowels are taught in connection with the two major rules governing their use.

Rule of the Silent e. In one-syllable words ending in a consonant with the vowel in the middle, the vowel is usually short—e.g., *mat, bit, cut.* However, when *e* comes at the end of such a word, it can make the first vowel say its own name. The pupils are then shown familiar words that change vowel sounds because of the silent *e*—for example, *can, hid,* and *mat,* which change to *cane, hide,* and *mate,* respectively. The children should be encouraged to formulate the rule for themselves.

Rule of the Double Vowel. When two vowels come together in a word, the first one is usually long and the second one silent, as in *paid*, *coat*, and *seat*. It is always good practice to present words and encourage the children to figure out the rule for themselves. A rule stated in their own words is frequently more meaningful. However, children should be told the rule if they do not see it for themselves. The important point is that they understand how it works and how to use it.

Diphthongs. It is usually sufficient for children with reading disability to be taught the short and long sounds of the single vowels. However, if pupils have difficulty with vowel combinations, these must be taught as well. Vowel variations are taught in the same way as are single vowel sounds. The teacher need not waste time teaching rare combinations. The most common diphthongs are listed below.

$\overline{oo}$ as in *moon*	*ay* as in *say*	*ow* as in *how*
$\breve{oo}$ as in *good*	*y* as in *my*	$\overline{ow}$ as in *slow*
oi as in *spoil*		*au* as in *fault*
		aw as in *saw*

Workbooks and games help to lighten the tedium in learning phonics and can be a supplementary device for practice. As already stated, phonics must be applied and used in reading as much as possible after any isolated practice is completed. A complete listing of phonics games with sources will be found in Appendix C.

In teaching phonics to children with reading problems we must be careful not to overemphasize its applicability to reading as it is only one of several approaches needed to develop competence in reading. The following case of Neil shows how he used the letter sounds he had learned but applied them indiscriminately. Here is the way one of the authors handled him:

Neil—Reading at Second Grade Level in Third Grade

Neil, an alert, articulate boy with red, curly hair, came for testing toward the end of second grade because he was among the poorest readers in his class. He was keenly aware of his low status, because his classmates ridiculed him constantly and called him "stupid." He was socially at ease, spontaneous, and keen during the administration of the intelligence tests.

However, his demeanor changed perceptibly when he encountered items on reading tests with which he could not cope. At such times, his profound discouragement and anxiety were paramount.

Neil's developmental history was reported to be entirely normal, so that there was little in his background that could throw light on the reasons for his reading problem. Yet, test results showed a marked discrepancy between his functioning in reading and his superior intellectual level on the WISC. Reading scores were as follows:

	Grade Scores	Percentile Scores for End of Grade 2
Gray Oral Reading Test	2.3	
Metropolitan Primary II		
Word Knowledge	2.3	22
Reading	1.7	11

The *Roswell-Chall Diagnostic Reading Test* showed a fairly good grasp of basic phonic skills.

Neil did particularly poorly on both the sentence and paragraph reading portions of the Metropolitan test because of his limited sight vocabulary. When left to his own devices, he used a phonic approach for all unfamiliar words. Thus, both phonically regular and irregular words were handled the same way. This led to enormous frustration when the sounds did not correspond to their visual symbols.

The examination covered three one-hour sessions.[11] Part of each visit was devoted to working with Neil in a typical learning situation where methods and materials were presented that he could handle with a fair degree of success as described in Chapter 6, in the section "Trial Lessons as a Diagnostic Technique." During these periods, Neil's spirits lifted considerably. He was interested in the interpretation of findings where his needs were pointed out to him and where methods that would be suitable for helping him cope with his various areas of deficiencies were discussed.

In this connection, he was told, "You're a very bright boy, but like many others, you have some problems with reading. You know your consonant and vowel sounds, and you can usually put them together to form words, although sometimes you don't do it when you read parts of

14. Diagnostician and reading specialist for Neil was one of the authors.

words like *c-at-ch* and *m-us-t*, and then stop without making whole words out of them. You also try to sound out all words you don't know and frequently this doesn't work, because some words, called 'sight words,' have to be learned by looking at them and remembering them." Then it was explained how we would use the *Dolch Picture-Word Cards* and the *Dolch Basic Sight Vocabulary*, among other materials, for this purpose. Typical stories that would be presented were shown to him so that he got some idea of procedures and materials that would be used to help him overcome his reading problem. In this way, his problem was concretized for him, thereby lessening his feeling of having vague, overwhelming difficulties which he could hardly grasp.

At the conclusion of the examination, Neil initiated a request that he be tutored by the author and seemed most eager to get started.

Accordingly, we got off to a good beginning. At the outset, something had to be done to discourage Neil's overuse and misapplication of the phonic method. Therefore, emphasis was placed on the development of rapid recognition of many commonly used words. Games and other materials were used along with a considerable amount of story reading, starting with a simple second grade reader. However, games were employed judiciously to avoid the impression that the purpose of the sessions was merely for fun.

Neil was so enchanted with the folk tales and other stories he was reading that he begged to be permitted to take books home for supplementary reading. Borrowing materials for home use was at this child's request. The writer rarely makes home assignments because this can be counterproductive, whereas self-initiated activity is conducive to growth. Because of the wide amount of recreational reading which Neil did, his competency improved to the point where it was possible to introduce silent reading exercises in various workbooks at third grade level. New vocabulary was presented and concepts that were likely to be unfamiliar were discussed.

Occasionally Neil's anxiety became apparent when tasks appeared challenging and fear of failure loomed. He frequently remarked, "That's too hard," during the earlier sessions. Thus, the writer was constantly alert to this child's frustration tolerance and his resistance to difficult materials. At such times, he was assured that assistance would be forthcoming if necessary. It was further pointed out that dealing with unknown factors is how one learns, and that not knowing an answer was not to be considered as a failure but part of a process of exploring something new. This led Neil to feel free to try to handle questions without concern as to the number of right or wrong answers. In this type of trusting relationship where the writer showed confidence in Neil's basic capacities and he showed faith in her professional ability to teach, he progressed extremely well.

After 40 sessions, work was discontinued. Comparable test scores were as follows:

	May	December
Gray Oral Reading Test	2.3	4.4
Metropolitan Achievement Tests	*Primary II* (for grade 2)	*Elementary* *(for grades 3 & 4)*
Word Knowledge	2.3	5.0
Reading	1.7	3.9

These satisfactory changes within a few months were probably due to the interaction of many factors, all of which were important. The constructive relationship between instructor and child was of paramount significance. The well-planned sessions with a definite structure promoted learning and lessened Neil's wish to control the situation by requesting only the activities which he preferred. He frequently asked for games or frowned when given work materials. Nevertheless, he responded well to the limits that were set, especially since there was a balance during the session between materials that were highly appealing and those that demanded concentrated, independent effort. His need for structure and gentle firmness were observed by his classroom teacher as well. Our coordinated efforts helped the boy cope with his feelings of inadequacy so that he was able to try challenging assignments without complaining.

From the very beginning, Neil was helped to overcome his tendency to rely solely on a sound-blending method. Other strategies were stressed, such as acquisition of a sight vocabulary, use of large units within words, and finding of words through context. At the outset he read books containing folk and fairy tales at low second grade level. By degrees, he progressed to high second, third, and then fourth grade levels with materials always carefully chosen for their high interest value. Silent reading exercises in workbooks at third and fourth grade levels promoted independent work at the same time that they increased his word recognition ability, broadened his vocabulary, and provided subject matter similar to that found in textbooks at school. At each session, spelling was introduced in connection with simple tasks involving expressive writing.

Treatment

As implied throughout this account, the atmosphere during the sessions was informal and friendly, but basic concern for this child's need to function in a mature, effective manner precluded the prolonged use of games. Thus, they were introduced first for motivational purposes, but their use was decreased gradually and then discontinued in order to place the major emphasis on oral and silent reading. The reasons were twofold. First, there is little carry-over from isolated words presented in games, and second, the main goal is to encourage independence in handling meaningful activities. Many children with reading disabilities are immature and not at all task oriented. Therefore, the overuse of games and other game-type devices only prolongs the period of dependency and are of questionable effectiveness in instruction. Instead, we believe that the inner satisfaction that a child derives from accomplishment and enjoyment in reading books is a more powerful and significant incentive.

Additional Word-Analysis Skills

Structural Analysis. Structural analysis, according to Gray,[15] is ". . . the means by which we identify the parts of a word which form meaning units or pronouncing units within a word." It therefore supplements the methods described previously in this chapter and includes the teaching of such word endings as plurals, compound words, syllabication, and roots, prefixes, and suffixes.

Word Endings. For children with reading disability, it is generally sufficient to point out the various changes of words; overemphasis should be avoided; time should not be spent on endings that occur rarely. The children are shown the base word and add several endings to see how the word changes. The most common endings are *s, ed, ing, er, est, y,* and *ly.*[16]

Compound Words. Compound words are fairly easy for children with reading disability to master. In most cases they need only be shown that some words are made up of two separate words, as *up stairs, blue bird, pea nut.*[17]

---

15. W. Gray, *On Their Own in Reading* (Chicago: Scott, Foresman, 1948), p. 76.

16. Once in a while children become confused because *ed* sometimes sounds like *t* as in *liked,* at other times like *ed* as in *parted,* and at others like *d* as in *roared.* If the pupil does not grasp the sound from reading the word in context, the teacher must take time to explain the differences.

17. Authorities sometimes recommend that the child "find little words in big words." If this technique is used, it is advisable to conduct it orally because finding the short word can actually hinder recognition. For example, focusing on *get* in *together* or *cat* in *locate* is very confusing.

Syllabication. Stressing too many rules of syllabication can diminish rather than promote reading fluency. Pupils need to know how to divide words into identifiable small units. De-emphasis on rules is advisable. Syllables are presented most effectively at first by exaggerating the pronunciation of words so that the separate syllables are easily distinguished. Until the pupils learn to recognize the number of syllables in a word and understand that each syllable always contains one vowel sound, they cannot determine how to divide words into syllables. Oral work must be undertaken with the teacher until it is established that the children know where the separations come.

Root Words, Prefixes, and Suffixes. Knowing that certain base words can be combined with prefixes and suffixes may be an aid to word recognition. However, for the child with reading disability, this concept must be simplified in order to eliminate confusion.

In teaching base words and suffixes, the teacher might point out that whenever a standard ending appears in a word, a suffix has been added. She then shows the pupils how to distinguish between the root and the suffix, as in *jump-ing, fast-er, quick-ly.* Prefixes are taught in the same way. The base words used in teaching should be complete in themselves. For example, pupils quickly grasp that the prefix *dis* (meaning *not*) placed before the word *believe* results in *disbelieve,* and its changed meaning is clear. Obviously it would be confusing to use such words as *disdain* and *revoke,* for which there is no independent base word in English. Finally, the relationship between the prefix, the root word, and the suffix is demonstrated, as in *re-wind-ing, re-work-ing,* and so on. From their knowledge of the base words, the pupils may be able to discover that *re* means *again,* and so on.

The suffixes and prefixes that are taught should be chosen on the basis of consistency of meaning and frequency of occurrence. The following prefixes fulfill these criteria:

> com   dis   ex   pre   re   sub

We suggest the following suffixes, using these same criteria:

> tion   ment   ful   less

As the foregoing discussion implies, extensive practice with root words, prefixes, and suffixes is more suitable for pupils at upper levels. Further discussion of methods for older pupils is presented in Chapter 12.

Linguistic Methods. Some children who do not learn easily through the sight-word, phonic, or other methods sometimes profit from linguistic approaches as an introductory measure. The consistency of the word structure helps them experience success and they can then transfer to regular readers when they are ready.

Certain linguistic approaches resemble phonic procedures in that they introduce words which follow regular spelling patterns.[18] However, according to the linguistic methods referred to here, the children are expected to discover the sound-spelling relationships and are therefore not given instruction in separate sounds of letters and are never taught sounds in isolation.

According to the teacher's handbook in one series, the teacher writes a word on the board, reads it aloud, and has the children repeat it. She then writes other words illustrating the same pattern directly below the first such as *man, Dan, ran*. Pupils are asked to spell and then read each word as it is added to the list. These words are subsequently incorporated into sentences such as: *The man ran. Dan ran. I ran.* The presentation of the spelling patterns is controlled so that the most regular correspondences are introduced first. The child progresses gradually from simple to complex patterns. However, there is no uniform agreement among linguists as to whether the direct teaching of sounds should be omitted from beginning instruction; there are also other differences pertaining to methodology. Therefore, those who wish to employ these methods need to refer to the original sources from which the programs have been derived and also follow carefully the instructions in the teacher's handbook accompanying the particular linguistic readers.[19] A word of caution: Most children need only limited practice when they use such specialized books. They should be transferred as soon as possible to regular readers.

Dictionary Skills. Children benefit from learning to use a dictionary efficiently for pronunciations, meanings, and word usage. Dictionaries are now available at all levels, starting with the very easiest picture dictionaries and ranging on up through various levels. The teacher gives practice in any skills the pupils lack, such as finding entries, identifying word meanings, and using the pronunciation system. Among the excellent simple dictionaries are *The Dictionary for Children* published by Macmillan, *The Thorndike-Barnhart Beginning Dictionary* and the *Thorndike-Barnhart Junior Dictionary*, both published by Scott–Foreman and *Scholastic Dictionary of American English* published by Scholastic. They

18. R. Emans, "Linguistics and Phonics," *The Reading Teacher*, February 1973.
19. Linguistic readers include the following: C. Fries, *Merrill Linguistic Readers* (Columbus, Ohio: Charles E. Merrill, 1966); D. Rasmussen, and L. Goldberg, *SRA Linguistic Readers* (Chicago: Science Research Associates, 1972); Robinette et al., *Miami Linguistic Readers* (Lexington, Mass.: Heath, 1970); Williams et al., *Linguistic Readers* (Beverly Hills, Calif.: Benziger, 1971).

all include instructions for their use. Guides and workbooks for the teaching of dictionary skills are available from the various publishers. Exercises are incorporated in most of the workbooks that accompany basal readers.

Context. Usually children with reading disability have previously learned how to figure out a word from context. Too often, time that might profitably be spent on foundation skills is wasted on teaching the use of context. Many children, in fact, overemphasize the skill, with the result that they tend to rely on indiscriminate guessing. Their eyes flit back and forth from the word to the picture; they use the initial consonant, general configuration, or other means to help them. For example, if the child does not know the last word in the sentence "The book is on the *table*" the teacher might suggest that he look at the picture and the initial consonant to guess the word. If the picture is clear, the child is likely to guess correctly. Many times, however, the illustration is ambiguous, and if the child continues to rely on this means, his guessing may become wild and his reading more inaccurate than ever. If children are not familiar with the use of context, merely pointing out that words can sometimes be ascertained from the rest of the sentence or other clues is usually sufficient.[20]

Overcoming Reversal Errors and Inaccuracy in Reading. The group of skills described in this chapter constitute the minimal word-analysis techniques that are needed by reading disability cases. There are certain special problems, however, that frequently occur in children with reading disability. They may tend to reverse letters, words, or phrases. They may add, omit, or substitute words when reading a paragraph aloud. They often phrase poorly and have little expression in their oral reading.

Reversing such letters as *d* and *b*, *p* and *q*, is common in children with reading problems. In the first instance, it is sometimes helpful to show the pupil that he can change small *b* to capital *B* by adding another loop in the same direction.

Another technique has also been found useful. Children never reverse the *d* or *b* in cursive writing. Therefore, when they are puzzled as to which letter a word begins with, they might be told to trace the letter with their forefingers. A cursive letter *d* can be traced over a printed *d*, since it "goes" in the same direction. The same thing can be accomplished with the letter *b*.

20. Y. Goodman, "Longitudinal Study of Children's Oral Reading Behavior," *U.S. Dept. of Health, Education and Welfare, Office of Education*, Project #9–E–062 (Washington, D.C.: 1971).

With the letter *q*, it can be pointed out that *q* is always found with *u*.

Reversing letters in such words as *was* (*saw*) is also common. Sounding the first letter of the word should act as a correct clue for the whole word. For example, sounding *n* at the beginning of the word *no* should help to distinguish it from *on*.

A large arrow drawn at the top of the page may remind the children to read words and sentences from left to right.

Placing a zipper over a line of print and letting the child open it from left to right is another useful method. Young children especially enjoy unzipping it and seeing the letter or word appear.

Beyond these simple devices, the occurrence of reversals can be lessened by practice in reading and strengthening of all word recognition techniques.

Finally, two additional characteristics of children with reading disability—inaccuracy and lack of fluency in oral reading—may become habitual patterns of performance because of the insecurity and anxiety inherent in the situation. Developing rapport with a competent teacher, improvement in word recognition, and experience in reading suitable material usually alleviate these difficulties. (The case of Tina later in this chapter illustrates these points.)

Encouraging the Use of Word-Analysis Skills

The skills outlined in this chapter can be incorporated in regular class work, as is described in Chapter 9. The teacher's relationship with pupils who have reading difficulty is of the utmost importance. Spending even a short time with an individual or small group can make an enormous difference in their progress. According to a study made by the New York City Board of Education, "Even five minutes a day of . . . individual contact which engrossed the child's real attention was worth much more to him than one-half hour a day in a group reading situation which merely tapped his surface attention. Moreover, the teacher's concern and efforts in his behalf seemed to convince the child that she understood his difficulties and meant to help him."[21] Children with disability need the satisfaction of being singled out as individuals in positive ways, since too often they have been singled out only for ridicule or reprimanding.

21. New York City Board of Education, *Teaching Guides: Language Arts*, No. 2 (New York: Board of Education of the City of New York, 1955); reprinted in G. Natchez, *Reading Disability: Diagnosis and Treatment*, 2nd ed. (New York: Basic Books, 1971), p. 102.

Spelling

Most children with reading disability have even more trouble with spelling than with word analysis. Teaching spelling along with the teach- of letter sounds acts as an effective reinforcement for using phonics.

Before beginning instruction with children who have spelling disability, the teacher administers a standardized spelling test. Spelling subtests are included in most standardized achievement batteries. Some of these are listed in Appendix A.

The basis of spelling is the knowledge of sounds. Pupils must be aware of the connection between hearing a sound and reproducing it accurately in writing. In teaching spelling by the phonic method, for example, the instructor points out the connection between sounds and visual symbols. For irregularly spelled words, the visual-motor method can be tried. However, many children with spelling problems have difficulty recalling words visually but can remember them by means of kinesthetic clues. Furthermore, any approaches that draw special attention to spelling patterns or to roots or parts of words can also be helpful. For example, once a child learns *could*, he can be shown the resemblance to *would* and *should*. The student who wrote *mudgarity* for *majority* had no further trouble after he was shown that it was related to the word *major*. Pointing out that the word *science* is imbedded in *conscience* had a similar effect. In addition, many students need to be reminded of the correct pronunciation of words as *government*, *probably*, and *environment* to eliminate common spelling errors. Still another approach which students at all ages have found helpful is keeping their own special alphabetized lists of words that they have repeatedly misspelled in order to refer to them when needed. Then too, there are published lists of words most frequently misspelled by children in various grades, as well as spellers which facilitate studying particular words.[22]

Such lists are much easier for children with reading disability than looking words up in the dictionary, for they contain far fewer words and

22. J. Mersand and F. Griffith, *Spelling Your Way to Success* (Woodbury, N.Y.: Barron's Educational Series, 1974).

B. Gallagher and J. Colvin, *Words Most Often Misspelled and Mispronounced* (New York: Pocket Books, 1972).

V. Thomas, *Teaching Spelling* (Canada: University of Calgary, Gage Publishers, 1974).

D. Simon and H. Simon, "Alternative Uses of Phonemic Information in Spelling," *Review of Educational Research* 43 (1973): 115–37.

are much less confusing. Although dictionary skills are important, they can prove discouraging to individuals with spelling difficulties. For example, a pupil once asked the author, "How on earth do you spell *pearl?*—and don't ask me to look it up in the dictionary because I've already looked under 'pir,' 'pur,' and 'per' without finding it."

Pupils may also be taught spelling in connection with written compositions. However, the teacher should not correct misspellings in written work by underlining the mistakes, for that calls attention to the *incorrect* spelling. Instead, misspelled words should be crossed out and the correct spelling written above each error. The child keeps a record of these words and tries to learn them.

Students who wish to become better spellers must continue to use whatever approaches are most suitable for them. Despite conscientious effort, some of them have extreme difficulty in this area for many years. Whether this is due to a general language disorder or other factors is not known. Students and teachers, however, who realize how long spelling and reading disability sometimes persist, can at least view the difficulty constructively by using every means of compensation for it rather than feeling apprehensive and guilty if practice and application are not entirely successful.

Tina—Reading at Fourth Grade Level in Sixth Grade

Children who have reading difficulties sometimes have mastered all the word–recognition skills and still are not able to use them to read easily or to gather information. Tina is such a child.

Tina, 11 years of age, in sixth grade, with high average intelligence, read at fourth grade level. Diagnostic tests and other qualitative evaluation revealed an excellent background in phonics and complete mastery of a basic sight vocabulary. Yet when she read aloud, she made innumerable errors. She misread words, read haltingly, repeated words, or showed marked hesitation. However, when her errors were pointed out, she was able to correct them at once. Where such characteristics appear, three major causes seem likely: (1) Dealing with words in isolation is a simpler task for some children than reading. It allows the pupil to take more time with less familiar words and does not interfere with the rendition or with the thought processes that are necessary for understanding connected reading material. (2) Added tension due to many factors may interfere with the pupil's ability to read aloud smoothly. (3) Inability to retrieve words readily reduces confidence.

In Tina's case, there was no problem in retrieving words or in reading them in isolation. Even when they were presented in a hand-operated tachistoscope, Flash X, which exposes words at the rapid rate of $\frac{1}{25}$ of a second, she had no trouble. She saw, without question, that she knew the words very well indeed.

The second possibility relating to anxiety in the reading situation is extremely complex area to explore, particularly if one desires the child to develop a certain amount of insight. This can sometimes be imparted in terms the child can understand.

In talking with Tina, the writer[23] indicated that perhaps they might try to discover the sources of her difficulty. She pointed out how Tina was able to read words correctly with merely the briefest glimpse. Her problem was certainly not due to inability to recognize words. There must be other reasons. They discussed how she must have been embarrassed in front of her classmates when she read so poorly. She must also have been afraid of getting low marks on her report card and was probably very concerned about what her teachers and parents thought of her. Perhaps as she reads aloud now, some of these worries are still present. And, since she wants so much to do well but is still uncertain about her ability, she reads hesitantly and cautiously. Also, her fear of exposing herself in front of classmates, teachers, and her family might still upset her. This happens to many children with similar difficulties.

Tina brightened up as the discussion progressed. Perhaps she was relieved to find an explanation of her stumblings and repetitions. Perhaps she now felt that they were not altogether her fault. When she found out, too, that the writer was accustomed to uneven reading in many other children like her and that a perfect performance was not expected, she seemed to relax visibly.

As sessions continued, Tina's reactions were even more dramatic. Instead of mobilizing her forces to try harder and thereby intensifying her anxiety, she no longer had to pretend to be what she was not. Her tension decreased even more noticeably, and she began showing marked improvement in her oral reading. Since the writer knew that such a high level could not in all probability be maintained, she wished to prevent the

23. Tina was seen by one of the authors for diagnosis and treatment of her reading problems.

possibility of future discouragement. Also, she did not want Tina to be frightened at having to sustain a standard so high it might prove unrealistic. Hence, she rejoiced with Tina over her improvement, but told her, too, that everyone's performance varies; some days she would undoubtedly do better than on others.

In addition to oral reading, Tina practiced answering questions on silent reading exercises. These were carefully selected on the appropriate interest and ability level. She was able to do well on them, and her high scores gave her concrete evidence that she really could do creditable work. Success during remedial sessions in oral and silent reading bolstered her courage sufficiently so that Tina was able to contribute to class discussions. In fact, she reached the point after ten sessions where she volunteered to read answers to specific questions aloud in class and finally managed satisfactorily without extra help.

Tina's case would not always be considered strictly one of word recognition difficulty. Yet, this is one of the ways in which her anxiety, due to unfavorable past experiences with reading, was manifested. Tina's problem is typical of that of many pupils who are considered by teachers to have serious word recognition problems. In most cases, the remedial treatment consists of plying these pupils with exercises in all aspects of word analysis in the hope that a firmer foundation will improve their reading. However, such emphasis tends to intensify the child's problem. As one older pupil hopelessly recounted, "I went voluntarily to corrective reading classes, but all they did was drill me on sounds, prefixes, suffixes, and roots. Now I just can't stand to read anything."

The four cases presented in this chapter point out how teachers can choose essential reading skills and materials to fit each individual. Most of all, the teacher's support can carry these children through their academic difficulties.

In conclusion it is interesting to note how differently José and Randy, both of whom were nonreaders, were handled. José had many deficits in language, auditory discrimination, and memory. As was pointed out, his visual discrimination was his strongest point. He did not do well seeing and remembering letters or words, but he could learn from simple pre-primers. This was what spurred him on and gave him a spark of confidence. More important, it gave him actual proof that he could learn. His tutor's delight and encouragement increased his confidence too, but he knew for himself that it was not empty praise. Next, using a variety of easy materials escalated both his confidence and his skill. He was on his way.

Randy also needed to learn to read at a slow pace with a visual approach. In his case, however, we saw that the problem was increased because the school and family did not understand what was wrong. Their anxiety about a possible memory deficit was unconsciously communicated to him. He seemed to say to himself, "If I have no memory, I can't learn." We saw how the consultant was able to mitigate these negative factors first by talking with his family and second by suggesting to his teachers how to avoid overloading his information processing.

We found that Neil and Tina had mastered basic word-recognition skills but still read poorly and had low achievement scores. Neil overused phonics, and as a result he found that reading made little sense, while Tina felt insecure and stupid.

Thus it can be seen that remedial treatment covers a wide range and variety of problems. The remedial specialist coordinates his work with other workers in the field whenever indicated, helps in any way possible to foster competency in schoolwork, and, above all, promotes the very best qualities that are present in every individual. Remediation is more than imparting techniques; it is more than therapeutically oriented treatment. It is a situation that is personal and unique in all cases. Such experience can make the difference between a life of failure and a life of acceptance and harmony.

Suggestions for Further Reading

Bryant, D. "Some Principles of Remedial Instruction for Dyslexia." *The Reading Teacher* 18 (1965): 567–72.

Dallman, M., Reuch, R., Chang, L. W. C., and Deboer, J. *Teaching of Reading.* New York: Holt, Rinehart & Winston, 1974.

Durkin, D. *Teaching Them to Read,* 2nd ed. Boston: Allyn & Bacon, 1974.

Gibson, E., and Levin, H. *The Psychology of Reading.* Cambridge, Mass.: MIT Press, 1975.

Goodman, K., and Niles, O. *Reading: Process and Program.* Champaign, Ill.: National Council of Teachers of English, 1967.

Guthrie, J. *Aspects of Reading Acquisition.* Baltimore: Johns Hopkins University Press, 1976.

Guzak, F. *Diagnostic Reading Instruction in the Elementary School.* New York: Harper & Row, 1972.

Heilman, A. *Principles and Practices of Teaching Reading,* 3rd ed. Columbus, Ohio: Charles E. Merrill, 1972.

Levin, H., and Williams, J., eds. *Basic Studies in Reading.* New York: Harper & Row, 1970.

Treatment

Reich, R. "More than Remedial Reading." *Elementary English* 39 (1962): 216–19.

Spache, G., and Spache, E. *Reading in the Elementary School.* Boston: Allyn & Bacon, 1973.

Weber, G. *Inner City Children Can Be Taught to Read: Four Successful Schools.* Washington, D.C.: Council for Basic Education, 1971.

White, R., and Gagne, R. "Past and Future Research on Learning Hierarchies." *Educational Psychologist* 11 (1974): 19–28.

Zintz, M. *Reading Process: Teacher and Learner.* Dubuque, Iowa: William C. Brown, 1975.

Selected Research on Individualized Reading

Congreve, W., and Rinehart, G., eds. *Flexibility in School Programs.* Worthington, Ohio: Charles A. Jones, 1972.

Klausmeier, H., Sorenson, J., and Quilling, M. "Instructional Programming for the Individual Pupil in the Multi-Unit School." *Elementary School Journal* 72 (1971): 81–101.

Kozol, J. *Free Schools.* New York: Bantam Books, 1972.

Moss, J. "Growth in Reading in an Integrated Day Classroom." *Elementary School Journal* 72 (1972): 304–22.

Popp, H. "Current Practices in the Teaching of Beginning Reading." In J. Carroll and J. Chall, *Toward a Literate Society,* pp. 101–46. New York: McGraw-Hill, 1975.

Rosner, J. *The Development and Validation of an Individualized Perceptual Skills Curriculum.* Pittsburgh: Learning Research and Development Center, University of Pittsburgh, 1972.

Southgate, V. "The Language Arts in Informal British Primary Schools." *The Reading Teacher* 26 (1973): 367–73.

Watters, E. "Reading in a Family-Grouped Primary School." In H. Smith, ed., *Meeting Individual Needs in Reading,* pp. 29–35. Newark, Del.: International Reading Association, 1971.

Wisconsin Design for Reading Skill Development. Wisconsin Research and Development Center for Cognitive Learning. Minneapolis: Interpretive Scoring Systems, a division of National Computer Systems, 1971.

Selected Research on Linguistics

Bernstein, M. "Reading Methods and Materials Based on Linguistic Principles for Basic and Remedial Instruction." *Academic Quarterly* 2 (1967): 149–54.

Eimas, P. "Linguistic Processing of Speech by Young Infants." In R. Schiefelbusch and L. Lloyd, eds., *Language Perspectives,* pp. 55–74. Baltimore: University Park Press, 1974.

Elgin, S. *What Is Linguistics?* Englewood Cliffs, N.J.: Prentice-Hall, 1973.

Engle, P. "Language Medium in Early School Years for Minority Language Groups." *Review of Educational Research* 45 (1975): 283–385.

Goodman, K. *Theoretically Based Studies of Pattern of Miscues in Oral Reading Performance.* Final Report, Project No. 9–0375. Kent, Ohio: Kent State University, 1973.

Labov, W. *The Study of Non-Standard English.* National Council of Teachers of English, 1970.

Menyuk, P. "Early Development of Receptive Language: From Babbling to Words." In R. Schiefelbusch and L. Lloyd, eds., *Language Perspectives,* pp. 213–36. Baltimore: University Park Press, 1974.

Smith, F. *Understanding Reading: A Psycholinguistic Analysis of Reading and Learning to Read.* New York: Holt, Rinehart and Winston, 1971.

Smith, F. *Psycholinguistics and Reading.* New York: Holt, Rinehart and Winston, 1973.

Tallal, P., and Percy, M. "Defects of Non-Verbal Auditory Perception in Children with Developmental Aphasia." *Nature,* (1973): 468–69.

Selected Research on Phonics Instruction

Ammon, R. "Generating Expectancies to Enhance Comprehension." *The Reading Teacher* 29 (1975): 245–49.

Brown, E. "The Bases of Reading Acquisition." *Reading Research Quarterly* 6 (1970): 49–74.

Goodman, K., and Niles, O. *Reading: Process and Program.* Champaign, Ill.: National Council of Teachers of English, 1970.

Groff, P. "Reading Ability and Auditory Discrimination: Are They Related?" *The Reading Teacher* 28 (1975): 742–47.

Hammill, D., and Larsen, S. "The Relationship of Selected Auditory Perceptual Skills and Reading Ability." *Journal of Learning Disabilites* 7 (1974).

Posner, M., Lewis, J., and Conrad, C. "Component Processes in Reading." In *Language by Eye and Ear*, ed. J. Kavanaugh and I. Mattingly. Cambridge, Mass.: MIT Press, 1972.

9

Application of
Word-Recognition Techniques

CHAPTER 8 has described the major word-recognition skills for children with reading disability. It was suggested briefly that these techniques be incorporated in reading material wherever possible rather than
taught in isolation. In this chapter we will describe some of the general
approaches that may be used in the actual teaching of word-recognition
to a group and to individuals in or outside the classroom.

Oral Reading

Although rarely considered a method, oral reading is one of the best
means for practicing word recognition. Many words, especially sight
words, are repeated again and again. The teacher can supply those that
the child does not know. He repeats them in the course of reading and,
in this way, gradually learns to recognize them. Although this is sometimes called "incidental" teaching, it is a sound and valid way for reinforcing words. Where indicated, the teacher can also help the pupil to
sound the words out and use structural analysis and context while reading. In this way, the pupil learns the words he does not know not just as

an entity, but he sees them embedded in many different contexts. For example, a child may know the word *there* in isolation, but it seems to be less recognizable when interwoven in different sentences where the individual gestalt appears altered. Therefore, as long as the oral reading is not allowed to become laborious, the pupil has a better chance of strengthening his word-recognition ability in this natural and less taxing setting than he has through meaningless drill. Also, the teacher can determine from the oral reading the pupil's progress in word recognition and what skills he still may need.

Phrasing and Expression

Before any attempt is made to practice phrasing or improve expression, the child should be reading within the scope of his ability and have mastered all the needed word-recognition techniques. Otherwise there are too many skills for him to consider at once. In any beginning foreign language class, for example, it takes a high degree of mastery before the pupils—regardless of their age—can read the text fluently or with expression.

To improve children's performance in reading, several procedures can be tried. The teacher might alternate with the pupil in reading paragraphs or pages, or she might try choral reading (reading simultaneously with the pupil). Thus the pupil may be able to imitate her example. She might use a tape recorder so that the child can hear how he sounds. For many pupils, tape recordings provide added incentive for improvement. For others, however, tape recording renditions are a threat, particularly those whose performance is very poor.

The most effective means of all is to encourage as much supplementary reading as possible. Most children with reading disability shy away from independent reading and therefore rarely gain the practice needed for a fluent performance. They should be guided toward exciting stories at a level that they can handle. More and more high interest, low vocabulary books with mature content are becoming available.

Comprehension in Oral Reading

For children with reading disability who are functioning on a primary level, the authors do not treat comprehension in connection with their reading in the manner recommended by the standard manuals for developmental reading. Since these pupils are usually reading material containing concepts designed for much younger children, they rarely have trouble with the meaning unless they have a language problem or an extremely limited experiential background. Their major problem stems from difficulty in recognizing words. Therefore, to follow the widespread practice of answering questions about the content, looking back to substantiate answers, finding explanatory phrases or paragraphs to elaborate specific points, is not only inappropriate, but it smothers any spark of interest that may have been aroused. In fact, some of the deep resistance to reading that the authors have encountered with such children has been due to the endless questions they were asked which ruined any delight in the story itself. Imagine how a child feels who is struggling with word recognition, feeling clumsy in reading aloud, and worrying lest he sound utterly absurd. Then at the end of this wretched experience he must think up answers to comprehension questions! Instead of concern over understanding the material at this stage, the teacher seizes every opportunity to promote pleasure in completing the story. Wherever there are strong reactions to the ideas themselves, she of course encourages spontaneous discussion. More often than not on the lower reading levels, however, the teacher and children finish the story with brief comments and go on to the next procedure.

The Place of Word Analysis in the Remedial Program

After oral reading and discussion have been completed, some extra practice on the separate skills may still be needed. The children learn consonant sounds, vowel sounds, consonant combinations, and so on by the methods described in Chapter 8.

As we have noted, only those word-analysis techniques that are most essential are emphasized with children who have reading disability. Because they usually have become discouraged as a result of previous failures and tend to carry over these negative attitudes, the teacher attempts to show them that certain basic skills will increase their reading ability quickly and effectively. She names the skills to be learned and explains how they are used. This encourages a collaborative spirit and sets concrete and realistic goals. Rather than plowing through endless lists and countless exercises, the pupils can learn a streamlined version of word analysis and proceed as rapidly as possible.

In working with such children, the teacher should not expect 100 percent accuracy. She knows their prolonged tendency to mistake sight words and confuse letter sounds. Whether this is due to word-finding difficulty, perceptual disorder, anxiety, or other factors related to reading disability is not known. What we do know is that many children with reading disability experience difficulty over a long period before they are able to achieve accuracy in word recognition. Instead of expecting perfection, the experienced teacher strives for steady improvement. If the teacher shows understanding and acceptance of the fluctuations in the child's progress, the child's anxiety about making mistakes usually lessens. This in turn tends to decrease his errors and gradually results in smoother and more proficient reading.

The Classroom Library

The ultimate objective of teaching word recognition is to develop the pupil's reading ability. To promote this aim, the teacher should have a large selection of appropriate reading materials on hand in the form of a classroom library.

Although many classrooms have libraries, children with reading disability usually are reluctant to use them. They have been discouraged long ago by their unsuccessful attempts to read any of the volumes. When these children are assigned outside reading, their major criterion is the slenderness of the book. In order to try again, they need a great deal of encouragement.

The teacher can foster more positive attitudes toward reading by providing a wide variety of materials with controlled vocabulary but high interest.[1] If only a limited amount of money is available, books can sometimes be borrowed in quantity from the public library. Another possibility is to purchase a number of short-story collections at varying levels. These can sometimes be cut up into their separate selections.[2] The children can help to prepare the material and to make suitable covers for each story. The result is hundreds of attractive booklets that offer pleasurable reading to many children at different stages of reading competency.

1. A large number of paper backs are available with high interest and modified readability levels. See Appendix D for representative listings.
2. F. Roswell, "When Children's Textbooks Are Too Difficult," *Elementary School Journal* 60 (1959): 146–57.

Treatment

To facilitate the pupils' choice of suitable reading matter, the teacher might code the books according to level, marking them conspicuously on the back binding or cover with an appropriate symbol. For example, if letters are used, the pupils are told which "letter" books are most sensible for them to read at present. A similar system can be used having different colors to represent the different levels. If such a procedure is used, the children should be told the reason for it: it is good to find books that are enjoyable; they cannot be appreciated if they are too difficult;[3] therefore, they are coded for convenience just as in regular libraries.

The teacher might check on the pupils' reading by asking them to tell what part of a story they liked best or found funniest. If a story seems suitable for other children as well, she might ask them to share it with the class. This practice is accepted enthusiastically by most children. It seems to effect an improvement in the attitude of the poorer readers in particular. Disheartened readers often become interested in exploring the possibilities of the library when they find out they can really read and derive pleasure from books.

Illustrative Cases at Primary Levels

A teacher may be knowledgeable about methodology and familiar with research concerning the teaching of word-recognition skills to poor readers yet find that this knowledge fails to help some children. A child's reactions may run the gamut from anxiety to outright negativism. If the child has had repeated experiences of failure in school the continued frustration can become unbearable and learning is impeded. Ruth was a nonreader who had begun to give up as early as first grade. The tutor discovered after some months that Ruth was worried about failing through school like her older sister Joline, who was still having a hard time in junior high.

Ginger knew most basic skills but needed an approach slightly different from the customary one, because of her high resistance. Roy, in contrast, had difficulty with specialized vocabulary and found his textbooks and various subject matter material too difficult for him.

The individual patterns of adjustment of these children and how

3. J. Chall, "Let Them Try the Book on for Fit," *The Reading Teacher* 7 (1953): 83–88.

their teachers were able to reach them are set forth in the following accounts. A description of background information has been kept at a minimum because the purpose is to point up ways of integrating word-recognition techniques into the reading program. Also, in many cases full background data is often unavailable to the teachers.

Two Sisters—Ruth and Joline

Ruth was referred at the age of 6 years 3 months to a remedial program conducted by a university tutoring center. She had spent three months in first grade and learned little; moreover, her teacher felt she was unusually slow and shy, yet prone to impulsive behavior. She was unable to read or even to identify letters of the alphabet and the teacher reported that she was fearful and uninterested during all class activities.

Her tutor,[4] however, found her eager to learn in an individual situation and aware of what was expected of her from the school. She was a bright-eyed, active child of average height and weight. A close relationship was formed with her tutor through which emerged an engaging personality, hardly shy or withdrawn but properly cautious and somewhat wary. From the first session, the tutor found Ruth asked many questions such as, "Are you going to teach me my ABC's?" which indicated that she wanted to read. She also responded to a story read to her with great interest and displayed her ability to observe closely and do many matching type exercises. It was obvious she had been aware of what was expected of her in the classroom, but fear of the teacher and her own inability to perform within a classroom seemed to be a major factor which prevented learning.

Ruth was the youngest of a family of five. The two oldest sisters had been brought up by the maternal grandmother and were at the time attending community colleges. Another sister was 13, and an 11-year-old brother was completing his second year at a residential correctional facility. The father had deserted the family three years previously. The mother, tired and bitter, gave up on Ruth and thought she'd do poorly in school like her next older sister and brother. She left Ruth's care to this sister, Joline. Joline was intelligent but depressed and doing poorly in

4. Virginia Miller, special education and learning specialist, Bank Street College Teacher Corps.

school. Ruth seemed fearful of becoming like this sister and worried about her.

Tutoring began in December once a week for the first two months, then twice a week through June. During the first few sessions Ruth and her tutor explored many areas of interest: food, her family, and music. The tutor adapted a song Ruth knew and particularly liked: "I Know An Old Lady . . . ," changing it to "Oh I Can See Ruth, She Swallowed a Cat . . . ." Together, tutor and child ate cookies in the shapes described in the song and followed the words printed in a special book made by Ruth. Ruth quickly memorized the words and realized for the first time what reading was all about. Soon she was able to recognize words out of context. Next she learned to copy the words and finally to print them from dictation.

The transfer from song to preprimer was relatively simple and Ruth was able to begin to learn the words in a series used in her classroom. At the same time, efforts were made to teach her the alphabet, using cue words, primarily food items, as well as alphabetizing the growing pile of sight words in a special box. Exercises and games with the words were devised and Ruth was soon able to choose from her word box and make her own sentences. At the same time, all attempts to teach a phonic system of word attack proved futile. However, initial consonants had not been difficult for her to learn through the alphabetized word cards and food cue words, so that Ruth could think of words beginning with various letters. She could then figure out how to begin to read a new word by connecting the sound of the letter to a familiar word beginning with the same letter. Emphasis was placed on how to say sounds and Ruth found feeling her jaw and looking in the mirror helpful. She could not, at this stage, discriminate vowel sounds nor blend sounds together. She was encouraged to guess a new word using initial letter sounds, context clues, and her good language ability. Efforts were also made to help her spell by having her slow down the pronunciation of a word until the separate spoken sounds were isolated. She could then very often connect the sound she said with a letter she knew and write it down. This was the beginning of preparing the blending process which was so difficult for her.

By the end of the first grade, Ruth had learned and could use a sight vocabulary of over 150 words. She had mastered the preprimers and much of the primer, but she had very little ability to attack new words. When presented with a new word, she would say, "I never saw it before."

During the second year of tutoring, she learned to recognize word families. Starting from words Ruth knew, games were played. For example, in playing the Concentration Game[5], we matched such words as *best-nest*. This helped her attention span as well as learning the words. At the same time, work was begun on vowel sounds in conjunction with reading the Primary Phonics Series (Educators Publishing Service, Inc.). Spelling patterns were emphasized rather than sounds which Ruth still could not blend. By the end of the year, Ruth was able to attack many new words somewhat independently by means of association with words that she knew in the same family. She was also able to do this with final consonants and blends. Vowel sounds and blending continued to give her trouble.

Ruth's growing trust in the tutor enabled her to talk about Joline, who was in such trouble at home and at school. Apparently Ruth's fear of falling into the same morass as the rest of her family prompted her to talk so much about her. For example, she would ask to call home during sessions knowing Joline would answer the phone. Even in reading exercises Joline's name came up—for example, in *at* word-family exercises. Ruth would say, "at-fat Joline." She would often draw pictures of Joline too.

The tutor finally realized how much Ruth was preoccupied with her home life and felt impelled to see Joline and her mother for a conference. At that time the tutor realized that they needed special help and suggested that they see a psychiatric social worker. After several sessions with this worker, many of the confusions were clarified for the family. At the same time Joline was referred to a clinic for psychological and educational management. Soon counseling was begun for the family at a neighborhood center, and Ruth was relieved that her family was finally getting help too. Tutoring sessions were cut down to once a week as Ruth's scores on paragraph meaning reached third grade level.

Thus, a child with a serious disability received early intervention enabling her to bypass her deficits in auditory discrimination and memory and use her considerable strengths. Despite a difficult family with many problems, she is progressing in school.

---

5. The Concentration Game is played with ten or more pairs of identical words which need practice. Words are printed on cards, shuffled, and placed face down on the table. Each player has a chance to turn up any two cards on his turn, one at a time. If he turns up two alike, he keeps them; otherwise he returns them face down. If a player "concentrates" on the cards as they are turned up and then replaced, he can remember where certain cards are and raise his chances of matching cards.

Word-Recognition Techniques for Pupils Reading Above Fourth Grade Level

In dealing with children who are reading at fourth grade level or above, the teacher is often preplexed by those whose basic foundation in word recognition is fairly satisfactory, but who still do not read as well as they are able. This may be due to many factors, such as insufficient development of comprehension and study skills; these are discussed in Chapter 10.

Very often, however, it is due to inability to utilize word-recognition skills properly. The case of Ginger and Roy follows. Both were nine years of age, and we describe how difficulties in this area were handled.

Ginger, who was in third grade, had a great deal of resistance to learning. She came to tutoring sessions because she wanted the teachers in her school and her mother to "leave her alone." She had her own way of handling the problem, as we shall see in the following account.

Ginger—Entering Third Grade, Reading at Second Grade Level

Ginger, reading at low second grade level, was first seen in September, at which time she was nine years old and attended third grade. She was a lively, charming young girl who was matter of fact about her schoolwork. "I don't do badly, but I'm not too good," was her statement. The school, however, was very concerned and the teacher claimed that, "She should be way ahead of her class. Instead she is one of the lowest." Her reading was scattered, inaccurate, and confused. She was erratic about her homework and sloppy in class. However, her social behavior and personality were delightful. The teacher recommended that she be tested and perhaps tutored individually.

The reading specialist[6] administered informal tests for several sessions. Results showed a child of superior intelligence with poor test scores but fairly good word–recognition skills; however, she would get stuck and give up easily if a sentence did not make sense to her. For

6. One of the authors handled this case.

example, if she ignored a period or could not figure out a word in a sentence, she was not flexible enough to recover her understanding of the story. This seemed partly due to her uncertainty about her reading and her anxiety about not achieving in school. To help Ginger with these difficulties, she was introduced to experiments, mysteries, biographies, jokes, puzzles, and project books with the hope of sparking her interest in reading outside of school and increasing her possibilities of success. She also talked with her tutor at length and she wrote some of her thoughts down in story form. Ginger liked this type of varied program. She also agreed to read at home for 15 to 20 minutes a night if it would help. The tutor said that they would look for a book that she really enjoyed so that she could gain ease in reading at the same time. After several tries they found a version of *Black Beauty* that she liked. She finished it and went on to other horse stories, such as *Three Dollar Mule* and *Wild Horses of the Red Desert*.

As the months passed it was important to introduce Ginger to comprehension exercises so that she could handle textbooks and gather information that she needed for school. Here her inaccuracy was particularly detrimental. Stress on word-analysis skills only made her more resistant, however. Instead, the tutor suggested that she read the paragraphs to herself first, when answering questions, and ask for any vocabulary or concepts with which she was unfamiliar. The tutor filled in the gaps in her background as needed. (Many poor readers have a dearth of information due to the minimal reading they are likely to do in or out of school.) She was asked to answer the questions aloud, however, so that the tutor could have a chance to see how she approached the material and where she might miss the point. It was interesting to see how Ginger used her high intelligence to compensate for misinformation. For example, in reading the article "Iron People" from *Reading for Concepts*, she read, "The *world* in the history that means *instruments used in fighting* is . . . ." (The actual sentence in the book was, "The word in the story that means . . . .") She immediately gave the correct answer, "weapons." The tutor pointed out how clever she was in knowing what answer was required even though she had mistaken some of the words. This gave Ginger some pride in her ability and at the same time called attention to her lack of precision which often got in her way, particularly in answers on tests.

In November, Ginger received 3.9 on the *Gilmore Oral Reading Test* and 2.7 on the *Metropolitan Primary II Test*, Form A, in word knowledge and 3.0 in reading. She was disappointed in the latter scores and became determined to raise them. She worked on pronouncing and spelling words accurately and began reading even more at home. By February she begged to take another test, this time the *Metropolitan Elementary*, Form B. (The tutor did not approve of her emphasis on tests, but realized that Ginger needed this type of motivation.) She received the same level in word knowledge, but earned 3.8 in reading. Work continued with attention paid to Ginger's attitudes, reactions, and learning processes. By May, she had achieved on the *Metropolitan Elementary Test*, Form C, 4.0 in word knowledge and 4.3 in reading. She was very proud of herself.

In considering Ginger, some of the factors that seemed to promote her growth were acceptance of her tendency to misread words and to compensate by checking her answers carefully. Her tutor encouraged her diligence. Mistakes were not considered "wrong" or "bad," but rather detriments to presenting herself advantageously at school. Her inaccuracy even interfered in daily experiences. For example, once she read a subway sign incorrectly, mistaking "Uptown" for "Up Down." Since she thought the stairway led to trains running in both directions, she came to the wrong platform and not only was carried uptown when she wanted to go downtown, but she lost the price of a subway token as well.

Secondly, her ability to master science experiments, magic tricks, and the like forced her to be accurate. In addition it won her status with her friends and family and made her feel wanted and accepted. Finally, her determination was a prominent factor. Her wish to improve her test marks was *her* request, not the tutor's. The tutor questioned so much testing with her. But she insisted and used the scores as a concrete goal for herself. The tutor told her how impressed she was by Ginger's use of tests even though the tutor herself would never have handled the sessions in this manner.

It is likely that Ginger's concentration on test taking was her way of saying, "Leave me alone! I just want to get through school. Stop bugging me." The truth is that as soon as her scores in school improved her teacher *did* stop pressuring her. Her teachers were amazed at her improvement. So, although the tutor's goal was to urge Ginger to value her pleasure in learning, Ginger was not ready for this. She has as yet not become an avid or even an interested reader. Instead she does just enough in school to get by. But allowing her to follow her self-imposed testing plan, despite her tutor's distaste for it, seemed to strengthen Ginger's confidence. Perhaps it was the first time that Ginger felt the full force of her ability to take hold of her schoolwork herself and was able to profit from the author's encouragement to assert her independence.

Roy—Reading at Middle Fourth Grade Level in Sixth Grade

Roy, aged 11, in sixth grade, in the bright normal range intellectually, obtained a score of 4.6 on the paragraph-reading section of the *Stanford Achievement Test*. His teacher reported that he was very alert in class and contributed much to group discussions. However, she could not identify the nature of his reading problem. She tested his word-analysis ability and found only a few gaps in his knowledge of phonics. She knew also that his comprehension of subject matter was satisfactory. Why, then, did Roy fall so far below grade level in this test and find his homework in geography and history so difficult?

The teacher consulted one of the authors regarding a program of remedial instruction for Roy which she could implement during brief sessions with him several times weekly.

In the course of informal testing, Roy read some passages from a textbook which he claimed just did not make sense. As he read aloud, his problem became quite clear. Some typical errors were *scoring* for *securing* and *revolution* for *resolution*. When he came to words such as *ancient*, *foreign*, and *alien*, he tried to figure them out phonically, grappled with them for a few seconds, and then continued reading. No wonder he lost the trend of thought so easily.

An analysis of the types of errors he made indicated that although his fundamental word-recognition skills were fairly satisfactory, he needed strengthening in the five major areas in word recognition: phonics, syllabication, context clues, specialized vocabulary in school subjects, and dictionary skills.

Even though Roy needed this type of remedial work, the way in which instruction was presented was most important so as to gain his cooperation. For example, merely using a series of exercises in each of these five areas would not have encouraged active involvement on his part, nor would there be any assurance of carry-over in his actual reading. The program had to be well balanced with some teaching of specific skills and some supportive help so as to prevent the work from becoming too tedious. Also, all the skills had to be interwoven into a total plan.

The writer and Roy's teacher set up a program with these goals in mind. First Roy was taught only the few phonic elements which he did not know. These he grasped quickly, as most bright pupils do who are reading above fourth grade level. Next, he was shown how to divide words into syllables. Practice in applying these principles was given through a device such as the Syllabascope and the game of Grab (advanced level). Roy, like many other children of his kind, enjoyed both of these techniques. The teacher then checked briefly to determine whether he was able to utilize these skills in handling class assignments. If he read *invitation* for *invention*, he was merely reminded that he now knew various means of figuring this word correctly including whether it made sense in the paragraph and was given additional help if he needed it. In going over words, Roy was helped to use many approaches. Words selected from his science and social study texts such as *insurrection* and *emancipation* could be figured out through syllabication, whereas *geyser*, *plateau*, and *drought* had to be looked up in the dictionary. He was not overburdened with such work. Instead, he was frequently told the pronunciation of unfamiliar words and given vivid descriptions of their meanings.

It took some time before Roy overcame his habitual manner of skimming over difficult words and guessing from their general shapes. However, because he knew that absolute accuracy was not expected immediately, and because the work was pared down to its essentials rather than remaining overwhelming, he was gradually able to incorporate his newly learned skills into his reading. Homework became less of a chore, and satisfactory gains were evidenced on achievement tests.

The previous cases point up the various ways in which we apply word-recognition procedures to children with particular problems. Each child has his way; each tutor has a way too. Thus we try to be creative and sensitive in matching the task to the individual pupil.

Suggestions for Further Reading

Athey, I. "Affective Factors in Reading." In H. Singer and R. Ruddell, eds., *Theoretical Models and Processes in Reading*. Newark, Del.: International Reading Association, 1970.

Coleman, J. "Education in the Age of Computers and Mass Communications." In Martin Greenberger, ed., *Computers, Communications, and the Public Interest*. Baltimore: Johns Hopkins University Press, 1971.

Comer, J. *Beyond Black and White*. New York: Quadrangle, 1972.

Finch, R. *The School and the Democratic Environment*. New York: Columbia University Press, 1970.

Lurie, E. *How to Change the Schools*. New York: Vintage, 1970.

Milgram, J., and Sciarra, D. *Childhood Revisited.* New York: Macmillan, 1974.

Rubin, L. *Facts and Feelings in the Classroom.* New York: Viking, 1973.

Skinner, B. F. *Beyond Freedom and Dignity.* New York: Bantam/Vintage, 1972.

Spiegel, J. *Transactions—The Interplay Between Individual, Family, and Society.* New York: Science House, 1971.

Taichert, L. *Childhood, Learning, Behavior, and the Family.* New York: Behavioral Publications, 1973.

Weber, L. *English Infants School and Informal Education.* Englewood Cliffs, N.J.: Prentice-Hall, 1971.

10

Basic Comprehension, Study Skills, and Vocabulary

COMPREHENSION is applying thought processes to reading; there are as many ways to teach it as there are variations in the pupils and their teachers. The main difficulty of pupils with reading disability who are reading at high third grade level or above usually lies in the manner of handling textbooks and the understanding of information found in reference books, newspapers, and magazines. They are less likely to have trouble comprehending simple narrative material. Thus, at this stage, the focus of instruction shifts. Instead of dealing with story-type material and word analysis, the remedial program is concerned mainly with comprehension and study skills. Work on word recognition continues where necessary, but greater stress is placed on reading to gain information. There is also more emphasis on silent reading than on oral, since eventually most reading is done silently.

In teaching comprehension and study skills, two broad aspects are kept in mind. One is helping pupils to apply the basic comprehension and study techniques wherever they are needed; the other is to overcome the distaste and aversion for schoolwork that most of them have developed over the years.

Of course adequate evaluation, as described in Chapters 6 and 7, should be undertaken as early as possible, since it determines ultimate expectations and suggests the areas which need special attention.

This chapter will discuss components and remedial procedures connected with developing comprehension and study skills in pupils of all ages. However, the older students in high schools and colleges who have particularly severe problems in comprehension and written expression are discussed in Chapter 11.

Teaching Comprehension and Study Skills to a Group of Pupils with Reading Disability

The most important factors interfering with comprehension are limited intelligence, insufficient familiarity with the basic concepts of the subject matter, lack of interest in the material, and meager vocabulary.

Comprehension should be taught in its entirety according to the demands of the topic. However, for purposes of clarification and emphasis, it is often discussed in terms of separate processes. Therefore, it is convenient to consider that the most important components of comprehension center on the following: (1) finding the main idea and important details, (2) following directions, (3) adjusting rate of reading to multiple purposes, and (4) vocabulary development. If the pupils have sufficient foundation in these four basic areas, the special subject teacher can develop others that may be needed in a particular course of study, such as finding inferences, critical reading, and interrelationships of ideas.

Thus teachers can develop comprehension in many ways. Simple stories usually present no problem. It is with texts and informational matter that the difficulty manifests itself. When comprehension techniques are focused on acquiring specific information in the subject areas, they are usually called study skills. In teaching such skills, the pupils need systematic guidance.

Use of Textbooks

In dealing with a text, the teacher might begin by familiarizing the pupils with the organization of the textbook. They might examine the table of contents, chapter headings, illustrations, and index to develop an overall conception of the major information that is offered in the book. Then the pupils might begin to practice using these aids to locate specific information.

In introducing a particular topic the teacher builds up understanding through extensive discussion. She explains unfamiliar concepts and vocabulary that appear in the selection. Then the pupils turn to the portion of the book under consideration. They are encouraged to use any aids the author supplies in the form of heading arrangements in different type, italicized words, charts, maps, and so forth.[1] It is sometimes useful to consider each subheading as a main idea and have the pupils turn it into a question.

The teacher is specific in her assignments. That is, she asks questions, the answers to which she knows can be easily found in or deduced from the text. This sets the purpose for reading and helps pupils work more efficiently. The more success the pupils gain and the more adept they become, the more advanced can be the materials they use and the skills they can learn.

Teaching Comprehension and Study Skills to a Group of Seventh Graders

Sometimes the textbook is too difficult and substitute material must be found. For example, a group of 12 seventh graders had difficulty with social studies. They worked as a group with the remedial specialist[2] at the school three times a week. After a conference with their teacher, the remedial specialist knew that they were currently taking up early explorers in North America. She substituted a fifth grade text for their regular one. She found that by showing the pupils how to use this book in ways similar to those described previously, she could develop the skills they needed. For instance, the pupils read to find the main idea and relevant details. As she helped them organize their work in notebook form, they soon had a rough outline of each chapter. This information paralleled the work being done in their regular classroom. It could be used for review purposes or even for test preparation. Such outlines were also used for teaching sequential reading. Thus not only did the pupils learn how to study, they were able to apply the content in their social studies period. This heightened morale and accelerated their learning. Eventually they were able to use the seventh grade text along with the rest of the pupils and did not need the extra remedial work.

Thus, comprehension and study skills cannot be taught in a vacuum.

1. F. Roswell and R. Adams, "Teaching Social Studies in a Remedial Program," *Intercom, a Publication of the Junior High Schools of New York City* 6 (1962): 14–19.
2. Ruth Adams, Associate Dean, City College of the City University of New York.

When the text is difficult, the teacher must offer help by way of building background and demonstrating efficient methods for finding meaning from the text. When material in the regular classroom is beyond the pupils, then special arrangements must be made to give added assistance in whatever way is possible.

Individualizing Factual and Fictional Reading Materials

Even though comprehension and study skills are best taught through using the actual material in connection with a topic under consideration, this is not always feasible. When dealing with pupils who have difficulty in comprehension, the teacher or reading specialist does not always have sufficient time to use the regular text, which may be broad in scope and coverage. Workbooks which contain a variety of interesting selections offer a convenient shortcut in developing comprehension and study skills. Also, they simulate other types of informational matter that the students will use. They are available at all levels of reading ability, from second grade level through college. The wide range of subject matter covered by these workbooks makes them especially valuable for pupils with reading disability, for it helps them to build up, in a relatively brief period, the foundation that so many of them lack because of their history of sparse reading. Also, the brevity of workbook selections is inviting to pupils who shrink from more lengthy works. In addition, they provide a basis for a systematic, periodic record from which the student can gauge his progress.

For example, workbooks were used as the initial source for developing comprehension skills in a sixth grade class supervised by members of the staff of the City College Education Department.[3] The children in the class varied in cultural, racial, and socioeconomic background. There was a wide range in intelligence and in reading levels. The class was divided into two groups: those reading between high third and high fifth and those reading above sixth grade level. They spent three hourly sessions a week reading selections from a wide variety of informational articles in workbooks at suitable reading levels. For the lower reading group, each pupil had simpler materials. The children read two selections at each session. Before reading them the teacher presented any new vocabulary and concepts that were necessary.

The more competent readers needed only a little direction from the

3. The project refers to one carried out by Professors Florence Roswell and Jeanne Chall of the City University of New York.

teacher. They finished the exercises more quickly than the other group, at which point they read library books. For this group it was not necessary to purchase a workbook for each child. Instead, two copies of each book were cut up into individual exercises, thereby providing a larger number of selections. The exercises were mounted on construction paper with answers recorded on the reverse side. The pupils prepared the material under the direction of the teacher, and they themselves took charge of distributing it. At every session each pupil chose two selections he had not read before. He then checked his answers with the key on the back and kept a record of which exercises he had read.

Whenever workbook exercises are employed, a plan is followed similar to the one described under "Use of Textbooks"; that is, the teacher builds up background, explains unfamiliar concepts and vocabulary, and so on. However, since the teacher has wide latitude in choosing selections, she is careful to preread articles in order to select those most appropriate in content and format. After the selection is read, the pupils can answer the questions orally or silently. If the work is written, however, the teacher must be sure to look it over so that the pupil has the benefit of her comments and suggestions to guide him in subsequent exercises. It is important at this time to make certain that the pupil understands the type of error he makes and is shown ways in which he might avoid it in the future. Also the answer key supplied with the workbook need not be regarded as sacrosanct; sometimes questions are ambiguous no matter how carefully they are selected, and more than one answer may apply. Therefore, if a pupil can sufficiently substantiate his answer, even though in disagreement with the key, the teacher should make allowances for it and explain the ramifications of the topic.

With very severe cases of comprehension difficulty, the teacher may need to participate more actively and introduce silent reading in gradual stages. For example, she might start out by reading an article to the pupils and have them answer the questions orally, so that she can see where they are confused and can clarify meanings immediately. In subsequent sessions, she can guide them to read the selection silently, but still have them answer questions orally with her so that she may keep a close check on their progress in comprehension skills. Finally, they can be encouraged to work more independently and be given help only as needed.

Throughout the period that workbooks are used, the teacher makes sure that the pupils know why they are working with them and how they may help them. Nothing is more unproductive for pupils than reading articles and answering questions mechanically without direction or purpose. The effective teacher does not expect workbooks to supplant instruction. By themselves, they never impart all that is needed. After they have served their purpose, the pupils must be guided toward transferring their skills to texts and other material.

If the teacher finds that her pupils are particulary weak in one of the comprehension skills, she may wish to teach it separately as a temporary measure. She then selects suitable material from texts or workbooks which lend themselves to practice in a specific area. Once sufficient practice on an isolated technique is accomplished, however, the teacher makes sure that it is integrated properly in a variety of materials used in regular classwork.[4]

Finding the Main Idea and Important Details

In discussing a main idea and its supporting details, the teacher might start by showing the pupils a picture or even by having them look out the window or around the room and then describe what they see. The teacher tries to get them to condense their thoughts into a few words or a sentence such as: "I see a country scene." This is the main idea. Then she asks them to list more specific aspects of this concept which form the details. For example: "Two boys and two girls are going on a picnic. They have a Thermos jug and a basket filled with food." These are the details. The pupils are helped to distinguish between the general concept and the details which they described by identifying the essential differences in the statements. Then the teacher explains that authors of paragraphs and selections have written down the main ideas and details that they wish to convey. Selections are then taken for illustration: Short paragraphs are best for purposes of clarity. For instance, the teacher might choose a paragraph similar to the following:

> Millions of years ago when the dinosaurs lived on our earth the North American continent was very low-lying. It was made up of seas and swamps. The climate was warm and humid and perfect for lush plant growth. The plant-eating dinosaurs would creep through the hot swamps continuously eating this vegetation. They required a tremendous amount of food for their huge bodies.

4. Suggestions for workbooks to practice finding the main idea and important details, following directions, adjusting reading rate, and developing vocabulary are listed in Appendix C.

The teacher would first explain any words that might be unfamiliar, in this case perhaps *continent, low-lying, lush, continuously,* and *tremendous.* She might ask if the pupils ever had been near a swamp and what they knew about dinosaurs. After the pupils had read the paragraph, she would ask them to state the main idea and supporting details. The teacher can then introduce short selections in workbooks in similar fashion and later show how to utilize this technique with books and reference materials.

It should be noted here that another way to practice the main idea and details is to explain the use of the topic sentence and its relation to the rest of the paragraph. As is well known, however, the topic sentence may be the first or last sentence in a paragraph or come somewhere in between. This variability often confuses pupils with reading disability who are not fluent readers to begin with. Hence, if taught at all, it should be delayed until they show evidence that they can profit from such practice.

Following Directions

Those who correct children's examination papers are well aware of the many points lost because the children made mistakes in following the directions. Pointing out this fact, plus other such dramatic examples as mistaking sugar for salt in a recipe, usually alerts the children to their problem. A variety of practice materials can be read from cookbooks, magic books, card trick instructions, mathematics problems, science experiments, and so on. An example of how an experiment might be used follows:

> Squeeze a lemon into an ordinary dish. Dip a toothpick in the juice and write a word. The toothpick won't hold much juice. You must dip it after every word. You can use any kind of white paper. To read the message, put the paper near a warm electric light bulb or iron.

The teacher can have the materials for the experiment on hand and have one pupil come to the front of the room for demonstration. Words such as *ordinary, message,* and *electric* are explained and pronounced when necessary. The pupils then read the experiment silently. The teacher asks them to watch the pupil who will demonstrate and check to see whether or not he is following directions correctly.

Adjusting Reading Rate

Adjusting the rate of reading to the material being read is usually one of the last skills to be taught. It is important to delay this skill until problems in word recognition, comprehension, and fluency have been mostly resolved. After children have relatively little difficulty in these areas, one can consider how to utilize their reading skills most effectively. Rate is not stressed per se but rather flexibility in reading that is adjusted to purpose. For example, even a "fast" reader does not read a technical report at the same rate or in the same way that he reads a mystery story. Nor should he. We consider, even if not consciously, what we want to get out of a selection and then read it accordingly. The one rate which the child may have used previously in stories will be inefficient for handling more mature types of reading matter. Thus pupils may have to be cautioned to read carefully just as much as they need to be taught to read more rapidly.

At every opportunity the teacher points out and gives practice in reading for a variety of purposes. When the class is studying social studies, for example, the teacher can ask for particular information and guide the children in deciding where and how to look for it, as well as how to approach the subject matter. For instance, finding the number of people living in Russia and where most of them live will require skimming, whereas discovering the major changes from feudalism to communism requires reflective, concentrated reading. Such contrast in different types of reading dramatizes the flexibility that must be developed for efficient reading.

Teaching Research Skills to Junior High School Students

In one junior high school, for example, the teachers complained that the students did not know how to use library references in connection with writing reports. The pupils not only were having difficulty finding information, but when they did come across relevant material, they tended to copy it indiscriminately. Although they had all been introduced to the use of the library, it was apparent that they could benefit from further guidance and the practical application which is necessary in research.

The reading consultant[5] and the librarian[6] undertook a joint venture

5. Ruth Gottesman, Albert Einstein College of Medicine.
6. Urania Fuller, Greenburgh Junior High School.

to teach research skills to these pupils. They formed several groups, each one differing in level of ability. (The minimum reading level for the lowest group was 5.0. Below this level the program would have been too difficult. More advanced groups ranged up to eighth and ninth grade reading achievement.) The groups met for approximately seven lessons; the slower groups had more, and the faster groups fewer, sessions. Some lessons emphasized where to find particular information, others how to keep notes of information obtained, still others how to use particular reference material. All the lessons were given in conjunction with regular reports that the children were required to write. After reports were submitted, the reading consultant and the classroom teacher evaluated them and looked for possible weaknesses in specific skills. These skills were then taught later on.

Some lessons emphasized how to use a "skimming" technique to gather information quickly and accurately. The *World Book Encyclopedia* was used for these lessons. Two sets of encyclopedias, 14 volumes each, were available in the school. Every pupil received a volume of the encyclopedia at random. A skimming quiz was available for each volume. After an orientation period in which "skimming" was explained and illustrated, the pupils worked individually on their quizzes. Assistance was available when needed. An example of one quiz follows:

Skimming Quiz for Volume A of the *World Book Encylopedia*

NAME: DATE:

GRADE:

1. Who was the wife of John Adams? When did she live?
2. What does air pollution cost the United States in damages each year?
3. What are the chief kinds of alfalfa grown in the United States?
4. How old are the oldest existing copies of almanacs?
5. What color does arsenic turn when it is combined with copper?
6. What are two kinds of asbestos?

After such practice, the pupils reported that they were better able to handle their research and homework assignments in their varied classes.

Teaching Comprehension in a Classroom

When teachers are faced with a class whose pupils show a wide variation in ability to utilize and master comprehension techniques, they often do not know how to provide for those whose foundation skills are weak. Sometimes the teacher can form teams of two or three pupils, each team with one good reader, to read the material that has been assigned. After discussion in class, the pupils are given questions for which they must find the answers. The good reader serves as a resource to help with words or passages that present difficulty. Of course the teacher uses her ingenuity in forming teams so that the more proficient member remains helpful and does not become domineering.

Other teachers handle the problem by having a collection of books, texts, and other material at different levels. Through the years they have developed a resource file on the main topics in the course of study. It includes sufficient variety to provide reading matter for both good and poor readers. Often teachers ask, "Doesn't this take a great deal of preparation?" It does. But, as one teacher said, "I'd rather spend one hour a day preparing materials and reap the sense of satisfaction of a happy, responsive class than be miserable five hours a day, five days a week."

Individualizing Teaching for a History Unit in Sixth Grade

One teacher,[7] whose sixth grade class was studying the American Revolution, used such a file to good advantage. He first discussed the lives of the people and government of that time. Then he raised the questions: "Do you think the American people treated England so unfairly that they were responsible for the events that followed? If you had been in the English Parliament would you have supported King George?" This led to research in which the more able pupils consulted English as well as American texts and had the startling experience of discovering that reputable English authors presented a strong case against the colonists. The less able pupils, in the meantime, read history texts at fourth and fifth grade levels and numerous simple pamphlets and articles that the teacher had collected in the past. Later, when the pupils decided on the unusual procedure of having a trial in the classroom to investigate

7. Donald Lonergan, Mamaroneck, N.Y.

whether King George and his government should have been held responsible for the American Revolution, all the pupils were able to acquire sufficient information to participate and contribute according to their ability. Thus comprehension skills were developed at different levels according to the stage at which each pupil was at the time. Since materials were also coordinated, poor readers could gain in knowledge and skill to the same degree as the others.[8]

Thus there are many ways to teach comprehension and study skills. The teacher must use her ingenuity and her interest in the subject to instill curiosity and excitement in the pupil. Once this kind of reaction is aroused, it is relatively simple to teach how to find the main idea and details, how to follow directions, how to draw inferences, summarize, or whatever else might be required in the course of study. The most important source for strengthening comprehension is reading books, but the difficulty in getting pupils with reading disability to read voluntarily is obvious. There are certain books, however, that are more tempting and have a better possibility for sustaining interest than others.[9]

Helping Pupils to Extend Their Vocabulary

It is well known that one of the ways of acquiring a large vocabulary is through wide reading. As we have pointed out, this avenue has usually been closed to pupils with reading disability. Thus the teacher continues to encourage them to read suitable supplementary material, although she recognizes that their reading difficulty may retard their vocabulary development for an extensive period.

To aid in vocabulary development, the teacher can try several techniques. She can encourage the pupils to use a more varied vocabulary in speaking and in writing. She can encourage using the dictionary. (But caution should be exercised in dictionary practice as it can become tedious for children who have to look up a great number of words and have not developed facility with using diacritical marks and accents or the use of syllabication.) Sometimes pupils need to be reminded to use the context in figuring out unfamiliar words. Also, in explaining new words, the

8. A. Robinson, *Teaching Reading and Study Strategies: The Content Areas* (Rockleigh, N.J.: Allyn & Bacon, 1976).
9. See Appendixes B and D.

teacher can make them more vivid and alive by using related audiovisual aids and connecting words with their own experiences wherever possible. Finally, she can extract words for practice that they will meet in connection with the subject matter that they read. These are referred to as technical vocabulary.

Origins of Words

Children can become more interested in extending their vocabulary by learning the origins of words. An enthusiastic teacher can communicate her interest in words and capitalize on dramatic examples. For instance, the word *Herculean,* of course, is derived from the name *Hercules.* Most children know the feats that Hercules accomplished, involving strength and prowess. Therefore, they can easily understand the meaning of *Herculean.* This and other interesting word derivations may be found in such books as *The First Book of Words,*[10] *Words,*[11] and *The Abecedarian Book.*[12]

Words with Multiple Meanings

Every subject employs its own vocabulary with special meaning. Therefore, words and concepts used in special ways must be explained. For example, *company* used as an economic term is very different from *company* meaning guests.

Children must also learn that even common words have more than one meaning. For the simple word *run,* which most young children think of as meaning "moving very rapidly," the *Thorndike-Barnhart Beginning Dictionary* lists about 40 different meanings. In one instance, the authors, while reading a story with a child, came across the word *bluff* used in the sense of a high, steep place, or cliff, whereupon the child seemed very confused and seemed to lose the sense of what he was reading. The child said, "I don't understand this. The word *bluff* means 'to fool somebody.' How could somebody fall off a bluff?" The fact that words may have many different meanings had to be explained to him.

These examples dramatize how experience is related to interpretation. They also point up the necessity for the teacher to develop multiple

10. S. Epstein and B. Epstein, *The First Book of Words* (New York: Franklin Watts, 1954).
11. M. Ernst, *Words* (New York: Knopf, 1951).
12. C. Ferguson, *The Abecedarian Book* (Boston: Little, Brown, 1964).

meanings of words and give considerable attention to extending them as an important aspect of vocabulary development.

Keeping Lists of Words

Asking children to memorize long lists of words with their meanings is usually ineffectual. Sometimes children remember the definitions for a short period of time. More often they confuse the definitions. Further, the rote method of learning gives the pupil no idea what the words really mean.

Instead it is better to have him keep a notebook in which he writes in sentences the words he does not know. When reviewing, he can use context aids in recalling their meaning. Care must be taken that this exercise makes sense to him and that he understands why he is doing it. Sometimes the ingenious teacher can develop sufficient curiosity in words or instill pride in acquiring a richer vocabulary. It is helpful also to ask the pupils to incorporate new words into their class recitations and into their written assignments as often as possible. Unfortunately, intrinsic interest in vocabulary development is rare, particularly for pupils with reading disability. Often they become interested in improvement only when they become aware of the importance placed on vocabulary scores on achievement tests. In any case they must have a clear-cut purpose for learning words before isolated vocabulary practice is at all effective.

Prefixes, Suffixes, and Roots

It has long been advised to extend vocabulary through the study of prefixes, suffixes, and roots, but this would seem to apply mainly to the brighter students free from reading handicaps. The writers have found, along with others, that this kind of word study is not very suited to pupils with reading disability. Therefore we rarely stress it.

When the occasion does arise for its use, we have found it best to teach only those prefixes and suffixes that are consistent in their meaning, such as the following examples:

Prefixes: *com, dis, ex, pre, re, sub*

Suffixes: *tion, ment, ful, less*

With pupils who suffer from reading disability, the writers rarely teach Latin and Greek roots. Instead we explain that certain main or base words can add prefixes and suffixes which alter their meaning. Attention is then called to the way in which words change. In the following examples, the meanings of the parts are mentioned; then the words are listed and gone over with the children.

way	subway
do	redo
help	helpful
fear	fearless

Workbooks that have provision for vocabulary development along with other comprehension skills are listed in Appendix C.

Supplementary Reading to Develop Comprehension and Vocabulary

It is obvious that the more books that the pupils read, the more competent their reading, the wider their vocabulary, the broader their background, and the more they will understand concepts in varied fields. Since pupils with reading difficulty find it laborious, they rarely engage in recreational reading. Teachers and parents sometimes become annoyed that students will not even attempt to go to a library or pick up a book in their leisure. Or if they do, they will not finish it. Exhorting them to read, urging them to get a book, nagging them continually, all prove fruitless. Instead the teacher might carefully select two or three books that she knows from past experience are likely to interest a particular pupil. Reading a few pages with him to help him choose among them sometimes turns the trick. Once the first few books are enjoyable he will be less reluctant to try others.

Also, a teacher is in a better position to help poor readers select books successfully if she becomes familiar with a large body of material appropriate for them. As she gets to know more and more such books, she has a better idea which ones are long-time favorites, which ones are likely to be accepted, what the readability levels are, and which pupils might appreciate them. Such familiarity also allows her to seize every opportunity to help a pupil select a book that he truly likes. Once a child has experienced pleasure from a book, she can encourage him to discuss it with the other pupils or in front of the class. Then others may be more willing to read it, since they often value their classmates' opinion above any other. Once the ice has been broken, the teacher can encourage the pupil to read additional books by the same author. This may lead, in turn, to looking up information about the author in the *Biographical Dictionary* and often initiates genuine interest in books and authors.

Sometimes even enjoyment of a brief article read in class can evoke interest in outside reading. For instance, after one pupil had read a short selection about Thomas Edison's life, he became so enthusiastic that one of the authors under whose supervision he was, introduced him to a longer story, "The Wizard of Menlo Park," in *Teen-Age Tales*, Book I. He read it avidly. This evoked further interest in other biographies. He then took home books about the lives of scientists, such as *Robert Fulton: Boy Craftsman* and *The Wright Brothers*. In this way he was started on the road toward reading for his own pleasure. Without some guidance, however, he might have chosen a book so difficult or so inappropriate for him that his small spurt of curiosity would have been smothered.

Even though enticing those pupils with reading disability to read for pleasure is a dubious venture, it can be done. Once the initial hurdle is surmounted the task becomes less and less difficult. As the teacher knows more about her pupils and the type of material that is available, she will find that many of them are able to read a book or an article with satisfaction and a feeling of accomplishment.

More and more books with strong appeal for older pupils but with ease of readability are becoming available. Some of the books and material that the authors have found most suitable for pleasure reading as well as to round out background and bring depth of understanding regarding general information and vocabulary are listed in Appendixes B and D.

Louise—A Junior High School Student Reading at Fifth Grade Level

Many children whose reading has been satisfactory in the elementary school suddenly become overwhelmed when faced with the type of reading required at the junior high school level. Louise, age 12½, with high average intelligence, experienced just such a problem. She read at about sixth grade level, but needed special direction in the skills necessary at the upper elementary and junior high levels. Louise was referred to one of the authors for remedial instruction when she was in grade 7. Her parents reported that her schoolwork was adequate throughout the elementary grades. Even though there were no complaints about her reading, her parents observed that she never went to the library or engaged in any recreational reading. However, when she reached seventh grade and had to write book reports and read difficult social studies texts, she seemed completely lost.

Louise, a very attractive girl with a vivacious manner, was friendly, warm, and charming. She showed a good deal of anxiety about school. She reported that she never got beyond the first chapter of any book because she became too discouraged with the task of reading an entire book. Furthermore, she became nervous and upset after English and social studies classes because her teacher rigidly upheld extremely high standards. The teacher said, "I am not concerned when I see adolescents fall apart as this girl is doing. She will have to pick herself up again. . . . It is my duty to prepare them. . . ." Thus coordination of private remedial tutoring with the school was difficult. It became necessary for the writer to help Louise accept the attitude of the teacher and to continue working with her on her basic reading problem.

Louise's test results were as follows:

	Grade Score
Gray Oral Reading Test	5.5
Metropolitan Achievement Test—Advanced	
Reading	6.5
Vocabulary	6.9

Louise's oral reading was highly inaccurate. There were mispronunciations, insertions, and omissions of parts or entire words. Her word recognition skills were well below average for seventh grade pupils. The fifth grade score, however, probably underestimated her ability to some extent because of her marked anxiety connected with reading. On the silent reading test her achievement was considerably better. However, when confronted with paragraphs which appeared difficult, Louise merely skipped over them rather than try to read them and experience failure. During a trial learning session, she appeared to be able to handle material between fifth and sixth grade level, but seemed to need a fairly long time to complete the work.

Louise had two 45-minute sessions a week for 30 weeks. The

remedial program stressed accuracy in oral reading and development of comprehension and study skills. Later on she was also given help in increasing rate of reading.

For oral reading, Louise was started on the story of *Homer Price and the Donuts*, fifth grade readability level. We have found that using humorous material at the outset has many values. It causes anxious children to relax, while those who are resistive become more amenable to treatment. After a few sessions, it was possible to use materials which paralleled the school curriculum in English literature. Thus she was reading an adapted version of *The Prince and the Pauper*. (The original book was a school assignment.)

Part of each session was spent working directly in her social studies text. Louise learned how to vary her reading according to her purpose—in some instances to prepare oral and written reports for class, in others to pass brief weekly quizzes, and, of most importance, to understand what the material in the text was designed to impart. Along with development of study skills, she needed help with the specialized vocabulary she encountered in the various content areas.

Silent reading skills were developed further through the use of comprehension workbooks. As Louise's power of comprehension and word-analysis skills increased, emphasis on ways of increasing her rate was gradually introduced. As her competence in all reading skills improved, the level of difficulty was gradually raised in both oral and silent reading materials. Louise's assigned readings from school remained difficult for her, so that for quite some time it was necessary to supply her with adapted versions of the classics such as *Ivanhoe* and *Lorna Doone*. Lack of flexibility in the school's standards of expectation kept Louise's morale and functioning at uneven levels. Her performance depended to a great degree on her teachers' and parents' attitudes. When they were critical, rejecting, and demanding, improvement was impeded. They seemed to feel that if Louise would only try harder her problems would be solved. Such attitudes placed a greater burden on the writer, who had the responsibility of counteracting them and keeping Louise on an even keel.

For example, Louise came in particularly discouraged one day when she received a grade of D in social studies on her report card. She blurted out, "I am a failure." This led to a discussion of the meaning of grades and the many factors involved in determining them. It was pointed out how teachers' judgments may be based not only on objective data such as test scores, but may also be influenced by impressions gleaned from pupils' behavior in class. As an illustration, they talked about two students who received the same grade of C on a midterm exam. One student chose to sit way off in a corner in the last row of the room, appeared very bored, and never volunteered answers to any questions the teacher raised. The other student sat toward the front of the room, evinced interest in what was going on, and occasionally asked to have a point clarified which she did not understand. When the time came for evaluating these students' work for report cards, if the teacher were in doubt about whether to give a grade of C or D, classroom behavior would certainly enter into such appraisal. The student whose attitude appeared to be negative and uninterested might receive a grade of D, whereas the teacher might be more kindly disposed toward the one who exerted some effort in class and give her a grade of C.

Louise appeared surprised at the idea that a report card mark was not an absolute rating of one's ability. As our relationship became more secure, it was possible to guide her toward more effective methods of studying and to point out ways in which she might participate more actively in class sessions. Furthermore, it was suggested that, as soon as she realized that she was unable to understand the subject matter being presented, she talk it over with her teacher after class.

At the following session, Louise reported that it took a great deal of courage to speak to her teacher about suggestions as to how she might improve her work in social studies. However, she considered the conference somewhat helpful in that at least her teacher probably modified the image she had of her as a totally uninterested pupil. On Louise's part, she recognized that she had to assume responsibility for her own achievement.

Thus, instead of seeing everything in terms of success or failure, Louise gained insight into her role in influencing her achievement and also the relationship between her approach to the school situation and her teacher's reaction to her.

There were many occasions when Louise felt disappointed in her performance. At such times some of the facets of her problem were talked about and possible ways of helping herself were explored. Frequently just sympathetic recognition of the difficulties she encountered in school helped to tide her over the humps.

The type of supportive handling described in this case can have a therapeutic effect. It can make the difference between prolonged failure, where the student appears to become frozen in a pattern of defeat, and the beginning of improvement. When some success is achieved, the process is gradually reversed and the student begins to adjust more satisfactorily in school. This is what happened in Louise's case. Further evidence of her progress is reflected in the results of comparable achievement test scores which follow:

	Seventh Grade	
	Oct.	*June*
Gray Oral Reading Test	5.5	8.0
Metropolitan Achievement Test—Advanced		
Reading	6.5	9.0
Vocabulary	6.9	9.6

When remedial treatment was discontinued, Louise was able to handle material above grade level and in line with expectancy for her mental age. Her rate was still slow, but certainly improved. She could handle her textbooks and read stories for recreation. However, of most significance, she had a more optimistic outlook and had developed some confidence in her abilities.

At the last follow-up, Louise was in tenth grade. Though reading is not among her favorite pastimes, she does pick up a book voluntarily now and then. Since her reading skills are good enough to enable her to function well in school, any deeper interests in articles, newspapers, and books may have to await a later stage, when she is more eager for them.

The case of Duane, age ten, which follows illustrates how a remedial specialist was able to help a very anxious, defeated boy develop competency in reading and a positive attitude along with feelings of self-worth. Her careful selection of materials, her cooperation with the classroom teacher and above all her understanding of Duane's needs led to a decidedly hopeful outcome.

Duane—A Fifth Grader with a History of Reading Difficulty since First Grade

Duane was referred for remedial treatment[13] when he was ten years old and in the fifth grade.

Duane had difficulty learning to read since first grade. In the second

13. Duane was tutored by Susan Blumenthal, Instructor, Dept. of Special Education, Teachers College, Columbia University.

grade he began to avoid it altogether. His teacher reported that although he seemed to understand what she taught, he applied none of the skills to his reading. His spelling was poor, his handwriting laborious.

Duane's problem was compounded by the fact that his two older brothers were excellent students. The pressure to match their achievements merely intensified his lack of faith in himself.

As he grew older, Duane's aversion to reading increased. When his fifth grade assignments began to include research reports, he rarely could get started. Because he was easily distracted, classwork was difficult. Outside of class, he did no voluntary reading.

While he avoided reading, spelling, and writing, he participated readily in discussions and was more articulate than the average child. However, he was popular with his classmates, perhaps because he was a particularly good athlete. Duane's test results were as follows:

Gray Oral Reading Test	5.4
Metropolitan Achievement Test—Intermediate	
Vocabulary	4.9
Reading	5.3
Spelling	3.4

Despite his difficulty, Duane managed to achieve reading scores which were on grade level. He was, however, referred for remedial treatment for several reasons. First, he was the poorest reader in his class (most children in his class were reading between the sixth and tenth grade levels) and he lacked a commitment to learning. Second, he exhibited an intense dislike for most of the routines of school. Third, and perhaps most compelling, an intelligence test showed that Duane had superior ability. Certainly there was a significant gap between his capabilities and his performance.

The reading specialist felt that Duane's major problems stemmed from his intense anxiety. He had apparently internalized his family's high standards and he seemed constantly tense. The more tense he grew, the more this appeared to ignite irritability and the more provocative he became in school. Sometimes he refused to touch his schoolwork.

The goals of the treatment were to help him feel competent, reduce his anxiety, and change his attitude toward learning.

Duane was seen once a week over a two-year period for a total of 50 sessions.

Duane had the same classroom teacher during the two years of treatment. She and the remedial therapist spoke on the phone periodically. The teacher was observant of Duane's moods, compassionate, and willing to adapt her approach to his needs.

A major turning point occurred when the teacher agreed to break long-range assignments into smaller units. For example, for a paper due the following week, she would first ask Duane to read a limited number of pages which might take one or two days. Duane would report when he was finished and she would praise him and assign more pages. Then, she would ask for a first draft. Finally, he would complete the paper. When Duane began to see that he was making progress his anxiety seemed to decrease and he became less provocative in school.

Since Duane was so resistant, the specialist intentionally chose materials which did not resemble school texts. Some of the more successful materials are described in the following paragraphs.

Duane enjoyed two adventure stories, *Running Scared*[14] and *Call It Courage*.[15] *Running Scared* was appealing because the story was exciting, relatively short, humorous, and full of realistic conversations. *Call It Courage*, whose theme is the overcoming of fear and discouragement, provided opportunities to discuss Duane's fears of achievement.

Children like Duane, who do little or no recreational reading, often have a restricted range of knowledge and vocabulary. *Point of Law*,[16] true law cases written for the layman, introduced novel and mature ideas. Each selection is followed by a range of possible judicial decisions, which encourages the reader to make critical judgments. Duane responded eagerly to the idea of weighing the evidence and argued fervently for his "clients."

Duane was interested—in fact, excessively fascinated by— catastrophes. The reading specialist wanted to use this interest to improve his reading skills, without exacerbating the emotions he brought to the subject. *Strange, Sudden, and Unexpected*,[17] factual accounts of singular natural events from the Smithsonian Institution's Center for Short-lived Phenomena, proved ideal. The straightforward reporting provided a calm, rational, scientific approach that Duane absorbed readily and with interest.

14. One of a series of soft-cover books with fine black and white photographs. The stories (levels 3 through 6) are derived from children's descriptions of activities and stories (New York: Cambridge Book Co., 1971).

15. A. Sperry, *Call It Courage* (New York: Scholastic Books, 1970).

16. M. Lipman, *Point of Law* (Baltimore: Avelon Hill Game Co., 1976).

17. J. C. Cornell, Jr., *Strange, Sudden, and Unexpected* (New York: Scholastic Books, 1972).

Finally, the *Guinness Book of World Records*[18] was useful for teaching Duane to locate information rapidly. Its collection of odd and interesting facts make it a book without peer.

The reading specialist selected articles that would appeal to Duane from *Getting the Facts*[19] (Books D, E, and F), *New Practice Readers*[20] (Books D and E), *Reading for Concepts*[21] (Books E and F), and *Timed Readings*[22] (Level I). Although he disliked making errors on the questions following the selections, he checked his own work and was encouraged to defend his choices against the answer key. If he gave a good reason for his choice, he was marked correct.

The Pocket Tac,[23] a hand tachistoscope, helped Duane overcome his discouragement about spelling. He could flick the lever as many times as required to get the spelling of a word before writing it. Knowing that he had as many "peeks" as he needed diluted his anxiety. He began to retain new words after three or four flicks of the lever—soon, after two or three.

As Duane began to see that he could learn new words, spelling became easier and this fact was reflected in his schoolwork. His teacher commended him and by the end of his first year of treatment he saw spelling as a task he could master.

When assigned factual writing Duane tended to worry that his facts might be incorrect, and he slowed down or stopped outright. To eliminate the problem, Duane was given short, nonfactual topics during the remedial session. The following topic sources were helpful:

The *Stop, Look, and Write*[24] series presents vivid black and white photographs of many subjects, supplying points of departure for descriptive and creative writing.

Making It Strange[25] workbooks encourage the imagination in writing short themes. Typical subjects: Which is louder, a smile or a frown? Why? Which is angrier, the kitchen or the living room? Why? What color is pain? Why? Other topics Duane liked were: Write a commercial selling a rainy day; write a commercial for the color blue; what is your

18. N. McWhirter and R. McWhirter, *Guinness Book of World Records* (New York: Bantam, revised annually).

19. R. Boning, *Getting the Facts* (Baldwin, N.Y.: Barnell Loft, 1963).

20. C. R. Stone et al., *New Practice Readers* (New York: McGraw-Hill, Webster Division, 1970).

21. W. Liddle, ed., *Reading for Concepts* (New York: McGraw-Hill, Webster Division, 1970).

22. E. Spargo and G. R. Williston, *Timed Readings* (Providence, R.I.: Jamestown Publishers, 1975).

23. Reading Institute of Boston, 116 Newbury St., Boston, Mass.

24. H. Leavitt and D. Sohn, *Stop, Look, and Write* (New York: Bantam, 1964).

25. Prepared by Synectics, Inc. Published by Harper & Row (New York, 1968).

favorite letter of the alphabet and why? If a topic did not appeal to Duane, another was used. The objective was to get him to write so that he could see that he could express his ideas and be interesting to others.

Important to the treatment was Duane's perception of the reading specialist, as his ally against pressure. He knew that the reading specialist had diminished school pressure by suggesting that assignments be broken down. When he went away for the summer, the specialist encouraged him to read only books he really liked. This was in contrast to previous summers which had been seen as a time to build reading skills.

Dramatic changes began to take place in the second year of treatment. Duane began to finish assignments before they were due. And where previously he had found it difficult to admit that there were things he did not know, now he was able to ask his teacher for help. He also began to show concern for other children in his classroom; if they had difficulty, he offered help.

At the end of the sixth grade Duane was retested and found to have a mid-seventh-grade reading level. He was ready to transfer to a new school and, although he admitted some worry, he said, "The new school may give me some problems, but nothing is too hard for me now."

Suggestions for Further Reading

Borton, T. *Reach, Touch, and Teach: Student Concerns and Process Education.* New York: McGraw-Hill, 1970.

Brown, G., "Affectivity, Classroom Climate, and Teaching." Washington, D.C.: American Federation of Teachers, 1971.

Guthrie, J. *Aspects of Reading Acquisition.* Baltimore: Johns Hopkins University Press, 1976.

Harris, A. and Sipay, E. *How to Increase Reading Ability.* New York: David McKay, 1975.

Robinson, A. *Teaching Reading and Study Strategies: The Content Areas.* Rockleigh, N.J.: Allyn & Bacon, 1976.

Schmuck, R., and Schmuck, P. *Group Processes in the Classroom.* Dubuque, Iowa: William C. Brown, 1971.

Smith, F. *Comprehension and Learning.* New York: Holt, Rinehart and Winston, 1975.

Tenney, J. "Development of Cognitive Organization in Children." Doctoral Dissertation, Cornell University, 1973.

11

High School and College Students with Marked Comprehension and Expressive Writing Difficulties

by Ruth G. Nathan*

THE underachieving adolescent and young adult in senior high school and college present a special challenge for the reading instructor. The problems of these older students, who have not been able to reach appropriate reading levels or achieve minimal competence in writing, require a complex approach. Skill development is only one aspect of the instructional process for students whose long history of language deficits has made them resistant and defensive, left gaps in their background knowledge, and, most important, deprived them of the basic organization tools.

This chapter is concerned with two important directions in dealing with the older student. One major focus is on ways to reach students who are discouraged about poor schoolwork. Another is on providing these students with means to cope with the immediate demands of academic life. Thus, it is necessary to stress techniques for teaching reading comprehension and expressive writing in ways which can be directly related to schoolwork.

* Instructor, Fashion Institute of Technology, State University of New York.

These older students carry with them the burden of years of persistent failure. Their instructors consistently describe them as "disorganized." Few are able to face up to their deficits, having invested a great deal of energy in denial or in heroic but inadequate attempts at compensation. When assigned to remedial classes they are often angry and resentful. They need to acquire insights into their difficulties which will allow them to learn. At the same time they need to be offered specific solutions.

Another general characteristic of these students is inability to distill essential meanings. Consequently, they show a fuzziness in their thinking which probably has been an important factor in preventing them from making appropriate connections in academic situations all through their school lives. The repetitive refrain of the disgruntled college student in a basic skills class is, "I had it in high school." This illustrates the plight of the underachiever, who indeed has been told throughout the years to find the "main idea," "central thought," and "theme," but has not been able to grasp these concepts.

The preceding profile of older underachievers emphasizes the special difficulty of working with these young people. The teenage struggle for identity and independence undeniably produces turmoil and tension. Nevertheless, there are positive developmental effects during these years. For example, they usually have more control over their behavior, so that the college instructors rarely complain of the discipline problems that characterize junior and some senior high school classrooms. Furthermore, the future is no longer a faraway fantasy but an imminent reality. Motivation, therefore, becomes stronger and more reality oriented.

Developing Reading Comprehension and Related Study Skills

The task of the instructor is to build on nonexistent or limited skills while giving the support necessary to enable students to approach learning with courage and confidence. These students need concrete procedures for dealing with reading and study skills. The types of materials which have proved the most useful in developing these processes are those which are expository rather than narrative. Textbooks and articles from newspapers and magazines make relevant and interesting practice material. For example, in one college classroom the instructor begins a process of orientation by using concrete examples. Producing a news magazine, she introduces a discussion of the cover picture. Parts of the picture are considered and weighed. Simple questions such as "What is the artist trying to tell us?" and "What makes you think so?" encourage analytic thinking.

The goals of these orientation sessions are twofold. It is important first to establish that acts of communication are about ideas. Second, access to these ideas is facilitated by the ability to break them down into parts and put them together again.

Cartoons are useful in reinforcing these principles. Analyzing the parts of cartoons, especially those with no written captions, can provide entertaining and useful insights into how the parts of an idea function. Covering up an essential part or detail of a cartoon and asking if it is still funny dramatizes the relationship of the parts to the whole.

In another class, the instructor distributed the words of a current popular song. The students read the words as they listened to the record. The lyrics reiterated a simple lament about man's destructive effect on his environment. Students were able to grasp the idea quickly, sort it into key ideas and supporting details, and repeat it in their own words. At subsequent sessions, the students brought in their favorite songs and enjoyed figuring out meanings in similar ways. Students and teachers alike discovered that seemingly absurd lyrics proved to be about ideas, which could be analyzed.

While working with the songs and cartoons, illogical thinking frequently became apparent. For example, one student responded to a cartoon depicting a presidential candidate debating with his opponent with the statement, "All politicians are crooks." Needless to say this concept was not implicit in the cartoon. Such irrelevant interpretations suggest that many students need fundamental orientation to arrive at sound conclusions. Lyrics and cartoons provide a concrete way to analyze material and separate logical inference from one's own opinion or bias.

Another teacher asked her college students with reading levels below the 6th percentile on a standardized reading test to make a collage to illustrate a complete thought without using words. The completed works were presented to the class for response and discussion. Some of the students with limited verbal skills were able to communicate visually on a highly sophisticated level. Among the collages submitted, for example, was one depicting the economic difficulties of a large city. Tumbling skyscrapers were surrounded by a shower of torn dollar bills.

The concept and its supporting details were clearly thought through and beautifully executed. In contrast, another student submitted elegantly structured pictures of natural phenomena. The content was so generalized that the only possible response from the class was simply "nature." Thus the assignment vividly demonstrated the difference between fully developed concepts and vague generalizations.

When students realize that media are concerned with grasping concepts, the next step is to analyze factual material. First, paragraphs are introduced as the smallest units of written communication. Good sources for practice paragraphs include the students' texts, current magazine and newspaper articles, and commercial workbooks such as *Reading Is Thinking*.[1] As they learn that each well-constructed paragraph is about one idea, students are often relieved. As they begin to feel more confident about finding the key ideas in single paragraphs, short selections composed of several related paragraphs are introduced. Current literature often provides good sources for such material. In one college remedial class, students subscribe to a weekly news magazine, which provides relevant, adult material for outside reading assignments.

Students are responsive to material which suggests provocative questions about human behavior. One example that elicited strong emotional reactions and lively discussions is a newspaper story about an infamous incident in which a large group of neighbors watched a woman murdered without calling for help or coming to her aid.[2] Another effective selection is a passage from the book *Alive* by Piers Paul Read found in *Topics for the Restless*,[3] which describes the plight of the victims of a disastrous air crash and an extraordinary moral dilemma which arose. The questions "What would you have done?" referring to either piece always provokes strong reactions, encouraging involvement and motivation in reading and provides interesting possibilities for written work.

Excerpts of this type[4] help students to recognize that articles can deal with serious and significant questions relevant to their own lives.

Another step in the further development of skills is to analyze textbook type material. Students need to use the same basic tools: breaking written material down into parts, understanding the relationship of the parts to each other, and discriminating among ideas.

1. R. Gedamke and N. Kropp, *Reading Is Thinking* (New York: Curriculum Research Associates, 1970).
2. A. M. Rosenthal, *Thirty-eight Witnesses.* (New York: McGraw-Hill, 1964).
3. E. Spargo, ed., *Topics for the Restless* (Providence, R.I.: Jamestown Publishers, 1974).
4. Ibid.

Taking Notes

One community college teacher[5] has developed a method called "study-note taking," which develops insight into logical processing and relates well to academic work. Her approach involves applying the techniques of surveying the material and analyzing the paragraphs of brief selections or chapters from textbooks. Students are given structured guidelines which direct them to include the title, headings, subheadings, and main thought of each paragraph in their own notes. Paraphrasing the main thoughts under supervision supplies the basis for a brief summary. As students see the written headings and key paragraphs shortened in the manner illustrated, they can actually visualize the skeleton of the major concept and its details.

Title	*Personnel Management*[6]
Subheading	*Recruitment* (to enlist [as an army] or to sign up new members for service).
1st Par.	A major task of personnel department is to keep an active file of *prospective* (future) employees who have the skills and education needed to carry out *diverse* (different) jobs in company. To do this, personnel department must *survey* (look over) all possible *sources* (origin or beginning) where future employees may be.
2nd Par.	*Advertising*: "help-wanted" ads in newspapers, radio and TV, magazines (disadvantage: no way to screen employees).
3rd Par.	*Public Employment Agencies*: Federal and state employment agencies will place all types of workers at no cost.
4th Par. & *5th Par.*	*Private Employment Agencies*: charge money to place individuals, such as large percentage of first month's *gross* (before taxes and deductions) salary, paid by either employer or employee.

Class discussion and model notes prepared by the instructor provide a concrete model for independent work. Students learn to understand

5. Betty Ford, La Guardia Community College, City University of New York.
6. Summarized from H. Pickle and R. Abrahamson, *Introduction to Business* (Palisades, Calif.: Goodyear, 1974).

and summarize the basic information in a paragraph. For further motivation, students are encouraged to use their study notes to predict possible test questions on the information. For example, an obvious question from the above paragraphs might be, "What are some of the sources the personnel manager of a company would use in order to maintain an active file on future employees?" The group discovers in a very practical way that distilling information leads to effective mastery of the material.

Taking notes on lectures, another skill requiring organization and concentration, is handled in a similarly practical and relevant way by a college professor of psychology.[7] She uses a series of two half-hour videotaped lectures on the subject of dreams.

Before the first videotape is presented, preparatory work establishes criteria for good lecture notes. It is often helpful for students to analyze the task, emphasizing the distinction between taking notes on written material, which is always available for reference, and the more immediate demands of listening.

First, awareness of a speaker's structure is encouraged. The speaker's language is also examined for clues, such as transitional words which signal his intention and organization. Another step uses both the auditory and visual modalities to remind students of the role played by body language in conveying messages and signals about the speaker's direction. Finally before the two videotaped lectures on dreams, students are asked to use a highly organized format based on the Cornell system[8] for taking notes. The page is divided into two columns, one wide one for notes, and a narrow one labeled the recall column. Soon after the video presentation, the students underline the important ideas and facts in their notes, using the recall column for brief summaries, key words, and phrases which should help them to "recall" the main ideas and important details. A practice quiz on the first lecture, "The Purpose and Mechanics of Dreams," is given in a subsequent class. The corrected quiz is returned and model notes are distributed and discussed, affording a novel opportunity to get feedback in the skill of note taking. The second videotaped lecture, "The Interpretation of Dreams," is used for further practice and gives students an opportunity to compare their two performances.

7. M. Rothman, Fashion Institute of Technology, State University of New York.
8. W. Pauk, *How to Study in College* (Boston: Houghton Mifflin, 1974).

Expressive Writing

Most of the older students described are likely to have a high degree of difficulty expressing themselves in writing. It is generally agreed that writing is the most complex of the communication skills and the most difficult to learn.[9] Furthermore, these students, with a long history of reading comprehension problems, have read very little and therefore lack experience with the organization and structure of written language. They approach writing tasks with great apprehension and confusion and often seem paralyzed when confronted with written assignments.

Again the problem for the instructor is to find concrete and workable ways to overcome these defeated and defensive attitudes. Many instructors have observed that writing tasks such as paraphrasing and summarizing based on the well-organized writing of others are effective and nonthreatening introductory assignments. Even students with adequate reading comprehension who have specific deficits in their writing are encouraged by this approach.

For example, factual articles on provocative topics of current interest such as feminism, environmental problems, and psychological phenomena are chosen from magazines such as *Psychology Today* and *Reader's Digest*, as well as upper level reading texts.

A first step in teaching writing is to develop the ability to paraphrase. The difficult struggle to put an author's ideas into one's own words has two important results. First, the student gains deeper insight into the communication process. Searching for an author's meaning and trying to rephrase it often clarifies the basic concept that writing is an act of communication.

Second, paraphrasing requires a complete understanding of the words used by the author. Students who habitually skip over long and unfamiliar words are required to be alert to word meanings. This can provide an excellent framework for teaching vocabulary in a meaningful and practical way. Developing dictionary skills and encouraging the use of a thesaurus are appropriate skills to teach in this context.

Progressing from simple paraphrasing to longer summaries of brief selections, the students have the experience of producing well-organized written work, often for the first time. Furthermore, they can apply summarizing directly to answering essay questions in school assignments.

9. D. Johnson and H. Myklebust, *Learning Disabilities* (New York: Grune & Stratton, 1967).

Perfect accuracy, conciseness, and clarity are rarely achieved at this point, but the basic goals of logical expository writing are clarified.

Further practice is provided by asking students to write brief reaction papers based on interesting reading material. These papers, limited to one or two paragraphs, enable students to move toward independence in writing within a structured framework. Experiential or creative writing is often too sophisticated and demanding a task for students at this level.

Another aspect of the writing component is grammar. Only a limited number of strategies are needed for students with writing problems. The sequence is adapted from sector analysis grammar[10,11] and is designed to give students concrete ways of dealing with some of the most basic writing problems, such as sentence fragments, verb agreement, and mistakes in tenses. The techniques are fully developed in the works cited. What is important to note here is that these methods do not require prior grammatical knowledge, and so students can learn immediately to edit their own work. The concept of editing helps these students who have formerly found traditional grammar too mystifying. Many teachers have noted that inexperienced students are often astonished by the revelation that editing and reediting are intrinsic to writing. In discovering that accurate, clear writing often needs many drafts, students gain understanding of the writing process.

The case of Joshua[12] illustrates an application of these writing techniques with an older student who was referred specifically as a writing problem. Joshua, a 17-year-old senior in high school, was a good reader with superior intelligence. His spelling was poor and his handwriting almost illegible. His written work was disorganized and expressed in fragmented sentences and disconnected thoughts.

Joshua seemed unable to recognize the seriousness of his problem, focusing instead on his handwriting as a major factor. He presented himself with an air of truculence and defiance. This strong hostility and resistance made it seem doubtful that Joshua would be able to involve himself sufficiently in learning to write.

The writer saw Joshua twice weekly. We began in a very directed way, with Joshua reading and discussing brief selections. Since reading comprehension did not present a problem, articles from upper level com-

10. R. Allen, *English Grammars and English Grammar* (New York: Scribner's, 1972).
11. M. Schwartz and C. D. Spinelli, *Writing, A Discovery Approach* (Dubuque, Iowa: Kendall Hunt, 1976).
12. The tutor in this case was Ruth G. Nathan.

mercial texts, such as *Reading Power*[13] and *Developing Reading Proficiency*,[14] and material from the New York *Times* and other periodicals were used.

A special effort was made to find materials that were stimulating enough to overcome some of Joshua's resistance. Articles about moral dilemmas, problems of human behavior and critical issues of the day elicited mature and thoughtful responses. Excerpts from an anthology devoted to the theme of the relationship of men to machines[15] were of great interest to him. An article about nationwide writing problems in a current news magazine proved particularly meaningful as Joshua realized the extent of the problems which plagued him.

As Joshua became more involved with ideas his ability to structure his own thinking increased; his anger and hostility lessened. Progress was slow but he began to produce clear written work. A growing sense of mastery resulted in a positive and dynamic change in attitude which made it possible for him to participate in the difficult work with an unexpected degree of serious commitment and concentration.

As the instructor and Joshua discussed significant ideas, he began to feel a sense of intellectual involvement. The instructor's interest and respect for Joshua's own thinking provided the dramatic impetus which stimulated him. Gradually he began to summarize, evaluate, and synthesize the writing of others on an independent level. As his competence and confidence continued to develop he was eventually able to make realistic plans for attending college.

The case of Joshua illustrates many characteristics which are noted in other college students. Many instructors recognize that finding concrete methods of dealing with apathy and inability to focus are crucial to the development of basic comprehension and writing skills. The change in attitude which accompanies involvement and increasing self-confidence and the reduced anxiety which lessens resistance are important factors in freeing students to move toward thinking and responding logically.

13. J. I. Brown, *Reading Power* (Lexington, Mass.: Heath, 1974).
14. B. Schmidt et al., *Developing Reading Proficiency* (Columbus, Ohio: Charles E. Merrill, 1971).
15. A. Lewis, ed., *Of Men and Machines* (New York: Dutton, 1963).

Suggestions for Further Reading

Allen, R. *English Grammars and English Grammar*. New York: Scribners, 1972.

Burmeister, L. *Reading Strategies for Secondary School Teachers*. Reading, Mass.: Addison Wesley, 1974.

Kahn, R. *Teaching Reading in High School*, 2nd Edition. Indianapolis: Bobbs-Merrill, 1972.

Pauk, W. *How to Study in College*. Boston: Houghton Mifflin, 1974.

Schwartz, M., Spinelli, C. *Writing: A Discovery Approach*. Dubuque, Iowa: Kendall Hunt, 1976.

Walker, M. "Setting Realistic Goals for the Ethnically Different Student." in Nacke (ed.) *Interaction: Research and Practice for College-Adult Reading: 23d Yearbook of the National Reading Conference* 8 (1976), pp. 265–67.

12

Remedial Techniques for Older Pupils with Severe Reading Disability

THE SEVEREST CASES of reading disability are those pupils in junior and senior high school who may be nonreaders or significantly below grade level. Although the method of handling these pupils is similar to the one used with others, they present certain special problems. First of all, attitudes ranging from apathy to antagonism are extremely pronounced. The older the pupils and the lower the achievement, the more defeated, frustrated, angry, or fearful they become; finally they are unwilling to try, or pretend not to care whether they learn to read or not. They often become the hard-core discipline problems of the school and are a tribulation to all those who deal with them. Not only are they a blight on the school's record, not only are they blatant troublemakers for all concerned, but no one is certain how to cope with them in a school setting. Even when a teacher tries to work with them, these pupils usually proceed so slowly that the teacher's patience is sorely tried and she may feel like giving up, too. Although working with them one at a time is beset with heavy enough problems, teaching a group is even more taxing. In dealing with such pupils, the teacher must consider ways to overcome interfering reactions and find suitable methods and materials so that they can benefit from schoolwork.

This chapter will discuss ways to improve these pupils' attitudes toward reading and ways to teach them through adapted methods and special materials.

Improving Attitudes toward Reading

Teachers who try to help such pupils must first of all have confidence that all is not lost. They need not despair, even when they gaze upon distraught, belligerent, tormented youngsters. Despite their utter misery, their lack of surface appeal, they can be transformed. Not only can their façade be penetrated, but they desperately need a forceful, inspiring influence in their lives—much more perhaps than their more fortunate contemporaries. Such an influence can cause them to drop their armor and start afresh.

The teacher who is determined realizes that such pupils need someone to care about them and believe in them enough to help them help themselves. When the pupils see that there are all kinds of useful and meaningful things to learn and that they can actually master them, they begin to feel competent. Through the teacher's respect, through reaching their basic desire to know and to grow, through connecting schoolwork with their personal lives and feelings, these pupils may finally emerge as earnest and resolute.

Ways to Handle Severely Retarded Readers

Besides overcoming entrenched resistance and finding qualified teachers, the major considerations in handling severely retarded readers center on setting realistic goals and finding ways to reach them in a learning situation. It is not that these pupils need anything so different from other young people. They have the same strivings for self-exploration and knowledge of the practical and esthetic world as others. It is just that their poor academic skills have alienated them from school. To bring them back, we need to have a realistic view of their problem and adapt the program to their present situation. They may then absorb the essentials that will carry over into their life after they leave school and at the same time enable them to experience the joy of a job well done in the classroom. Each school and each teacher must plan and improvise according to the pupils' stage of development, the subject matter to be taught, and the materials available. Therefore, no specific prescriptions can be offered. Instead, some over-all suggestions will be stated concerning goals, adaptation of the program, and the finding of suitable reading matter. These suggestions can then be modified to fit the particular pupils that a teacher may face.

Setting Realistic Goals

As in all cases of reading disability, diagnosis determines individual expectations and circumscribes the goals that are realistic. Diagnosis has been discussed in Chapters 6 and 7. However, for pupils with severe difficulty, more reliance should be placed on informal rather than standardized measures. Trial lessons, as described in Chapter 6, are particularly suitable in evaluating the needs of such pupils. Also, prognosis should be tentative because these pupils have failed for so many years that they are likely to have developed antipathy toward formal examinations of any kind, and test scores and to underestimate their ability.

Therefore improvement—even though very slow—is the realistic goal. Even those pupils who are far behind can and should be able to improve. Perhaps their extreme disability will prevent their ever reaching their potential, but they can move ahead; their poor foundation and years of failure may cause severe handicaps, but they can be surmounted to some extent[1] Perhaps they will never reach the ideal; perhaps they will never even rise to average standards. But they can do better. Hopefully these pupils can all be brought up to at least sixth or seventh grade reading level before they leave school. This is the minimum for getting along in our world. But even if this minimum is not reached, every effort must be made to prepare them to fit into society, to help them better their vocational chances, and to see that they get as much out of school as they can.

The cases of Karl and Dirk which follow describe two boys of the same age and reading at about the same grade level according to standardized tests. However, they needed very different kinds of teaching. Karl could follow accepted procedures for remedial instruction, and Dirk needed a special program.

1. R. Gottesman, I. Belmont, and R. Kaminer, "Admission and Follow-up Status of Reading Disabled Children Referred to a Medical Clinic," *Journal of Learning Disabilities* 8 (1973): 642–50.

Karl and Dirk—Both 12 Years of Age, Reading at Third Grade Level: A Contrast in Treatment

Karl, aged 12 years, 5 months, had a long history of school problems. He had particular difficulty in absorbing reading instruction. During the testing,[2] he was pleasant and friendly but unable to give consistent or sustained effort to any task. Questions and instructions had to be repeated over and over. Karl's responses were incomplete, poorly expressed, and accompanied by the almost constant refrain, "I don't know that one." He seemed to anticipate failure and had so little faith in his abilities that he felt that there was no use trying. Thus he needed an inordinate amount of encouragement to keep functioning.

His intelligence was within normal range with deficiencies noted particularly in his background of general information and ability to define words. His reading test scores were as follows:

	Grade Score
Gray Oral Reading Test	3.6
Metropolitan Achievement Test— (Elementary Battery for Grades 3 and 4)	
Word Knowledge	3.2
Reading	2.2
Wide Range Achievement Test	
Word Pronunciation	3.8
Spelling	3.2
Arithmetic	4.7

The *Roswell-Chall Diagnostic Reading Test* showed a good grasp of phonic skills but difficulty in handling polysyllabic words.

It was found that when the author sat alongside Karl, he could work reasonably well. However, when independent effort was required, his concentration span was extremely short and little was accomplished. Furthermore, as soon as he encountered challenging tasks, he gave up.

Yet in a typical learning situation when the author discussed the subject matter with Karl and it made sense to him, the results were noticeably better. It was clear that on his own he read everything in a vague, unfocused, general way, which probably accounted for his very low silent reading score. He stated that if he had to answer questions about a passage, he would have to read it many times over. Thus, when

2. By one of the authors.

a new selection was introduced, Karl was given an idea of its contents. Difficult concepts and unfamiliar words were explained, and poor questions in the workbook were eliminated. For example, in presenting an article entitled "Wetlands, Wildlife, and Wells,"[3] discussion centered on the meanings of *swamp*, *reservoir*, and *wildlife*. Then Karl was asked to read the article to find out why it is important to preserve swamps. With this type of preparation, his comprehension of the selection was quite good.

For oral reading, materials at fourth grade level seemed suitable. It was not difficult to find books that interested this boy because he was quite immature for his age and reacted well to stories that generally appealed to younger children. During the trial learning session he chose several books that he would like to read. (These were subsequently suggested to his tutor.)

At the completion of the examination, Karl seemed interested in the author's explanation of what he needed in reading, spelling, and expressive writing, and he appeared willing to receive individualized instruction in these areas. Accordingly, arrangements were made with a reading specialist to work with him twice a week. Regular conferences were to be held with his classroom teacher so as to coordinate their efforts.

Remedial Instruction

Karl's tutor reported that it was necessary to plan in terms of two levels. The first was to try to help the boy overcome his deficiencies, especially in comprehension; the second was to assist him with his schoolwork. The latter was implemented by means of communication with the classroom teacher, either by telephone or through messages taken by Karl to or from his teacher whenever clarification of assignments or remedial instruction was indicated. This led to the boy's developing a sense of collaborative efforts on his behalf. Whereas previously he had a feeling of being on the fringe of his class, he now had a sense of being cared for which resulted in his gradual willingness to enter into group activities. He was also encouraged to take full responsibility for his homework, thereby freeing his parents from constantly having to check up on it. In time, his parents' anxiety diminished as they recognized that Karl's instructional needs were being met. Therefore, they could focus on other ways of spending time with their son which could be both pleasurable and instructive. For example, it was suggested that when

3. W. Liddle, *Reading for Concepts*, Book C (New York: McGraw-Hill, Webster Division, 1970).

taking Karl to special exhibits, they talk over what they were viewing or, on trips, call to his attention the name of cities they were in or states they were passing through. His tutor felt this would strengthen his geographical concepts and lessen his vagueness in relation to trips he took with his family.

In the beginning of remedial work, materials at third grade level were used. When reading aloud, Karl and his tutor read alternate paragraphs, thereby helping him with phrasing, expression, and learning new words. For silent reading, he was given a good deal of preparation, as outlined previously, before introducing a selection. For recreational reading, only short stories were used at the outset. Then longer stories divided into short chapters were introduced, and finally, toward the end of the year, Karl completed several full length books at about fifth or sixth grade reading levels. There was also emphasis on developing spelling and writing skills, starting with simple sentences and progressing to simple paragraphs. Words taught in spelling were regularly reviewed by means of dictating them in sentences. It was found that Karl needed a great deal of reinforcement because of his poor ability to recall what he seemingly learned. Another area in which he showed conspicuous deficits was orientation with regard to time and spatial concepts, so that various games and devices to improve such concepts were presented.

Karl developed an excellent relationship with his tutor, who observed that along with progress in school, there were discernible changes for the better in his posture and stance and degree of independence in many areas. Even his tendency to shrug his shoulders accompanied by "I don't know," decreased markedly. Improvement was steady but uneven, with occasional lapses in one area or another which then required patient reteaching and review. Yet overall gains were apparent both at school and at home. Nevertheless, it seems likely that Karl will need supportive help until a higher level of competence and independence are achieved. Furthermore, at some point, consideration might also be given to supplementing his curriculum through avenues of approach other than reading, as discussed in the case of Dirk which follows.

Dirk

Dirk, aged 12 years, 8 months, reading at third grade level, was referred to one of the authors by his school for guidance in connection with educational planning, as he was becoming increasingly resistive to reading instruction.

For several years, Dirk had been placed in special classes for children with learning disabilities where he had accepting, specially trained, competent teachers. Yet he was a very frustrated boy who said that he was "completely turned off" by reading and reading materials designed for pupils with reading problems. Examination revealed some indication of neurophysiological dysfunction. His mother described him as a child who asked bright questions at a very early age but could not remember names of anything for many years and could not even remember different names of colors at five years of age.

On the WISC, Dirk's verbal scale I.Q. was high average, performance scale very superior, and full scale I.Q. in the bright normal range. The subtest scores revealed wide variability in his intellectual functioning with extremely high abilities on most performance tests and striking deficits on tests involving short-term memory and learning of new symbols. Similarities and vocabulary were average because of some difficulties with abstract thinking. Dirk's reading test scores were as follows:

	Grade Score
Gray Oral Reading Test	3.2
Metropolitan Achievement Tests— (Elementary Battery for Grades 3 and 4)	
Word Knowledge	3.3
Reading	3.0
Wide Range Achievement Test	
Word Pronunciation	1.7
Spelling	2.0
Arithmetic	4.5

The *Roswell-Chall Diagnostic Reading Test* revealed lack of mastery of basic phonic skills.

Informal procedures indicated that Dirk could handle materials at about third grade level. Even though he could give a fairly good oral report of what he had read, he had enormous difficulty in rendering information in written form. As indicated by his score, his spelling problem was severe. He used a phonic approach solely in his attempts at writing. For example, he wrote *ej* for *edge* and *citchn* for *kitchen*. Furthermore, even though he could succeed with some of the spelling approaches used during the trial learning session, he indicated that he found them too tedious to apply.

Dirk was charming, pleasant, and cooperative during the testing sessions, but was totally frank about the fact that he disliked heartily the books customarily used for pupils like him.

Making recommendations for Dirk posed a real problem because of his strong negative attitudes towards the usual practices and materials that are helpful. Therefore, it appeared that we were dealing with the type of child who needs a nonreading supplementary curriculum that would not rely on reading as the principal means of gathering information. Such an approach is described by Wiseman.[4] Other media would need to be used to encourage learning, such as cassettes, recorded books, tape recordings, TV, films, film strips, and slides. For example, in the areas of science and ecology, rich sources of materials are now widely available. Teachers have always used trips to museums for all kinds of firsthand information. Such experiences for Dirk would need to be expanded so as to meet his individual needs.

Accordingly, the school was advised to develop a nonreading curriculum to the extent possible, also to encourage any activities that would utilize this boy's unusually good manual skills and creativity. Fortunately, the school was equipped with facilities for various kinds of woodwork. This was an area in which Dirk excelled. Since he felt surfeited with remedial materials, the school was advised to deemphasize their use and instead to present reading incidentally in connection with his shop work. Technical vocabulary could be selected from directions for assembling units or whatever type of work he was engaged in. Spelling and writing might be introduced gradually wherever actually needed.

Thus, for Dirk, alternative ways to educate him had to be explored until he reached the point where he would willingly participate in some form of remedial program. The authors have encountered many such students who have become more amenable to help in later adolescence where plans for their future became realistic and the need for learning became more compelling.

In a follow-up study one year later it was found that through family counseling both Dirk and his mother discovered that his dyslexia was being used as a means of maintaining a close, dependent relationship. Dirk learned further that he had been perpetuating many immature patterns of adjustment by clinging to his dyslexia. This also provided an excuse for not having to exert effort in coping with the demands of an academic curriculum.

As his insight deepened into his unfruitful defensive adaptations, he

4. D. E. Wiseman, *The Nonreading Parallel Curriculum*, from "The Child With Learning Disabilities," ACLD 1971, 8th Annual Conference, pp. 111–17.

decided to enter into a program for improving his school performance. The medium which provided the greatest motivation proved to be the use of recorded books. He found these talking books, which were at a mature level, fascinating and, according to his mother, "gobbled them up." As he began to recognize that he did not always have to succeed and that failure was part of the learning process, the possibility of failure became less threatening. Gradually his rationalizations about his inability to learn lessened and he was willing to engage in reading and related activities again. The recorded books, in addition to providing pure enjoyment and interesting information, introduced Dirk to literature as it was originally written. They also aroused his curiosity to learn more about a wide variety of subjects, and his outlook broadened in innumerable ways.

Recorded books can be particularly valuable for students with reading disability because reading matter which is designed especially for such students is usually quite limited in depth and scope. Thus, we have counseled both parents and teachers that education for children with learning disabilities needs to be implemented through whatever media and firsthand experiences are feasible in order to broaden their knowledge, stimulate their thought processes, and keep them in touch with what is going on in the world around them.

The Teacher's Role

Karl and Dirk are typical of the large number of older pupils with severe reading problems. In helping these pupils understand their various subjects, the teacher first presents material orally, visually, and concretely. For example, some adults have neither the time nor patience to wade through complicated material, but will be able to go back to it after they have, let us say, seen a movie on the subject. Likewise, pupils can gain the needed information when the teacher presents the subject in ways that help them compensate for their lack of foundation skills. In other words, reading fits into the total framework, but the teacher cannot count on independent use of books the way she can with better prepared pupils.

Thus the teacher depends heavily on films, recordings, recorded books, television, cassettes, dramatic productions, oral discussion, and the like for elaboration of the subject before books are used and tries in every way to humanize the material. This usually gets the pupils thinking and responding actively and helps them surmount their listlessness and resistance. Although they need to develop a broader background and vocabulary and to extend their skills just like other pupils, this cannot be done in the usual ways. In fact, formal practice on techniques, such as finding the main idea and important details, rate, and so on, must be delayed until the pupils learn to apply their thoughts and efforts to the subject matter under discussion, regain sufficient confidence and discipline to undertake study-type reading, and develop enough competence to proceed more independently. When they reach this point they can benefit from instruction similar to that described in Chapter 10. In the meantime, the teacher assumes an active role and wherever possible evokes interest in the topic, relates factual material to their personal lives, and shows them that discovery of the information can have real value.

Those who work with such pupils are well aware that most of them have little desire to learn academic subjects. They are usually not even willing to undertake them for secondary goals, such as a means toward higher education or improvement of their status. So they need presentations that come alive and emphasize those aspects that make sense to them at their present stage. Later on they may be able to absorb more abstract approaches, but their attitude at the beginning is usually "What does this mean to me?"

The teacher can introduce the text by building concepts and new vocabulary and raising questions. Then she guides the class to find the answers. However, with such poor readers, she places emphasis on discussion and oral reading in order to compensate for their minimal reading ability. She postpones expectation for more independent work until they are capable of doing it.

These pupils can also engage in a certain amount of simple supplementary reading. Books of historical and informational interest with low vocabulary are becoming more available. These books are less difficult than their regular texts. Publishers such as Garrard Press, Bobbs-Merrill, Webster, and Scholastic have developed many such books. Naturally, the pupils cannot be expected to do extensive research, particularly in the beginning. But they can be encouraged to do more than they have ever done before. When assignments are clear-cut and properly circumscribed, they can experience the satisfaction of finding answers without fruitless effort and discover that they actually can obtain information they wish from reading material.

After the preparatory discussion, collaborative textbook work, and supplementary reading, the teacher helps the pupils organize information into a logical and useful order. That which the teacher and class consider sufficiently important can be compiled into notebooks for future reference. This helps them remember what they have learned and can also be used for review purposes and for tests.

The Place of Test Taking

The taking of tests by pupils with severe reading disability deserves special comment. Their general attitudes of extreme indifference or acute anxiety apply here also. Some of the children, for example, have failed for so many years that another failure rolls off their backs. Others have a great deal of apprehension about attaining the required reading level for promotion. Or, as graduation looms near, still others may have a great stake in passing tests, either because getting a certificate or diploma has intrinsic meaning or because it is crucial for their future job placement. Whatever the ramifications, passing tests creditably can play a specialized role with such pupils. The new experience may be, for instance, an added factor in renewed effort; it may be concrete evidence that they really are not as stupid as they have always felt; best of all, it can engender personal pride and satisfaction.

Therefore, it is important that the teacher explain the purpose and place of tests. If the pupils perceive a test as something punitive or devastating, she tries to relieve their fears. She explains that the test will be used only as a measure for assessing understanding of the subject matter and to help clarify ambiguous points. The teacher makes certain that the pupils know that tests will be based directly on their work in class. They should be familiar with the content because of their previous class discussions and notes.

Short quizzes, oral or written, with two or three simple questions can serve as a start. Tests may be objective or essay, closed or open book, depending on the teacher's preference. The important point is that they be related directly to the material covered in class and formulated in such a way that the pupils have every fair chance of doing well on them. As short a time as possible should intervene between taking tests and learning the results. Tests can be corrected in class by the pupils themselves and marks deemphasized. Questions which are answered incorrectly may be discussed in class, or pupils can be directed to sources where they can find the necessary information. Ultimate knowledge of the material, not right and wrong answers, is stressed, so that the pupils come slowly to care about what they are learning and how they are improving.

When the pupils realize a measure of success through competency on tests and increased understanding of the subject matter, they may feel an entirely new sensation—a sharp sense of accomplishment. It may not be outstanding according to some standards, but for them it is remarkable.

As pupils have concrete evidence that they are learning and becoming informed about different issues and individuals, they have a chance to develop some dignity. This may diminish their outbursts and their antipathy toward school. When they consider, in addition, that they are no longer second-class citizens and that they are improving beyond their wildest expectations, they react with untold pride. Too often in the past, they have been relegated to the jobs of errand boy, chalkboard washer, or bulletin board monitor. In a situation designed to compensate for their difficulties and promote competence, this need no longer be. Instead of standing on the periphery or failing abysmally, these pupils become an integral part of their group. As they acquire further knowledge, skill, and insight, they begin to gain a feeling of triumph. This enhances their concept of themselves and their status in relation to school. From angry, unruly pupils they can slowly pull themselves upward and can develop a sincere desire to learn more on their own.

Choosing Suitable Material

Interesting material for older pupils with very low reading ability is necessarily extremely limited. The lower the level of readability, the narrower the choice and the less appealing the story is likely to be. For authors to write interesting, let alone mature, reading matter with very few words which must be repeated constantly is next to impossible. Therefore, it is impractical to rely on content to tempt the pupil. Instead, it is best to choose reading matter that is as acceptable as possible and to depend on skillful presentation. For example, when a teacher starts working with a 15-year-old who is practically a nonreader, there tends to be a minimum of embarrassment and resentment if she offers pamphlets and books that are designed especially for adults. Operation Alphabet[5] and stories in *Reader's Digest Skill Texts*, at approximately first and second grade level, are ostensibly for teaching English to adults. Older pupils generally react favorably to such material perhaps partly because of the

5. All materials listed in this chapter, graded according to reading level, can be found in Appendixes B, C, and D.

illustrations and characters which represent adults and partly because of their relief on discovering that people even older than they have serious reading problems.

Such material should be presented as an introduction only to give the pupils the boost they need and to crumble some of the hard, ingrained distaste for reading. This clears the way for accepting any books that must be used. Changing the material frequently is advisable also. Indeed, prolonged use of any one book at this level usually proves undesirable because so many of them have limitations. Sometimes the teacher might wish to present articles chosen from school newspapers, such as *My Weekly Reader* or *Scholastic Magazines*, at beginning reading levels. As soon as some basic word recognition skills are developed, a simple collection of sayings for autograph albums like *Yours Till Niagara Falls* can prove appealing. It offers ideas for signing yearbooks and the like and is popular with pupils who have no sign of reading difficulty. *Bennet Cerf's Book of Laughs* can add some spice and humor to the program. In other words, the structure must of necessity include a great deal of experimentation together with artful handling in order to compensate for the serious problems involved.

At second grade level, choices of books are similar to those described above. Books in all the series mentioned go up to at least third grade level. One series, *The Deep-Sea Adventure Series*, start at high second grade level. It is particularly attractive to those who enjoy finding out about the mysteries of ocean life. In addition there are excellent materials which can be chosen from *SRA* (Science Research Associates) *Box IIIA*, *Reader's Digest*, and comprehension articles published by *Scholastic*. There are also appropriate school newspapers with reading levels from elementary grades through high school. At all levels, selections can be chosen that relate to curriculum topics.

Coordinated with this type of material should be workbooks containing practice material for teaching word recognition. Among those best suited for older pupils are *Conquests in Reading, Across and Down,* and *Ways to Learn Words*.

Books written at third grade level provide a somewhat wider choice. Also it is possible at this stage and onward to select reading matter more directly related to basic information and the more significant aspects of our cultural heritage. This emphasis is important because we want to round out, as stated in previous chapters, the foundation and background knowledge that these pupils have missed. For example, there are many biographies which may be tied in with various periods in history. Among those offered at third grade level are *Abraham Lincoln, Martin Luther King, Samuel F. B. Morse,* and *Leif the Lucky.* For pleasure reading, there are sports, mystery, and adventure stories. Each of the following books at third grade level, for example, is one of a series with at least one other book on the same level and several on higher levels: *Mystery of Morgan Castle, Ten Great Moments in Sports,* and *Pilot Jack Knight.*

Pupils who can handle fourth grade reading matter and above can be treated in ways similar to those described in Chapter 10. Of course, where methods or materials are too immature they should be avoided. More grown-up stories concerned with teen-agers' personal problems, such as dating, cars, and so on, are particularly apt. Some at fourth grade level are *Directions, Crossroads,* and *Something Else.* Sources which build up background include comprehension workbooks, rewritten classics, and biographies of inventors, scientists, nurses, pioneers, and other historical figures.[6]

Thus in choosing suitable books for older pupils with severe disability, the main goal is to whet their appetites, to pick subject matter that is of general significance as well as related to topics being studied in school, and to find material that is not too overwhelming. Some of it may be frowned upon because it is rewritten and does not follow the richness of style and ideas portrayed by the original authors; some of it may be considered inconsequential. However, anything that can help pupils who have a serious reading difficulty get started serves an important function. Just as a convalescent may need to be coaxed to eat by means of attractive trays and special tidbits, so children with reading disability must be lured to read by providing them with exciting but uncomplicated reading matter. Books that are inherently too complex and involved quickly discourage pupils whose reading power is weak, and they end up reading nothing.

The ways in which two teachers handled group situations with severely retarded readers in junior and senior high school follow. The programs can be adapted to similar school situations. Their accounts show graphically how, even under the most trying circumstances, difficult pupils can be salvaged.

6. See materials at fourth grade level and above listed in Appendixes B and D.

An Individualized Program for Junior High School Students with a Wide Range of Reading Ability

A teacher[7] in a New York City junior high school was confronted with a group of 23 pupils in eighth grade. Not only were most of them extremely retarded in reading, but they were resistant to learning and had disciplinary problems besides. His own account follows:

"My most immediate need was to establish a classroom atmosphere in which discipline could be maintained without resorting to dire threats and punishments to which the boys had long become inured. I attempted to establish rapport by getting across the feeling that I was keenly interested in each member of the class. Various devices that had a noticeable effect in a relatively short time included visits to homes when pupils were ill, monthly birthday parties, and my participation in punchball games in which the boys could demonstrate their proficiency. Fortunately, I acquitted myself creditably on the ball field and gained status in their eyes. My position was made secure when, drawing on my musical ability, I performed rock and roll music for them at our parties! Day by day there was an improvement in class morale and deportment.

"A study of the pupils' record cards revealed a reading range of second to fourth grades. An informal textbook test, however, indicated that one boy was on a preprimer level, four were on first grade, and 18 ranged from second to fourth grade reading levels. Results of the *Roswell-Chall Diagnostic Reading Test* revealed severe lacks in almost all word-recognition skills. The I.Q. range was from 66 to 104, and ages from 13 to 16.

"I set up three reading groups, using the *Reader's Digest Reading Skill Builders*, but I soon realized that this plan would not work. I had no suitable material for the slowest group, nor had I the knowledge of how to devise my own. The two other groups had both been exposed to the *Skill Builders* in years past, and resented the grading on the covers. Furthermore, discipline problems arose because the groups could not work independently. Out of this confusion and frustration came the idea of an individualized reading program.

"I broached the plan to my principal and found a willing and sympa-

7. Louis Simon, Associate Professor, City College of the City University of New York.

thetic ear. Unfortunately, the purchase of books for this class was not possible since funds for the current year had already been spent. Asking the boys to bring books from home was out of the question. Most of them had never owned a book, and if they had, these probably would not have been suitable for this class.

"I finally reached a compromise solution by arranging a trip to the public library. Peace was made with the authorities by the payment of accumulated fines for past transgressions, and that afternoon my class returned to school with 23 library cards and a collection of books.

"The next four months were spent in reading library books during the English periods. Pupils were encouraged to recommend books that they found interesting, and these were freely exchanged. Volunteers for the privilege of reading a third grade level book, *Curious George*, or a book on magic to the five slowest readers were plentiful. The boys in this group would then read to each other, with assistance from me or another pupil.

"My time was spent in individual conferences during which I assisted with vocabulary, comprehension, and word recognition skills. The chief benefit lay in the opportunity for giving encouragement and individual attention. Almost magically, reading had become a 'good' period.

"Pupils were called for conferences in alphabetical order. We sat together at a desk in the rear of the room. A conference usually included some oral reading, a brief discussion of what the story was about, and some direct teaching or review on a needed skill.

"If little Helga was laboriously reading word by word, our conference time might be devoted in part to taking turns in reading so that her interest in the story might be maintained. At the same time, I provided a model for more fluent reading. I also made a note to assign a page in a workbook to help her in phrase reading.

"If Dominick was deeply absorbed in a book that was on his independent reading level, our conference might be merely a brief discussion of what had happened so far, a conjecture as to how it would end, and an admonition to be sure to let me know how the story turned out. But I made a note to steer Dominick to something more challenging for the next book, or the one after that.

"Each conference was an opportunity for diagnosis, skill teaching, vocabulary enrichment, and oral communication in a relaxed one-to-one relationship.

216

"I found that a touch of humor each day was of inestimable value in getting activities started or keeping them moving. One of the most effective devices was the 'daily chuckle.' Written with brush pen, a two- or three-line joke taken from a magazine or jokebook was displayed in the front of the room before the class arrived. The class looked forward to this little treat and vied for the privilege of reading or acting out the joke. Of course this could not take place until everyone was seated and ready for work.

"With a little practice, I developed a feeling for the type of humor which the children enjoyed most. The following are typical:

NED: What are you doing with a pencil and paper?
ED: I'm writing a letter to my brother.
NED: Who're you kidding; you don't know how to write.
ED: Sure, but my brother doesn't know how to read.

VISITOR: Why is your dog watching me while I eat?
HOST: Maybe it's because you're eating out of his plate.

"After a while pupils brought in jokes, and I appointed a rotating committee to select those to be posted.

"I learned that asking what was funny about a joke was not the unpardonable sin that it would be with a more sophisticated audience. The discussions that followed provided an ideal opportunity for oral communication, comprehension development, vocabulary enrichment, and exchanges of experiences in an atmosphere that was light and comfortable.

"Since there were many stages of learning going on at the same time, I found that a record for each pupil's progress was advisable. An anecdotal account of each conference, results of diagnosis, assignments, and subjective evaluation of progress in skills and attitudes were kept in a notebook. A page or two was devoted to each pupil and was invaluable in helping my planning.

"Two records were maintained by the pupils. One was a mimeographed form on which the student indicated the title and author of the book being read, the number of pages read each day, the kind of reporting activity planned, new vocabulary, and a brief sentence or two on their reactions to the book. This form was helpful in eliminating squabbles about who was reading a particular book and also enabled me to maintain a check on the amount of reading being done.

"The other record was a large wall chart which listed the names of all the pupils and the titles of books they had read. Separate colored slips were available to paste next to each pupil's name. On the slip, pupils wrote the title of the book that they had completed and its author. Each color signified their opinion of the book. For example, a blue slip meant the book was 'excellent,' green indicated 'good,' yellow, 'fair,' and so forth. This device served as a record of accomplishment for each student and also guided other members of the class in their choice of a book.

"In January, after four months of individualized reading, standardized tests revealed some satisfying results. The average gain for the class was one year. Individual gains ranged from 2 months to 2.6 years. Fourteen pupils had scores over the 5.0 mark necessary for promotion to the next grade, as opposed to 23 pupils who began the term reading between preprimer and fourth grade level.

"Other evidences of progress were equally heartening. The number of books each student had read ranged from four to 14. There was a decided improvement in fluency in written and oral communication. Most encouraging were the evidences of positive attitudes toward reading. It is a heart-warming sight to see a child linger in the room after the bell has rung, regretfully return his book to the cart,[8] and say as he leaves, 'Gee, that's a good story!' "

Dr. Simon's report shows what a devoted teacher can accomplish. It shows how a serious condition, which is prevalent in many urban areas, can be successfully handled. Certainly the needs of his pupils did not call for the level or type of teaching generally expected in the junior high school. But this is neither the pupil's, the teacher's, nor the school's fault. When confronted with such an unfortunate situation, the teacher must rise to the occasion or collapse in despair. Granted that many of us could not make home visits, play punchball in the yard, or play rock and roll music as did this teacher, but each one can find a way to teach his pupils after his own fashion, if he so desires.

Individualizing Reading for High School Dropouts

The pupils in the next instance were 16 to 18 years of age in an ungraded class at a special school. They had been given up by almost everyone in the area. Their parents insisted that they get a high school diploma, so

8. With the assistance of the shop teacher, pupils built two bookmobile carts, so that books could easily be shared by many classes.

they were forced to remain in school beyond the usual age limit. The pupils all read at about fifth grade level. Their intelligence fell within normal range, 90–110. They were uninterested in school, surly, and unmanageable. The first day was spent amidst frequent explosions from firecrackers, "hot foots," and "cherry bombs." That night the teacher[9] contemplated, not lesson plans, but a scheme that might capture the hearts and feelings of these youths.

The next morning they were told that they would all be given a "diagnosis" to help them and the teacher to find out what they could do well and where they needed help.

The pupils were told that the test would not "count" for their school marks or as an official record of any kind. In fact the test booklet could be thrown out as soon as it had served its usefulness if they so wished. They were told that the test consisted of items which increased in difficulty; therefore they might find it harder to answer questions as they went along. In any case they would not be expected to get all the answers correct. The important thing was to assess the kinds of errors they made so that they could be taught to avoid such mistakes in the future. The process was compared to a physician's examination in which the patient might be told that his weight and height were proportionate, his general health good, but he was somewhat anemic. Just as a doctor would prescribe a regimen for bodily improvement, they, too, would be apprised of a way to increase their achievement.

The *California Reading Test—Elementary*, for grades 4, 5, and 6, was chosen. After the students completed the test, they took turns coming to the desk for their "diagnostic interpretation." In contrast to orthodox procedure, the test was scored immediately with the pupil, so that he could be shown exactly where his strengths and weaknesses lay. This took the mystery out of the test taking and engendered a feeling of collaboration and self-respect in the student. Of course this had to be handled most skillfully to avoid undue anxiety regarding failure. Each one came away with as much concrete, constructive information as possible. For example, one child did very well on answers requiring factual information that was imparted in the paragraphs, but could not "read between the lines" for implied data. Another was excellent at understanding the main idea, but poor on recall of details; another showed misunderstanding of directions but strong vocabulary; whereas two boys

9. The teacher in this case was one of the authors, who taught in a special school for dropouts in an urban area.

received a high degree of accuracy in responses but were penalized by time, and so on. Each child was given some immediate suggestions for overcoming his difficulty and shown some of the materials he might be working with for practice. They were told that time would be set aside to practice each day in class.

The effect of this procedure was electric. There seemed to be two important reactions. First, the students felt that someone might really be trying to help them, and second, the selections offered indicated that there might be something of true interest for them. It was not "the same old hard, boring stuff," as one student commented later.

From that day forward, discipline problems diminished, although they never disappeared completely. But it was clear that a spirit had been captured; from dispirited, disruptive young people, they were willing to try again. In order to keep up their morale, the teacher continued to foster feelings of competence. Periods in social studies, English, science, and math were conducted in a group, and the particular skills were practiced individually for a half hour, three times a week. At that time the teacher helped with and checked their work. Besides using some fourth and fifth grade comprehension workbooks, they worked with materials such as crossword puzzles specially prepared for those with reading disability, directions for card tricks, fortune-telling cards, magic books, simple science experiments, and *Weekly Reader* and *Scholastic Magazines* at appropriate levels. Simple books with high appeal, such as *Alec Majors*, *The Trojan War*, and *The Spanish Cave* helped develop more fluency and speed in their reading. Such material proved dramatic, compelling, and sufficiently different to stimulate their curiosity. In addition, they were encouraged to bring in anything with which they wished help, such as driver's manuals, menus, and the like.

In each subject area, lively discussions and explanations preceded every reading lesson. The pupils learned a wealth of facts and ideas pertinent to the subject matter before reading the text. In this way, demands never became overwhelming. The pupils used textbooks to fill in their knowledge rather than as a source for independent gathering of information. Many times subject matter was related to personal experience in order to evoke attentiveness. For example, when learning about the Food and Drug Administration, the students were asked, "Have you ever seen the purple stamp on meat? Have you ever, to your knowledge, eaten meat without this stamp?" Sometimes discussions combined general student attitudes and subject matter. For example, in discussing the Constitution of the United States, the students thought that perhaps a class constitution would help them maintain better order. Thus, they decided to draw up their own class constitution. It is reproduced here in its original form, including errors:

CONSTITUTION OF CLASS ———

ARTICLE 1 There shall be no throing of books, erasers, chalks, pensils,
Sec. 1   can openors, paper airplanes and spit balls and other thing that go in that category.
Sec. 2   There shall be no giving hot foots handeling of other persons while class is being conducted and you can do as you wish as long as it doesn't affect any one else. There shal be respect for the person in charge and Prophanity shall be kept to respected minimum. This constatution shall be respected by the person kuo sines this, and if not respect shall leave the class.

Through communicating to the students her desire to help them and by making available actual means for improvement, the teacher helped these boys to make slow but steady progress during the term. Although they never turned into "model" pupils, they became a cohesive unit willing to listen, reasonably well behaved, and with a less antagonistic attitude toward learning.

Handling the Most Severely Retarded Readers

Sometimes pupils have suffered such severe difficulty that they need prolonged special attention. The case of Lloyd describes remedial treatment of an adolescent who was a nonreader and never managed to attain average standards. Whatever gains he made proved to be extremely significant in his adjustment to life. On the other hand Frank, who also had enormous difficulty learning to read, attained a much higher level of achievement. This was probably because his problem was identified at an early age and he had consistent remedial help over a long period.

Lloyd—A Nonreader, Age 15, Suspended from School

At the age of 15, Lloyd, a student with borderline intelligence, was still a nonreader. He was unruly and rebellious, on the road to becoming a hardened delinquent. The psychiatrist at the mental health clinic which Lloyd attended had many interviews with him but considered psychotherapy contraindicated. He concluded that what Lloyd needed most was to learn enough to be able to get a job and take care of himself in a satisfactory fashion. Since no school would accept him, he was referred to one of the authors for individual instruction. During remedial sessions, he acquired sufficient reading and arithmetic skills to find a job. More than that, he slowly dared to hope that he could improve. Through his relationship during remedial sessions he came to feel that all was not lost for him—that maybe he could make a new start. Lloyd was suspended from school permanently at 12 years, 8 months of age because the school considered him lazy, disturbing, defiant, and uninterested. The school reported that they could not keep him because he "has no respect for authority. He cannot be trusted at any time. He is bold, insolent and does not accept corrections. He sulks, pouts, lies, and never admits he is wrong. He is failing in all classwork, does not appear interested, is untidy and disorganized." It was the school's recommendation that behavior and achievement were so deviant that arrangements should be made for institutional care for the boy.

The psychiatrist at the mental health clinic did not agree that Lloyd should be institutionalized. He tried to work out educational plans for the boy. He found Lloyd very eager to cooperate. However, the one school that was willing to accept him would do so only if they might place Lloyd, then 14, in a third grade class. The psychiatrist felt that despite the boy's drive to gain some education sitting in a third grade class would have been too humiliating for him, especially since he was an important member of a group of boys in his neighborhood who planned many activities together.

It was immediately clear why Lloyd could not do his homework and experienced so much difficulty in school. Not only was his intelligence low, but there was definite evidence of neurological impairment on psychological tests. This finding explained Lloyd's inability to develop effective word-analysis techniques throughout the years. Reading tests revealed that he was a total nonreader, unable to read even the simplest material at preprimer level. Because of his poor visual and auditory memory and inability to synthesize sounds, both the visual-motor and phonic methods were found entirely unworkable. The only method by which Lloyd could learn was a whole-word approach.

After reading the school's reports, the author who treated Lloyd was prepared to deal with a hostile, aggressive, resistive boy. Instead she found a very cooperative one, serious in attitude and eager to learn. Even though this boy had far to travel, he always arrived early. Indeed, these sessions seemed to be the only source of order and meaning in his life at this time.

Lloyd had three sessions a week for one and a half years, excluding summer vacations. He was so eager to learn that it was possible to start with the regular published materials at preprimer level. The correlated workbooks were used to give additional practice in the new words learned. Because of his poor auditory discrimination, some time was spent at each session on developing phonic readiness. Pictures of common objects were cut out of newspapers and magazines and pasted on cards. The name of each object was printed underneath its picture; on the reverse side the word appeared alone. Lloyd enjoyed learning in this way and was most responsive as he gradually saw evidence of progress. He was also able to learn consonant sounds by associating them with representative pictures. As soon as his knowledge of consonant sounds developed, he could learn by a word-family procedure. Thus, if he knew the word *light*, he was able to figure out *sight*, *right*, *fight*, and so forth.

The level of difficulty in the graded series of readers and workbooks was increased gradually. Because it was so difficult for Lloyd to remember, learning to read was a slow process for him. He never was able to blend sounds together, despite his persistence in trying to do so. Thus his ability to develop independence in word recognition was limited. Every bit of achievement entailed real effort on his part. Yet he did not become overly discouraged.

By the time Lloyd read at second grade level, he started taking home simple books which he was able to read by himself. He was now past 16 years of age, and a new approach was introduced. He was taught words which he would be likely to encounter on signs, labels on foods and medicines, menus, and help-wanted advertisements. He responded enthusiastically to this approach and seemed to derive great satisfaction from his attainments. Each word had to be taught not only in capital letters but in lower case as well, since there was no carry-over in his learning. It was as if he were learning two different languages. Some of the words taught this way were:

Help Wanted	Men	Employees
Boy Wanted	Women	No Smoking
Danger	Boys	Fire Escape
Poison	Girls	Doctor
Keep Off	Fire Extinguisher	First Aid
Keep Out	Live Wires	Employment Agency
Stop	Bus Stop	Wet Paint
Go	Beware of Dogs	Hands Off
Walk	Out of Order	Elevator
Don't Walk	Glass	Telephone
Wait	In	Box Office
Entrance	Out	Thin Ice
Exit	Hospital	
Up		
Down		

Since the summer was approaching and instruction would be interrupted, Lloyd had become interested in finding a job. He started reading the want ads, such as:

> Boy Wanted—Dishwasher
> No experience necessary
> Call at 765 North Street
> Between 3 and 5 P.M.

He had reached the point where the little reading knowledge that he had was being applied in a practical and constructive way. This proved highly significant in his future adjustment because he could connect it directly with his daily experiences. Since Lloyd was never accepted at any school, it was imperative that he have some meaningful way of applying his reading outside the remedial sessions. This was accomplished by using word lists that served as a source of protection and assistance to him. Thus, even the meager ability he acquired in reading simple materials afforded him some personal satisfaction and a sense of achievement.

Toward the end of remedial treatment, Lloyd expressed the hope that he would be able to get a job working with his brothers for the telephone company. The mental health clinic which was following his progress confirmed this as a job possibility. Therefore, *telephone wires, electric plugs, cable,* and other related words were added to his growing functional reading vocabulary. An illustration of material which the writer made up for Lloyd to read follows:

Today is Thursday, June 5th. This is the last month that I will be coming here. I have learned to read and to add and subtract. When I leave here, I will go to an EMPLOYMENT AGENCY that says HELP WANTED, because I want a summer job. I will walk in and say, "Good Morning.

My name is Lloyd Brown. I am looking for a job." "What can you do?" "I can wash dishes, help in the kitchen, and be very handy."

After I leave the employment agency, I will take an ELEVATOR to the first floor. If I am very hungry, I will go to a DINER and eat some lunch. This is what I will have: Tomato soup, Ham sandwich, Milk, and Cake.

My brother has a friend who will help me get a job next winter working for the telephone company. These are the signs I will have to look out for: LIVE WIRES, LOOK OUT, KEEP OUT, KEEP AWAY, STOP, LOOK, DANGER, WATCH OUT.

If I hurt my hand, I will go to a box marked FIRST AID. I will look for ALCOHOL, COTTON, and BAND AID. I may also want ASPIRIN.

At the end of a year and a half, remedial work was terminated. Lloyd had shown growth in every way. The remedial treatment appeared to have alleviated the strong feelings of inferiority that resulted from his school failure. It seemed likely that Lloyd would be able to find work. At this point, there was no question of institutionalization. Had he experienced continued rejection on all sides, however, and remained totally illiterate, he might have committed antisocial acts, become a burden to himself and society, and becomes less amenable than ever to change.

Frank—A Nonreader after Repeating First Grade

Frank, of low average intelligence, with neurologic impairment, was first seen when he was 7½ years old. He repeated first grade and still was a total nonreader. He could not understand basic concepts in arithmetic either. Because of his extreme difficulty in learning, Frank's prognosis for improvement was unfavorable. However, Frank did learn, albeit slowly. This case describes the procedures and materials used for remedial treatment and includes follow-up information until Frank reached 19 years of age.

Frank was an only child. His father was in the advertising business. His mother was a conscientious woman who worked as a secretary.

Frank's mother reported that her pregnancy was normal but labor was prolonged and difficult. During Frank's first years, there was evidence of delay in all areas of development, including teething, sitting, standing, walking, and talking. Frank's parents considered him a nervous and restless child. He did not play well with others.

Treatment

Although Frank had been in first grade twice, he still could not grasp even the simplest instruction in schoolwork. His experiences in school had been most unfortunate. An extremely unsympathetic teacher demanded work which was far beyond his capacity. She was impatient with him because "he refused to learn."

Frank was referred to one of the authors by a psychologist who reported an I.Q. of 88 on the *Stanford-Binet Intelligence Scale*. The Rorschach record at that time revealed an unstable personality. There were indications that Frank's approach to reality was confused and distorted. Some of his responses suggested the possibility of organic brain damage. His reactions were those of an extremely immature boy with a marked learning disability. A severe memory defect, together with reactions resembling anomia (difficulty in retrieving words) confirmed the Rorschach impressions of neurological impairment, as did the *Bender Visual Gestalt Test*. Therefore, Frank was referred for a neurological examination. The findings revealed brain damage.

The neuropsychiatrist considered psychotherapy inadvisable. Instead he recommended remedial teaching, along with an educational program adapted to Frank's level of functioning and his adjustive needs. Consultations with several neuropsychiatrists over a period of time continued to confirm these recommendations.

Frank was seen for remedial reading twice a week. (His mental age was 6 years, 8 months at the time.) Each session lasted about 45 minutes and was divided into very brief activities so as to maintain Frank's interest and attention. He reacted very favorably from the outset. A good relationship was established easily and has been maintained throughout the years. The author who worked with him remained as educational consultant to Frank and his family. Reevaluation was undertaken annually long after remedial instruction was discontinued.

When remedial work was started, Frank was given very simple materials at preprimer level. It was evident almost immediately that he could not cope with them. Thus, reading readiness materials were substituted. These he accepted readily. Because of Frank's extreme immaturity, he responded enthusiastically to such materials. He would clap his his hands like a young child to show his pleasure and delight as he performed the simple tasks required in these readiness books. He experienced success at each session and was most responsive to encouragement.

Because of Frank's poor muscular coordination, readiness activities were an integral part of the program. Exercises in visual discrimination were introduced at the simplest level. Gradually he was given increasingly difficult items, until he reached the point where he was able to recognize words through associating them with pictures. Similarly, exercises in auditory discrimination were presented so as to integrate work in both visual and auditory perception.

A typical session would include (1) cutting, pasting, drawing, and matching exercises in readiness books; (2) work in auditory and visual discrimination, presented through game-type procedures; and (3) reading to Frank, which he enjoyed immensely. The latter served many purposes. It provided experiences of sheer delight in listening to stories, thereby engendering awareness that books contain something pleasurable and worthwhile. This served to counteract the very traumatic experiences related to reading which he had in school. Some of the stories offered therapeutic possibilities as discussed in Chapter 5. The tutor noticed that Frank was particularly delighted with stories selected from *It Happened One Day*, such as "The Lion and the Mouse," where the little mouse comes off victorious; "Jack and the Beanstalk," where Jack conquers the giant; and "Drakesbill,"[10] where a little duck eventually triumphs over a king. Apparently Frank identified in each instance with the helpless creatures who became heroes in the end and seemed to sigh with relief as each one overcame his lowly status.

Thus each session provided feelings of success and well-being for Frank. He came for his sessions regularly and willingly. He always put forth excellent effort and felt he was gaining in achievement. Along with the reading, help was also given in arithmetic.

Gradually, Frank developed a sight vocabulary. He also learned to read the names of colors connected with concrete illustrations. But abstract words such as *here, the, get, this, will,* and so forth, were impossible for him to learn as yet.

Difficulty in recalling names and in associating words with pictures persisted for the first two years of tutoring. Frank frequently groped for names of animals or objects with which he was completely familiar. For example, he looked at a picture of a cow and after being unable to name it said, "Eats hay"; for "top" he said, "Spinning thing"; for "barn," "You find it on a farm." And vice versa when he saw the word *cow* in print, he said, "I can't think of its name, but I'll find its picture." He quickly glanced through the book and said, "It's this." Also, when he saw the word *elephant* in print and could not name it, he said, "I know what it is, let me draw it." He sketched it hurriedly and then suddenly called out, "Elephant!"

10. Miriam Huber, *It Happened One Day*. (New York: Harper & Row, 1970).

Words that had seemed thoroughly learned were forgotten. Sometimes Frank could read a word correctly in four successive sentences and then fail to recognize it in the fifth sentence. In fact, various kinds of memory defects had been manifested repeatedly. He could not remember names of the characters in the books which he read. (They were always quickly supplied.) When he could not recall a word he would say, "Don't tell me what the word is. You're supposed to think of the right word." He would try to remember by such means as closing his eyes and trying to visualize the object. He would try very hard and become upset when he was unable to recall words. Again encouragement was given. The word would be supplied to him while he was told, "Soon you'll be able to remember it."

During this period, many methods of word study were tried, including the kinesthetic, but the only successful one was the visual, and this to a limited degree. Since he had no other means of figuring out words, he would continue to confuse words of similar configuration, such as *doll* for *ball*, *pig* for *big*, *pig* for *dog*, *letter* for *kitten*, and so on.

After nine months, there was improvement in his visual and auditory discrimination. At this time, a preprimer in a graded series was introduced along with its correlated workbook. He continued with the other preprimers in this series, and by the end of one year, he was ready for his first hard-covered book—a primer. He was also beginning to learn the names and sounds of letters. Correlated with this was work in writing, using material from the same publisher as his reader and sentences that were made up for this purpose. Even though Frank was in a special class, in which he had been placed following the outcome of the neurological examination, school still presented problems. Frank reported, "The other kids make fun of me. The teacher gets angry with me. Then I go home and pester my mother and father because I get so angry about what the kids did to me. My mother and father have a right to scold me because I pester them so much."

Frank continued to learn very slowly. There was much fluctuation and variability in his performance, but nevertheless learning gradually took place. When Frank was 9 years 6 months of age and after two years of work, he was able to handle a high first grade reader in most series. He enjoyed this book and found it " 'citing." His infantile speech patterns persisted as an integral part of his language disability. He was even more pleased when he could read *I Know a Story*, a first grade book which contained folk tales. When he was 10 years 3 months of age, he was given an easy second grade reader. At this point, he was actually capable of reading the folk tales in *It Happened One Day*, "The Lion and the Mouse," "The Three Little Pigs," and "Jack and the Beanstalk," which he had enjoyed so much when they were read to him. He still remained enchanted with these stories. He took home supplementary reading material at first grade readability level.

Around this time it was possible to introduce the word-family approach. He had learned letter sounds somewhat, through practice in the remedial sessions and in workbooks, but mainly he learned them by playing *Go Fish*. As soon as he learned these sounds, he discovered how new words could be formed by changing the initial consonants.

Some phonic workbooks were used in connection with the teaching of word-analysis skills; and the Group Word Teaching Game, played like Bingo, helped reinforce his learning of the Dolch 220 basic sight words.

It would be too cumbersome to mention all the materials used with Frank. Only those will be commented on when changes in procedures or levels took place. By the age of 11 years, 1 month, Frank could read *Aesop's Stories*, at third grade readability level. Word-analysis skills were improving. He was able to learn consonant combinations. Go Fish, Set II, was particularly helpful in this connection. But he still experienced difficulty in blending sounds together. Through the use of exercises in many different phonic workbooks, he was able to learn some means of figuring out phonically regular words, probably through word comparisons, even though he could not blend auditorily. Also, he was able to write regularly spelled words which were dictated to him. By the age of 11 years, 6 months, he was able to read a high third grade book.

Between the ages of 12 and 13, there was considerable improvement in his word-recognition skills. He was at last able to use a phonic approach. In all probability, some integration in the central nervous system had taken place which facilitated this ability. This is commented on further at the conclusion of this case. In addition, silent reading materials at third grade level were introduced. He showed decided interest in materials found in various workbooks and enjoyed reading them. The comprehension questions were simple enough for him and resulted in a high degree of success. His persistence and effort were maintained at a high level throughout the sessions. When Frank was 13 years of age in seventh grade, reading at fourth grade level, the regular weekly remedial sessions were discontinued, but contact was kept up with the school. Thereafter, Frank was seen about twice a year, then once a year up until age 18. Progress continued to be apparent as evidenced in the test results which follow:

Age in Years		Grade Score
8 to 10	For the first two years, Frank's reading was too low to be measured by standardized tests.	Nonreader
10	Metropolitan Achievement Test Primary I	2.3
12	Metropolitan Achievement Test Primary II	3.3
15	Metropolitan Achievement Test Elementary	4.6
17	Metropolitan Achievement Test Intermediate	7.5
18	Stanford Achievement Test Advanced	10.1

Roswell-Chall Diagnostic Reading Test administered at fifteen years of age showed mastery of phonic skills.

When Frank was 18 years old, he had completed his work at school, and satisfactory vocational plans were made for him. Reading was at tenth grade level, and arithmetic, which had presented an even more difficult problem for many years, was at seventh grade level.

This degree of proficiency meant that Frank could function adequately in the areas he needed. He could read popular fiction, biography, and current events, which would open new vistas, broaden his horizons, and continue his education. In this way he would begin to accumulate knowledge and become more and more sensitive to and understanding of the world around him.

In retrospect, this case shows the snail's pace at which severely impaired children learn. Had Frank been given up as hopeless during the period when evidence of progress was almost imperceptible, it is difficult to predict what might have happened. It might be surmised that his adjustment would have been totally inadequate and that most avenues in school and work would have been closed to him.

Figures 1 through 4 are reproductions of four *Bender Visual-Motor Gestalt Tests* administered to Frank between the ages of eight and 17 years. Marked changes in visual-motor coordination, perceptual development, and integrative capacity are apparent in his performance on successive records.

It is interesting to note that as Frank's development in these areas proceeded, it was not only reflected in his handling of the *Bender Visual-Motor Gestalt Tests*, but was also evidenced in his ability to synthesize sounds as well as perform better in other aspects of his reading.

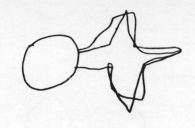

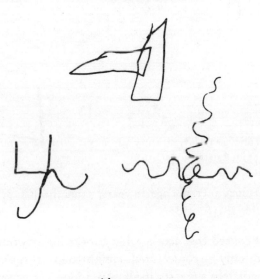

FIGURE 1. Frank: age eight years (59 percent of the size of the following figures). (Cf. pp. 225–230.)

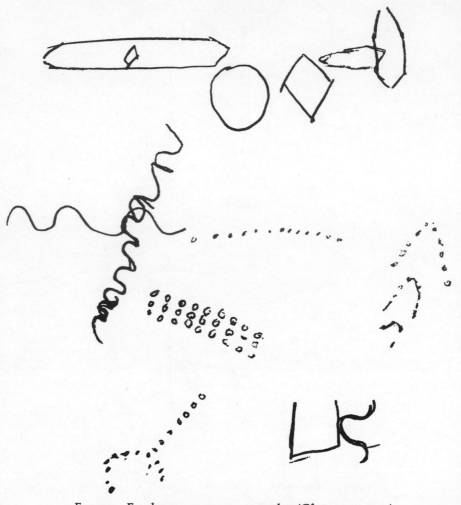

FIGURE 2. Frank: age 10 years, 3 months. (Cf. pp. 225–230.)

What caused this acceleration especially around preadolescence and beyond can only be conjectured. Heightened neurophysiological development immediately suggests itself. An added factor was probably Frank's ability to utilize all of his capacities more effectively. Hence, any one factor or the interaction of many could explain the striking changes in his achievement test results.

The foregoing accounts of students treated individually and in groups, show that extremely poor readers who have already given up are able to gain a fair degree of skill and confidence. Even though achieve-

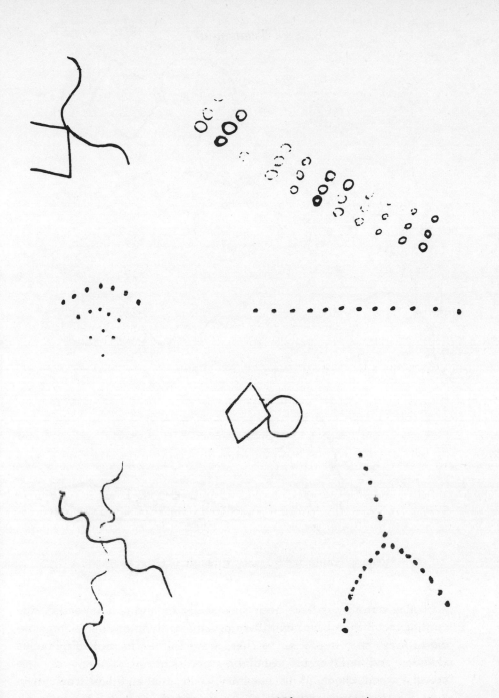

FIGURE 3. Frank: age 14 years. (Cf. pp. 225–230.)

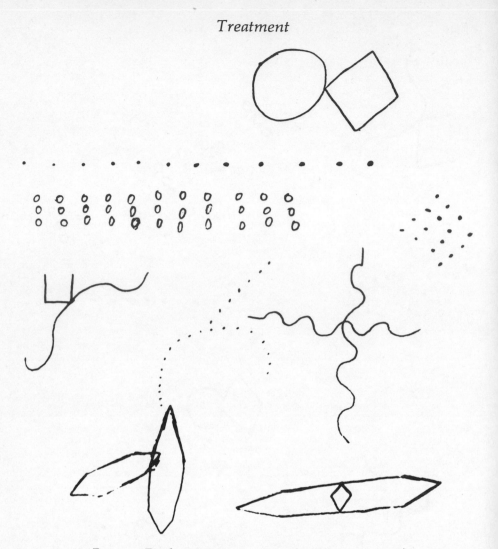

FIGURE 4. Frank: age 17 years, 1 month. (Cf. pp. 225–230.)

ment may not always have been spectacular in terms of potential, the startling fact is that these pupils became sufficiently interested to improve and to keep on trying. Their teachers were able to succeed despite the obstacles and unfavorable conditions prevalent in so many of our crowded urban schools. With ingenuity, dedication, and hard work, they were able to change attitudes of doom and degradation to those of anticipation and animation.

When such pupils are ready to leave school, they can be told that education need never stop. Once they are out in the world they can always seek admission to programs now available to adults of all ages.[11,12] Some may eventually reach their intellectual capabilities even though it takes them many years to do so. Some may yet enter college when they themselves wish to work hard enough for it; some may enter careers which require exacting academic preparation. If they have learned the rudiments of academic skills, they no longer need to scoff at educational pursuits. But if they lack the barest essentials they may indeed be absorbed into the morass of delinquent, antisocial, and wretched people with whom urban societies are becoming more and more familiar.

Suggestions for Further Reading

Bailyn, B. *Education in the Forming of American Society.* New York: Norton, 1972.

Bronfenbrenner, U. *Two Worlds of Childhood: U.S. and U.S.S.R.* New York: Russell Sage Foundation, 1970.

Brown, C. "Literacy in Thirty Hours: Paulo Freire's Process in Northeast Brazil." *Social Policy* 5 (1974): 25–32.

Caplan, N. "Delinquency and the Perceived Chances for Conventional Success." Institute for Social Research, Ann Arbor, Mich., unpublished manuscript, 1974.

Feigelson, N., ed. *The Underground Revolution: Hippies, Yippies, and Others.* New York: Funk & Wagnalls, 1970.

Giorgi, A. *Psychology as a Human Science: A Phenomenologically Based Approach.* New York: Harper & Row, 1970.

Horn, T. *Reading for the Disadvantaged.* New York: Harcourt, Brace & World, 1970.

Jourard, S. *The Transparent Self.* New York: Van Nostrand, 1971.

Kagan, J., and Coles, R. *Twelve to Sixteen—Early Adolescence.* New York: Norton, 1972.

Kiell, N. *The Adolescent Through Fiction: A Psychological Approach.* New York: International Universities Press, 1974.

Mead, M. *Culture and Commitment.* Garden City, N.Y.: Doubleday, 1970.

Mussen, P., Conger, J., and Kagan, J. *Child Development and Personality.* New York: Harper & Row 1969.

Weiner, I. *Psychological Disturbance in Adolescence.* New York: Wiley Interscience, 1970.

11. P. Fielding, ed., J. Moss, consultant, *A National Directory of Four-Year Colleges, Two-Year Colleges, and Post High School Training Programs for Young People with Learning Disabilities,* 2nd ed. (Tulsa Okla.: Partners in Publishing, 1975).

12. S. Slaver, *Non-Traditional College Routes to Careers* (New York: Simon and Schuster, Julian Messner Division, 1975).

13

The Bright High School Student Who Is Not Achieving up to Capacity

---

THE BRIGHT high school student who reads up to grade level but still is not functioning up to his potential presents a reading difficulty of such a subtle nature that it has probably gone undetected until he has reached high school. He was able to continue up to this point and obtain fairly satisfactory marks despite his lack of interest, his dearth of outside reading, and his minimal application to his studies. The more rigorous requirements of high school, however, often bring his difficulty to light for the first time.

In educational parlance, such a student is called an underachiever. His teachers consider him uninterested and difficult to reach. The pupil himself is at a loss to know where the trouble lies. He is weary of being told by parents and teachers alike "You could do much better if you only applied yourself. You have the potential; why don't you use it?" These empty phrases only arouse more anxiety and guilt in the student because he knows that he is not stupid, yet he realizes that something seems radically wrong.

Evaluation

The first step in helping such a student is to assess the problem. Techniques used in this connection are discussed in earlier chapters. For the convenience of the examiner, tests such as the *Iowa Silent Reading Tests*, Levels 1, 2, and 3, for grades 6 through 12 (1972 ed.), and the *Nelson-Denny Reading Tests*, Forms C and D for grades 9 through 16 (1973 ed.) offer evaluation of reading efficiency or rate in addition to vocabulary and reading comprehension. The *Iowa* reading efficiency subtest is designed to measure the student's ability to read easy material rapidly and with understanding, using a modified cloze procedure which requires the student to complete sentences within each passage. The allotted time is four or five minutes, depending on which level is used. On the *Nelson-Denny Test*, the time of one minute allowed for measurement of speed is too short to be a reliable gauge of reading rate. (For additional tests at these levels see Appendix A.)

A more adequate method of estimating rate of reading is through the use of informal measures introduced during the trial learning session. For example, several articles at the student's reading level, including both narrative and expository material, are presented. A record is kept of the various rates employed and degree of comprehension shown, based on objective questions. In this way, reading efficiency and flexibility according to the nature and difficulty of the material can be evaluated. The use of both standardized tests and informal measures are illustrated in the cases of Carol, Lucy, Tod, and Ralph described in this chapter.

Wherever possible, test results are interpreted to the student in a constructive manner. The teacher might find that the student displays a high degree of accuracy in his answers but is penalized by time or that he has misread words that look alike, and so on. As the pupil becomes aware of his ineffective approach and finds out what he can do about it, he becomes more interested in receiving help. In this way, diagnosis lays the groundwork for future cooperation and sustained effort.

Dealing with Adolescent Underachievers

The approaches necessary for effective assistance include finding ways to help the student overcome his basic distrust of himself, locating reading matter and workbook exercises to surmount weaknesses in reading, and assisting with any other aspect of his schoolwork which interferes with his functioning. These include handling assignments, improving rate of reading, and the like.

It is not always possible for underachievers, even with help in reading, suddenly to obtain the grades or test scores predicted for them. In fact, if overemphasis is placed in this direction, it may produce even lower scores because of increased tension or resistance. Instead of repeatedly admonishing them to improve and reminding them of their untapped possibilities, the authors discuss with the students the ways in which they might handle their problems. We also indicate the various alternatives available even if their achievement scores do not rise appreciably. We point out that their lives will not be ruined if they fall short of the high standards set for them. We may mention that famous scientists, presidents of colleges, and other outstanding men did not receive high grades in high school or attend well-known universities.[1]

Furthermore, we have observed that although many with whom we have worked eventually ranked high in their classes, achieved outstanding scores on their college boards, and entered the colleges of their choice, these incentives rarely were effective at the outset. Thus, the student is helped to gain insight into his strengths and his deficiencies. He is shown how he can improve his skills and cope with the problem at hand.

Choosing Narrative Material

The teacher chooses stories, classics, novels, and the like that touch upon universal human experiences. The most important objective is to find something that will impress the student sufficiently to read further on his own. A story that directly relates to a personal need or problem can have a powerful influence. Not only can it heighten his interest in reading, but sometimes it can be forceful enough to help him relate better to other individuals and to his most important responsibility—schoolwork.

Sometimes the teacher must search long and diligently through

1. L. Thompson, "Language Disabilities in Men of Eminence," *Journal of Learning Disabilities* 4 (1971): 34–45.

anthologies, comprehension exercises, and workbooks before she can find material which will move the students. But when she does, the impact will be unmistakable. Then their inherent interest will carry them along. But many times this does not happen. The student reads grudgingly or merely to improve his school grades. This is an acceptable start. Reading to obtain higher marks can improve the student's functioning in school and can open the door to future academic plans that are more in line with his ability. Rather than deplore such an attitude, the teacher accepts it for the time being and realizes that as the student matures, he may develop sounder goals. In the meantime, every effort is made to find appealing short stories and articles that will serve as a springboard to other books.

Sometimes one brief, dramatic story will have a lasting effect and inspire the student to read more. For example, an adolescent boy who rarely read for pleasure or enjoyment completed a short story by Steinbeck in an anthology. He became fascinated with Steinbeck's style of revealing a character's secret thought. Before this he considered that he alone had "bad thoughts." He felt that he was the only one who said one thing and thought another. The story made such an impression on him that he began reading everything by Steinbeck that he could find. He finally became an avid reader of a variety of authors.

The case of Carol, which follows, shows how careful choice of subject matter was significant in changing her discouragement with school and her fear of doing college work eventually.

Carol—in 11th Grade, Discouraged and Unable to Cope with Advanced Reading Skills

Carol, in 11th grade, with superior intellectual potential, felt very discouraged about her prospects. She had had reading instruction from time to time, but nevertheless obtained fairly low scores on her *Scholastic Aptitude Tests*. She was not at all certain that she wished to enter a reading program again, and she also wavered as to whether or not she wanted to attend college. The one area in which she showed some talent was painting.

Carol made a few tentative appointments for instruction with one of the authors. They agreed that she would be free to cancel them should she decide against receiving help. Her only reason for coming was that she felt she read extremely slowly, but she seemed skeptical that any instruction could help her.

Carol presented a challenge to the author to search painstakingly for subject matter that might be meaningful and relevant to her present situation. Accordingly, along with many selections of a generally interesting nature, Carol was also given articles on subjects that might be of special interest to her. Her responsiveness was indeed striking.

For example, an excerpt from *The Psychology of Consciousness*[2] on the modes of operation of the two hemispheres of the brain was particularly intriguing. Being artistic, she was fascinated with the explanation that the right hemisphere was responsible for spatial orientation, artistic endeavor, and probably intuitive thinking, among other things. This kind of information was new and stimulating and was an area that she stated she would like to learn more about. An article by John Holt, "Admission to College,"[3] elicited positive reactions also. Holt discussed the unrealistic standards of admission to colleges in contrast to the policies of public libraries. He pointed out that librarians do not quiz people on books to ascertain whether they can understand their contents, nor do they refuse to lend records of serious music to individuals before learning whether they are educated enough to appreciate such music. He regretted the fact that young people start living under the shadow of universities almost as soon as they are born.

This article led to a very serious discussion of the many college programs now available that do not rely heavily on SAT scores, but which meet the special needs of individuals. Still another article which had particular meaning was "Four Choices for Young People," by John Fisher.[4] Fisher made several points: (1) A student could drop out. This was the oldest expedient. It was used by Hindus, mystics, Buddhist cults, monastic orders, and those who took hallucinogens. (2) One could flee. Ever since civilization began, individuals have tried to run away. (3) One could plot a revolution. (4) One could try to change the world gradually. The latter was described at great length. This article brought forth the response from Carol, "I guess I have only one choice—to go to college."

These are just three examples of a large number of carefully chosen articles which kept Carol involved and interested in continuing on a

2. R. Ornstein, *The Psychology of Consciousness* (New York: Viking, 1974).
3. In B. Schmidt et al., *Developing Reading Proficiency* (Columbus, Ohio: Charles E. Merrill, 1971).
4. In M. Schumacher, *Design for Good Reading* (New York: Harcourt, 1969).

regular basis. In time, she became motivated enough to ask for help in vocabulary development and spelling, in addition to working on rate of reading. One area in which she functioned consistently well was comprehension. However, as in the case of Lucy described later in this chapter, flexibility in handling different types of materials had to be stressed.

Probably even more significant than her progress in reading was the fact that Carol was able to think in terms of constructive educational plans and furthermore had developed sufficient confidence in herself to pursue her goals.

Thus, dramatic changes occurred in this student, who at first had claimed that she was so fed up with the scholarly demands of her school that she planned to quit at the end of 12th grade. Yet, before instruction was terminated, she asked, "Do you think that some day I could work with children with problems, because I really know how they feel?" Even the thought of graduate studies did not faze her.

Selection and Use of Workbook

In addition to compelling narrative material, it is important to use a variety of comprehension exercises dealing with separate fields. This offers the student a wealth of background information and new vocabulary in a short span of time. Besides broadening background and vocabulary, which the student decidedly needs, these selections develop flexibility in reading. Also, choosing articles from social studies, science, current affairs, and the like, approximates the reading that the student needs for his textbooks; hence it develops study skills as well. (Of course the student who does not transfer these skills to actual texts needs further supervised practice.)

Articles are selected with care so that time is not wasted on irrelevant or poorly constructed ones. The main criteria for selection include intrinsic interest of the subject matter, a wide choice of content and style, clear exposition of paragraphs, and properly constructed questions. If the teacher makes it a practice to preview the articles and answer the questions herself, she can soon discover which are most suitable. She may also discover which to discard as too difficult, ambiguous, or inappropriate.

The instructor shows the students how different articles will be used. Some selections are very short; others are a thousand words or longer. They include newspaper articles, technical reports, informational material, and so forth. The types of questions vary also. Some are followed by one or two questions that seek the main idea; others have about ten questions that search out details. Some questions are reflective, others inferential, and so on. In handling these materials, the student practices shifting his pace from one to the other. He learns when to read carefully and when to skim. He aims for efficiency in reading rather than increased rate per se. (A more extensive discussion of rate is offered on pages 242ff of this chapter).

After the student has completed a selection and corrected his work, he may find that keeping a record of his accuracy or his rate of reading score is a beneficial incentive for improvement. But another student might find it too threatening, since there is apt to be wide fluctuation in performance. Some derive benefit from working under the pressure of a stop watch; others find that this detracts from their concentration. The student experiments under the instructor's guidance until the latter finds the method that best suits the student. Also, it is enlightening for the student to discuss the nature of his errors after he has completed the comprehension exercises. For example, did he misunderstand a question due to its ambiguity or insufficient familiarity with the subject? If so, he might be told to leave such questions out in the future and answer the rest. (Perhaps he will have time at some point to use an encyclopedia or other source to obtain the information.) If he makes wild guesses, he must learn to read more accurately. If he confuses his personal reactions or past knowledge with the information specifically stated in the paragraph, he must learn to make the distinction between them. If he tends to read every word, he can be encouraged to read for ideas; if he skims too rapidly and loses the details, he should be shown the value of becoming more precise.

The student continues working in this way for as long as necessary. For many students, ten to twenty sessions are sufficient to show them what they need and how to proceed independently. After completing instruction, a student can always return for occasional practice whenever he feels the need. But the more responsibility he assumes for incorporating the skills he has acquired into his general reading and school assignments, the more he should be able to improve his reading efficiency.

Vocabulary Development

Many high school students with limited vocabulary find themselves at a disadvantage compared with their more articulate peers. Frequently they wish, for the first time, to improve their vocabulary because they have either reached the point where they recognized the value of expressing themselves effectively or because of the weight given to vocabulary subtests on the *Scholastic Aptitude Test* for college entrance. In helping such students enlarge their vocabulary a multifaceted approach is needed. At the simplest level merely keeping an alphabetized notebook in which new words are written with their definitions and use in simple sentences has proved helpful. However, systematic study of the most common Latin and Greek roots, prefixes, and suffixes can increase vocabulary considerably. The older student needs greater emphasis on this aspect than the younger ones described on p. 179. Furthermore, exposure to new words may be accelerated through the reading of articles on a wide variety of subjects which introduce specialized vocabulary and new concepts. These may be found in many of the excellent workbooks available for high school and college students. Most of the books include accompanying exercises with words that are likely to be unfamiliar in the articles. In addition, dictionary practice with specific reference to choosing appropriate definitions from the multiple meanings is still another way. In this connection it has often been found that even capable students need specific instruction in order to decipher diacritical marks and use the pronunciation key at the bottom of most dictionary pages. Least effective is assigning lists of words to be memorized because students learn the lists for specific sessions or tests; unless the words are incorporated into their speech or written expression they are promptly forgotten.

Rate of Reading

Today more than ever, a great deal is heard about rate. Some reading centers claim that they can increase an individual's rate of reading to the upper hundreds and even thousands of words per minute. To achieve or maintain such astronomical speed is in our experience most unusual. Besides, rate should always be governed by purpose and be assessed in conjunction with comprehension.[5] There is no "normal" or average rate of reading. For general reading, some authorities have considered 300 words per minute fairly adequate. Very good readers read 500 to 600 words per minute and occasionally there is one who reads at the phenomenal rate of 1,000 words per minute or faster, but this is rare.

How do we determine rate, and how do we decide who should have training in it? Rate is measured on some subtests of the regular reading

5. N. Smith, *Read Faster and Get More For Your Reading* (Englewood Cliffs, N.J.: Prentice-Hall, 1958), p. 3.

tests listed in Appendix A. It is but one portion of a diagnosis which includes evaluation of advanced word recognition techniques, vocabulary, comprehension, and so on. Rate scores must always be evaluated in connection with comprehension. For instance, students who score in the 90th percentile in rate and the 20th percentile in comprehension are bound to run into trouble in high school and college, obviously not because of rate, but because they get so little from their reading. In addition to looking at the scores of rate and comprehension, it is important to investigate the student's own thoughts on the matter. Is he spending an inordinate amount of time on his homework? Does he consider that his rate in general is excessively slow?

If the test results or informal measures confirm the impression that rate improvement is indicated, then the instructor works out an appropriate program with the student.

Students who need to speed up their reading and are able to work on their own may profit from a workbook which explains the theory of efficient reading at the same time that it measures the student's rate and comprehension. Some students find that this is all the work that they need. However, these students are in the minority. Most individuals wish for some direction and guidance. This is where the teacher can provide the necessary stimulus and the systematic checking that keep the student going. If he is motivated adequately, he can make good progress.

The program consists of practice with appropriate material. All the reading matter suitable for practice in comprehension is also appropriate for rate and vice versa. However, for correcting answers and measuring words per minute, it is convenient to have material that contains the number of words in the selection, conversion tables for finding rate, individual answer keys, and the like.[6]

In addition to such practice, the student must agree to undertake some independent reading at home which he does regularly for approximately a half hour. It is recommended that the student choose reading matter that does not make excessive demands on concentration. Magazine articles, short stories, novels, fiction, and so on are suggested. He forces himself to read these as fast as he possibly can, making certain that he understands reasonably well what he reads. Several weeks or months of such practice usually result in facile reading ability. For further discussion of procedures for an individual with a slow rate of reading, see the case of Lucy which follows.

6. College level materials for bright high school juniors and seniors and college students are listed in Appendix C.

Most students are able to read more rapidly after they undertake the program just described. However, there are always some who do not increase their rate to a satisfactory degree. Such students may develop so much concern about the number of words they read per minute that their progress is often impeded. Where this occurs, the instructor may help the student by discussing some of the ways in which he might compensate for his slow reading. For example, he might set aside a little more time for daily studying than he ordinarily does. Or he might take four courses rather than five a year, or he might take additional credits in summer school. Adopting these alternatives would provide him with enough time to study so as to complete assignments without working under undue pressure. Apprising the students of such choices serves to decrease his anxiety about his inadequate rate of reading. As he gains a more realistic attitude toward his problem, he is usually able to function more effectively.

The case of Lucy is that of a bright 16-year-old girl who was serious about increasing her rate of reading. The program she followed was fairly close to that set forth in the preceding pages.

Lucy—An 11th Grader with a Slow Reading Rate

Lucy, aged 16 years, 9 months, in 11th grade, was referred to one of the authors for testing because she did poorly on the PSAT (examination) despite the fact that she was considered bright and her school grades were generally good. Lucy's view of her problem was that she understood what she read, but felt that she read "at a snails pace."

Lucy's intelligence was in the superior range. On the *Iowa Silent Reading Test*, level 2, she achieved the following scores:

Vocabulary	91st percentile
Reading Comprehension	89th percentile
Reading Efficiency	43rd percentile

During the trial learning session, her rate of reading was exceedingly slow, even on narrative material. When she tried to read more rapidly, her comprehension suffered. Therefore, it was clear that she needed to engage in a program that would help her develop more efficient patterns of reading. This Lucy agreed to willingly.

245

Treatment

She came once a week for instruction for only 12 sessions, at which point she felt that she understood the skills necessary for increasing her rate of reading and would, therefore, be able to proceed on her own. She learned, for example, that she needed to apply various rates depending not only on her purpose for reading a particular selection or book but also on the complexity of the material and her background of knowledge of the subject matter. Furthermore, her goal was not to read a specific number of words per minute, to which many students seem to aspire, but rather to develop many different rates.

Weekly instruction included reading articles covering a wide range of topics on many levels of difficulty with a careful check on comprehension.[7] In addition, Lucy practiced reading at home almost daily, trying to force herself to read faster than her customary rate. In this connection, she read short stories and various types of magazine and newspaper articles and editorials.

After about three months, sufficient progress was shown for her to be able to work independently. However, in order to maintain her gains, she borrowed several workbooks of the kind generally used in college reading centers, thereby enabling her to check regularly on her comprehension. She recognized that she needed to guard against any loss in her ability to comprehend while focusing on speed.

Lucy's total involvement in the program and her mature handling of her independent supplementary work resulted in her attainment of decidedly more effective reading skills.

The Place of Machines in Improving Rate

The subject of rate would not be complete without some mention of the use of machines. Various types of pacing machines, tachistoscopes, and other devices for quick exposure of words, phrases, and connected reading have long been in use. They have some desirable aspects as well as limitations. On the positive side, students are frequently intrigued by them. Thus they heighten motivation. They may give students the initial boost that they need in developing a faster rate, or they may help to overcome a long-standing habit of slow reading.

7. Some of the materials used were the following: L. Miller, *Personalizing Reading Efficiency* (Minneapolis: Burgess, 1976); J. Brown, *Reading Power* (Lexington, Mass.: Heath, 1975); J. Brown, *Efficient Reading*, Form B (Lexington, Mass.: Heath, 1976); B. Schmidt et al., *Developing Reading Proficiency* (Columbus, Ohio: Charles E. Merrill, 1971); D. Milan, *Modern College Reading* (New York: Scribner's, 1971).

However, there may be little carry-over from the machine to the normal reading situation. A machine represents an artificial learning situation and is rarely available outside of school. It also leads to some distortion in the reading process.[8] Furthermore, any program still depends on the person who leads it. Without skillful personal guidance, the use of machines is likely to develop into a meaningless procedure. Therefore, a period of guided reading without mechanical devices should follow any program that depends on machines.

Meeting Academic Requirements and Assignments

As is well known, high school requirements become more stringent as students advance. Students who are reading less well than they are able may find their assignments becoming more and more arduous. All the reasons that have been enumerated contribute to this predicament. The students' foundations may remain inadequate, their vocabulary insufficient, their rate slow, and their confidence low. Besides the suggestions described, it is sometimes profitable to give the student a little extra direction in assignments. For example, helping him to look for suitable references or guiding him in organizing the salient features for an outline can be beneficial. Concrete explanations as to the format and scope required in a term paper can bring about satisfactory results.

In organizing their studies, some students find the SQ_3R method helpful.[9] This formula stands for "Survey, Question, Read, Recite, Review." In essence, this technique suggests (1) glancing over chapter headings for major points; (2) turning paragraph headings into questions; (3) reading to answer the questions; (4) looking away from the book, briefly reciting to oneself, then writing down the information; and finally (5) reviewing the lesson for major points.

Whatever the method used, the student needs continued encouragement. One cannot always live up to theoretical potential nor work at the peak of one's efficiency. But a student can be helped to improve his techniques, accelerate his effectiveness, and increase his power of functioning. The cases of Tod and Ralph, which follow, illustrate this point.

8. For references regarding the use of pacing machines, see A. Harris and E. Sipay, *How to Increase Reading Ability* (New York: McKay, 1975), p. 566.

9. F. Robinson, *Effective Study* (New York: Harper & Brothers, 1961).

Tod—Adequate Test Scores but
Falling Behind in Ninth Grade

Tod, aged 14 years, 5 months, in ninth grade, was referred to one of the authors because he believed he had a serious problem understanding and recalling what he read. His teachers observed that he was participating less and less in class, and his parents reported that he found his home assignments extremely difficult and felt quite incapable of handling them. His feelings of inadequacy were further reflected in his tendency to withdraw from family conversations. His parents, concerned about his emotional adjustment, suggested some form of counseling, but Tod countered that he really needed help in reading.

During the testing, Tod was quiet, reserved, and strikingly unsure of himself. He approached items on the Verbal Intelligence Scale in a cautious, uncertain manner as though he expected to give the wrong answer. However, he related easily to the author and showed excellent effort and perseverance when thinking independently.

On the WISC, he ranked in the bright-normal group. His verbal sub-test ratings revealed superior comprehension and abstract reasoning, but his background of information and immediate recall were only average. His reading scores follow:

	9th Grade Norms for All Students	9th Grade Norms for Students Following College Prep Course
Iowa Silent Reading Tests (Level 2)		
Vocabulary	82nd percentile	67th percentile
Reading Comprehension	81st percentile	62nd percentile
Reading Efficiency	73rd percentile	57th percentile
Wide Range Achievement Test		
Spelling		10.5 Grade Level

The scores listed above indicate that Tod was reading in line with his level of intelligence. Furthermore, during the informal reading sessions, he showed good comprehension of articles presented at his grade level and, in addition, summarized one of the selections in a clear, concise, well-written statement. Thus, in a situation where he felt at ease, he functioned quite effectively.

Even though his Bender-Gestalt drawings were well-executed, the figures were tiny, which is often indicative of a sense of inadequacy. This characteristic was also found in his Human Figure Drawings.

In considering recommendations for Tod, it might be observed that, according to reading expectancy formulas, he could not be regarded as a reading disability. However, the author decided to take seriously Tod's impression of flaws in his reading, because she recognized that there are so many facets to mature reading skills that test scores alone cannot be used as the sole criterion. Furthermore, other factors influencing a student's functioning need to be assessed also. For example, in Tod's case, his problem was exacerbated by the inordinately high academic standards of the suburban high school he attended. Familial factors constituted another component. Tod had very capable parents and a younger brother who excelled consistently in all his academic work.

Since Tod emphatically stated that he wanted help, and according to our point of view needed it, arrangements were made for the writer to work with him on a once-a-week basis until he showed signs of feeling more comfortable in handling his schoolwork.

Tod was seen for a total of 20 sessions, and the outcome was most rewarding. He showed decided changes, not only in his reading, but in all aspects of his emotional adjustment. There was no question about his ability to cope with his schoolwork, and moreover, he no longer hesitated to express his opinions at home or to enter into discussions at school.

In considering how these constructive changes occurred, it is likely that the writer's attitude played an important role. Instead of agreeing with the guidance counselor at school that Tod had no problem and was doing as well as might be expected, she showed empathic understanding of the boy's feelings. Thus, his deep sense of inadequacy in his abilities was accepted. A program of instruction was discussed with him that would alleviate the specific difficulties he was experiencing. Thus he knew what steps would be taken to help him.

As for instruction, at the beginning he was given materials at about ninth grade level. Gradually the levels of difficulty and complexity of the materials were increased until Tod was capably handling reading selections designed for students attending college reading centers. He came to recognize that unevenness in performance could be expected because readability of materials depended on so many factors. From time to time, he brought along school assignments which were indeed difficult, but which were used as examples of the need to apply different reading skills to materials which required greater effort, concentration, and specialized knowledge. He began to grasp the need for flexibility in his approach. Some of the skills developed during the sessions are those described in Chapter 10 in the discussion of reading comprehension. In addition, there was emphasis on how to study. In this connection, he found the SQ3R approach helpful.

In view of the fact that it was reported that Tod was reluctant to express his own ideas both at home and at school, some stress was placed not only on what was stated in an article, but also on what its contents meant to him. Practice in formulating and expressing his own reactions orally was one of our major goals and probably of decided significance in his developing feelings of confidence. Special attention was also paid to the introduction of a wide variety of subjects because he showed gaps in his background of information on the intelligence test.

At the close, Tod felt that he had gained considerably from the sessions and was apparently applying his increased competency in reading and study skills to his schoolwork. This progress was reflected in marked improvement in his final grades and in his very good functioning reported in a follow-up interview one year later.[10]

Ralph—In Tenth Grade with Fluctuating Test Scores Depending on his Attitude

Ralph was sullen, passive, and uninterested and saw no need to be tested. He was noncommittal about school and his poor grades, but he was convinced that he did not have a reading problem. The school and Ralph's parents thought otherwise. They attributed his difficulties to inadequate reading comprehension and believed that evaluation by a reading specialist was advisable.

Throughout the administration of the intelligence test, Ralph was

10. In addition to Tod's own school texts, selected articles were chosen from the following materials:

M. Schumacher, et al., *Design for Good Reading*, Books B, C, and D (New York: Harcourt, 1969); SRA IIIA, *Rate and Power Builders*, levels 9 through 11 (Chicago: SRA, 1973); L. Miller, *Increasing Reading Efficiency*, 3rd ed., (New York: Holt, Rinehart, & Winston, 1970); E. Spargo, et a., *Timed Readings*, Book 6 (11th grade level), (Providence, R.I.: Jamestown Publishers, 1975); E. Spargo et al., *Topics for the Restless*, Olive, Brown, and Purple Books, (Providence, R.I.: Jamestown Publishers, 1974); E. Fry, *Reading Drills* (Providence, R. I.: Jamestown Publishers, 1975); J. Brown, *Reading Power* (Lexington, Mass.: Heath, 1975).

minimally cooperative and answered questions cryptically and in as few words as possible. In spite of his negative attitude, there were indications of superior capacities. On the other hand, the *Iowa Silent Reading Test*, Level 2, yielded a comprehension score in only the 30th percentile.

As Ralph began to recognize that he was doing well on the intelligence test, there seemed to be some thawing in his cold, resistive manner. Therefore, the specialist[11] risked a discussion of the many possible reasons for his problems and said that frankly she was puzzled. He undoubtedly was very bright, but his own assessment of his reading ability did not jibe with present reading test results, which were very low. Furthermore, the school reported that he needed to receive special reading help and was even considering having him repeat the grade. Ralph then admitted that he didn't really put forth much effort because he hated reading tests and thought that perhaps he read the test items too quickly. It also dawned on him that decisions in the large public school he attended might be based on the outcome of this examination. Thus, he became amenable to the suggestion that at the next session he be given an alternate form of the same test along with additional evaluation of his reading skills. Sure enough, at the following visit Ralph came prepared to exert appropriate effort. This time he scored at the 81st percentile on an alternate form of the *Iowa* test and showed further evidence on informal measures in both oral and silent reading of being capable of handling work at the upper high school levels.

These results buoyed Ralph's spirits considerably, and he became more open about discussing his problems, which proved to be numerous. Therefore, he required not only some modifications in his curriculum, but also attention to personality aspects.

This case illustrates the need to use a variety of measures in evaluation of reading skills together with interpretation of test scores in the light of the student's degree of cooperation and effort while taking the tests. If extended analysis had not been made, the school would have continued to prescribe reading help which Ralph did not need and his resistance to it would have mounted. Moreover, attention to the deeper sources of his problem would have been overlooked.

Coping with Examinations

Another problem of major importance concerns pupils who often become overconcerned and panicky over intensive examinations. Particu-

11. One of the authors.

Treatment

larly in the latter years of high school, tests such as the *Scholastic Aptitude Tests* cause heightened fear and anxiety. Students who have minimum achievement become particularly unnerved by them. They may react similarly to class tests, too. Although there is no cure, there are certain things that have proved alleviating. The teacher and pupil can discuss the latter's approach toward taking tests. Does he "freeze"? Does he make "careless" errors in mistaking directions? They can discuss how many people "go blank" when faced with an important test; in fact, it is almost universal for everyone to have anxiety before, during, and even after taking tests. The student can then take actual examinations for practice. This makes the ordeal more commonplace and lessens some of its overpowering tension. In addition, he is advised to exert reasonable effort on each test item, but not puzzle too long over any one of them. If there is time, he can always return to a question he left out. If an answer is omitted, the student learns caution in placing the next mark properly. (Too often a "skipped" question throws off subsequent markings.) On an essay-type examination, he is encouraged to read all the questions first; this sometimes yields valuable hints for answering several of them. Learning to gauge time correctly is also of paramount importance. After practice tests are taken, the teacher and student can score them jointly. Incorrect responses can be accounted for on the spot. Reviewing his errors can help the student gain insight into the nature of his mistakes. Finally, assuring him that there are still colleges that accept students without examinations takes away the unrealistic fear that his whole life depends on a test.

Fallacy of Prediction from Test Scores Alone

Evaluating ability and suggesting choices for the future entail the use of predictive measures. That is, they include mapping out courses of study and future academic plans on the basis of test scores and teachers' evaluations of the student. But foretelling human outcomes is at best a risky undertaking. The largest factor, motivation, still remains a mystery. Demosthenes, the severe stutterer, became an accomplished orator. Winston Churchill reportedly failed English composition three times; yet his prose is impeccable. Those considered "most likely to succeed" in high school yearbooks often turn out to be miserable failures. Furthermore, the growth spurt from late adolescence to maturity makes prophecy hazardous.

Therefore, let us not in this overtesting age be influenced by quantitative scores and other mechanical measures alone or misled by the assessment of a student who, in his present stage, shows less academic aptitude than is considered desirable. Those who deal with reading problems are still puzzled over outcomes. Some mediocre students whose test scores suggested that they were not college material have become sufficiently interested at a later date to seek college admission. There they have made creditable and even brilliant records. Or they have taken advantage of junior colleges or special programs geared for those whose needs deviate from conventional scheduling.[12,13] Other students whose "verbal" scores were significantly higher than their "math" scores on scholastic aptitude tests were sometimes advised against pursuing the science, mathematics, and physics studies which attracted them. Yet many who ignored this counsel have turned out to be successful in these fields. There are some students who have suffered from reading difficulty throughout their first 12 years of schooling and are still miserable spellers. Through sheer determination and adherence to their goals, they have become doctors, lawyers, engineers, or whatever else they wished. We have known pupils who were told to give up the idea of college completely. Against this advice not only did they go to college but, in many cases, they went on to graduate study.[14]

The opposite situations have also obtained. Students who were scholarship material in high school have failed in college; those who were told that they would make excellent Ph.D. material never were able to withstand the academic strain. Thus an experienced teacher or counselor imparts as many of the skills as possible. When a certain amount of failure seems unconquerable, the "door must be left open." The situation is assessed as fairly as possible, but decisions remain tentative. Tremendous change can occur outside the confines of formal education. Life circumstances, inspiration, and growth processes between 18 and 30 years of age and even older have yet to be investigated. No one knows when maturation reaches its zenith. People continue to learn throughout their lives. Our most important contribution to those who have academic difficulty is to lessen their sense of failure so that they have an opportunity to make use of whatever abilities they may have.

12. P. Fielding, ed., J. Moss, directory consultant, *A National Directory of Four-Year Colleges, Two-Year Colleges and Post High School Training Programs for Young People with Learning Disabilities*, 2nd ed. (Tulsa Okla.: Partners in Publishing, 1975).

13. S. Splaver, *Non-Traditional College Routes to Careers* (New York: Julian Messner, Division of Simon and Schuster, 1975).

14. L. Thompson, "Language Disabilities in Men of Eminence," *Journal of Learning Disabilities* 4 (1971): 34–45.

Treatment

Suggestions for Further Reading

Alschuler, A. *Developing Achievement Motivation in Adolescents*. Englewood Cliffs, N.J.: Educational Technology Publications, 1973.

Brown, G., ed. *The Live Classroom*. New York: Viking, 1975.

Bruner, J. *Beyond the Information Given: Studies in the Psychology of Knowing*. New York: Norton, 1973.

Cahn, S. *The Philosophical Foundations of Education*. New York: Harper & Row, 1970.

Erikson, E. *Identity, Youth, and Crisis*. New York: Norton, 1968.

Feathersone, J. *Schools Where Children Learn*. New York: Liveright, 1971.

Gattegno, C. *The Adolescent and His Will*. New York: Outerbridge and Dienstfrey, 1971.

Griffith, W., and Hayes, A., eds. *Adult Basic Education: The State of the Art*, Washington, D.C.: U. S. Govt. Printing Office, 1970 (ERIC–ED. 051475).

Hellmuth, J. *Cognitive Studies*. New York: Brunner/Mazel, 1970.

Henry, J. *On Education*. New York: Vintage, 1972.

Isaacs, S. *Troubles of Children and Parents*. New York: Schocken Press, 1973.

Kagan, I., and Coles, R. *Twelve to Sixteen: Early Adolescence*. New York: Norton, 1972.

Rancier, G., and Brooke, W. *An Annotated Bibliography of Adult Basic Education*. Ottowa: Queen's Printer, 1970.

Rogers, C., and Stevens, B. *Person to Person*. New York: Pocket Books, 1973.

Rubin, L. *Facts and Feelings in the Classroom*. New York: Viking, 1973.

Skinner, B. F. *Beyond Freedom and Dignity*. New York: Vintage, 1972.

Sheldon, S., and Schwartzberg, H. *The Human Encounter*. New York: Harper & Row, 1969.

Silberman, C. *Crisis in the Classroom: The Remaking of American Education*. New York: Random House, 1971.

APPENDIX A

Representative Tests[1]

Reading Readiness Tests[1]

Clymer-Barrett Prereading Battery
(Personnel Press, 1969)
Range: First grade entrants
Forms: 2

Gates-MacGinitie Readiness Skills Test
(Teachers College Press, 1969)
Range: K–1
Forms: 1

Jansky Screening Index
(in *Preventing Reading Failure*,
   Harper & Row, 1972) Screening
   Index Kit, Matthew Jansky, 120 E.
   89th St., N.Y.C. 10028
Range: K (spring term)
Forms: 1

*Kindergarten Evaluation of Learning
   Potential* (KELP)

(McGraw-Hill, Webster Division,
   1969)
Range: K
Forms: 1

*Metropolitan Readiness Test
   Levels I & II*
(The Psychological Corp., 1976)
Range: K–1
Forms: 2

Monroe Reading Aptitude Test
(Houghton Mifflin)
Range: K–1
Forms: 1

*Murphy-Durrell Reading Readiness
   Analysis*
(The Psychological Corp., 1965)
Range: K.8–1.5
Forms: 1

---

1. The tests were compiled by Barbara Goldberg, reading specialist, in consultation with the authors.

Reading Tests

Adult Basic Learning Examination
  (ABLE)
(The Psychological Corp., 1970)
Group tests designed to measure adult
  achievement in basic learning.
Range: 1–12
3 levels
Forms: 1

Botel Reading Inventory
(Follett Publishing Co., 1970)
Four tests include word recognition,
  opposites, phonics, and spelling re-
  placement.
Range: Depends on specific test
Forms: 1

California Achievement Tests
(McGraw-Hill, 1970)
Group test consisting of several sub-
  tests.
Range: 1.5–12
5 levels
Forms: 2

Dolch Basic Sight Word Test
(Garrard Publishing Co., 1942)
A listing of the 220 Dolch Basic Sight
  Words to determine children's abil-
  ity to recognize them.
Forms: 1

*Doren Diagnostic Reading Test of
  Word Recognition Skills*
(American Guidance Service, Inc.,
  1973)
Range: 1–4
Forms: 1

Durrell Listening-Reading Series
(The Psychological Corp., 1970)
Provides a comparison of children's
  listening and reading abilities.
Range: 1–9
Forms: 2

*Durrell Analysis of Reading
  Difficulty*
(The Psychological Corp., 1955)
Individually administered.
Range: 1–6
Forms: 1

Gates-MacGinitie Reading Tests
(Teachers College Press, 1972)
Group tests
Range: 1–12
7 levels
Forms: 3

Gates-McKillop Diagnostic Test
(Teachers College Press)
Detailed diagnosis of deficiencies.
17 individually administered tests.
Range: all grades
Forms: 2

Gilmore Oral Reading Test
(The Psychological Corp., 1968)
Individually administered.
Range: 1–8
Forms: 2

Gray Oral Reading Tests
(Bobbs-Merrill, 1967)
Individually administered.
Range: 1–12
Forms: 4

Iowa Silent Reading Tests
(The Psychological Corp., 1973)
(New Edition)
Group silent reading tests that include
  measures of vocabulary, reading
  comprehension, and speed of read-
  ing.
Range: 6–14
3 levels
Forms: 2

Metropolitan Achievement Tests
(The Psychological Corp., 1970)
(scheduled revision for 1978)
Six batteries of group tests. Separate
  booklets for reading tests available
  for 2.5–9.5.
Range: 1–9.5
Forms: 3

Nelson-Denny Reading Test
(Houghton Mifflin, 1973)
(Revised Edition)
Group test measuring vocabulary,
  comprehension, and rate.
Range: 9–16 and adults

Nelson Reading Skills Test
(Houghton Mifflin, 1977)
Range: 3–9
Forms: 2

*Peabody Individual Achievement
  Tests*
(American Guidance Service, Inc.)
Screening test to survey basic skills
  and knowledge.
Range: Preschool–adult
Forms: 1

Roswell Chall Auditory Blending Test
(Essay Press, 1963)
Individually administered. Evaluates
  ability to blend sounds into words.

*Roswell-Chall Diagnostic Reading
  Test*
(Essay Press, 1976)
(Revised Edition)
Individually administered.
Evaluates basic word anaylsis skills.
Determines reading deficiencies at all
  levels.
Range: 1–4
Forms: 2

*Screening Tests for Identifying
  Children with Specific Language
  Disability* (Slingerland)

(Educators Publishing Service, Inc.,
  1973)
Range: 1–6
3 levels
Forms: 1

*Sequential Tests of Educational
  Progress* (STEP)
(Educational Testing Service, 1972)
Group tests
Range: 4–14
4 levels
Forms: 2
(Also available in Braille and large
  type from American Printing House
  for the Blind)
1839 Frankfort Ave.
Louisville, Ky. 40206

Sipay Word Analysis Test (SWAT)
(Educators Publishing Service, Inc.,
  1974)
17 individually administered tests.
Forms: 1

Slosson Oral Reading Test (SORT)
(Slosson Educational Publications,
  1963)
Word pronunciation at different levels
  of difficulty.
Range: 1–high school

Spache Diagnostic Reading Scales
(McGraw-Hill)
(Revised edition)
Range: 1–8
Forms: 1

Stanford Achievement Tests
(The Psychological Corp., 1973)
Six batteries of group tests. Also avail-
  able in separate reading tests.
Range: 1.5–9.5
Forms: 2
Stanford Diagnostic Tests
(1966–69)
Range: 2.5–13
3 levels
Forms: 2

Wide Range Achievement Test
(Guidance Associates of Delaware,
 1965)
Word pronunciation, spelling, and
arithmetic computation.
Range: Preschool–adult
2 levels
Forms: 1

Special Tests

*Ammons Full-Range Picture
 Vocabulary Test*
(Psychological Test Specialists)
Individually administered.
Age range: Preschool–adult

*Beery-Buktenica Developmental Test
 of Visual-Motor Integration*
(Follett Educational Corp.)
Age range: 2–15
Forms: 2

Bender Visual-Motor Gestalt Test
(The Psychological Corp.)
A test involving copying visual de-
signs.
Age range: 6–adult

Benton Revised Visual Retention Test
(The Psychological Corp.)
A test involving recall of visual de-
signs.
Age range: 8–adult

*Frostig Developmental Test of Visual
 Perception*
(Consulting Psychologists Press)
Tests various aspects of visual per-
ceptual functioning.
Age range: 4–9

Goodenough-Harris Drawing Test
(The Psychological Corp.)
Age range: 3–15

Harris Tests of Lateral Dominance
(The Psychological Corp.)
Tests of hand, eye, and foot domi-
nance.
Age range: 6 and up

*Illinois Test of Psycholinguistic
 Abilities* (ITPA)
(University of Illinois Press)
Evaluations of linguistic strengths
and weaknesses.
Age range: 2–10

Peabody Picture Vocabulary Test
(American Guidance Service)
Individually administered.
Age range: 2.6–adult
Forms: 2

*Stanford-Binet Intelligence Scale,
 Form L–M*
(Houghton Mifflin)
Age range: 2–adult

*Wepman Auditory Discrimination
 Test*
(Language Research Associates)
1973, Revised
Age range: 5–8

Wechsler Adult Intelligence Scale
 (WAIS)
(The Psychological Corp.)
Age range: 16–adult

*Wechsler Intelligence Scale for
 Children* (WISC–R)
(The Psychological Corp.)
Age range: 6–17

*Wechsler Preschool and Primary
 Scale of Intelligence* (WIPPSI)
(The Psychological Corp.)
Age range: 4–6.5

APPENDIX B

Selected Books by Grade Level

In using any compilation of graded books, the teacher's judgment plays an important role; no estimate of the reading level of a book can be entirely accurate. Many factors—the author's style and sentence structure and the child's interest in the subject matter, his experience, and his understanding of the concepts—affect the ease or difficulty of a book for a particular child. Nor is the score a child achieves on a standardized reading test always a reliable indication of the level of book he can handle. Therefore readability levels, including those indicated on this list, should be used only as guides. To be sure that a book is appropriate, the teacher must try it out with her pupils. Sometimes, however, teachers have difficulty deciding on the reading level of a book. They know they cannot always rely on publishers' estimates either. Thus it is helpful to use certain readability formulas which rate a book according to grade level.[1]

Beginning at the fourth grade, teachers who deal with children who have reading disability have specific requirements for book lists. They often wish to know which books contain short stories and brief articles suitable to class and individual work, which books can be recommended for independent reading, and at which level certain classics have been adapted. Thus for fourth grade and above, the following list has been divided into these three

1. Those which are most widely used at the primary level are G. Spache, "A New Readability Formula for Primary-Grade Reading Materials," *Elementary School Journal* 53 (1953): 410–13. At elementary and advanced grades, those worthy of consideration are E. Dale and J. Chall, "A Formula for Predicting Readability," *Educational Research Bulletin* 27 (1948): 11–20. Some compilations based on readability formulas that may be helpful to the teacher in selecting children's books are G. Hanna and M. McAllister, *Books, Young People and Reading Guidance* (New York: Harper, 1960), N. Larrick, *A Teacher's Guide to Children's Books* (Columbus, Ohio: Charles E. Merrill, 1960), G. Spache, *Good Reading for the Disadvantaged Reader* (Champaign, Ill.: Garrard Press, 1975), and D. Fader and M. Shaevitz, *Hooked on Books* (New York: Berkeley Publishing Corp., 1966).

categories. In compiling the books in these categories, the authors have borne in mind the resistance that many children with reading disability show toward full-length books. Such pupils frequently read brief articles and stories, then become engrossed in longer works. To entice the pupil to read full-length books independently without becoming overwhelmed by them, the authors have chosen those which many such pupils have found absorbing.

Many simplified classics are available at a variety of reading levels. Sometimes the same classic has been adapted by several publishers at levels ranging from fourth grade to senior high school. Only a small sampling of these classics is presented here. For complete listing and information regarding levels, such publishers as Globe; Sanborn; Scott, Foresman; Webster; Random House; Garrard; and Laidlaw, who are well known for adapting the classics, should be consulted.

For further differentiation as to characteristics and suitability of books, the following symbols have been used:

*   Reading level as indicated; especially useful for junior high school students.

**   Reading level as indicated; mature format and contents, especially useful for senior high school students.

·   Part of a series; other books on various reading levels.

LOW FIRST GRADE

Author	Title
· Hurley	*Dan Frontier* (Benefic)
· ———	*Dan Frontier and the New House* (Benefic)
· Wasserman	*Sailor Jack* (Benefic)
· ———	*Sailor Jack and Eddy* (Benefic)
· ———	*Sailor Jack and Homer Potts* (Benefic)

FIRST GRADE

Author	Title
· Chandler	*Cowboy Sam* (Benefic)
· Dolch	*Dog Pals* (Garrard)
· ———	*Tommy's Pets* (Garrard)
* Gibson and Richards	*First Steps in Teaching English* (Pocket Books)
Guilfoile	*Nobody Listens to Andrew* (Follett)
· Huber	*I Know a Story* (Harper & Row)
King	*Mabel the Whale* (Follett)
· Rambeau	*Jim Forest and Ranger Don* (Field Pub.)
· ———	*Jim Forest and the Bandits* (Field Pub.)

*	Robertson	*Veteran's Reader* (Steck)
**	————	*Operation Alphabet* (Noble & Noble)
*	Wasserman	*Sailor Jack and Bluebell* (Benefic)

SECOND GRADE

Author	Title
Angelo	*Just Be Patient* (Winston)
* · Bright and Mitchell	"The Home and Family Life Series": *Making a Good Living* (Croft)
· Cerf	*Book of Laughs* (Random House)
* · Coleman et al.	*The Sea Hunt* (Field Publications)
Dolch	
· ————	*Circus Stories* (Garrard)
· ————	*Dog Stories* (Garrard)
· ————	*Folk Stories* (Garrard)
· ————	*Horse Stories* (Garrard)
· ————	*Irish Stories* (Garrard)
* · Goldberg and Brumber	"Rochester Occupational Reading Series": *Gas Stations* (Syracuse Univ.)
· Hoff	*Danny and the Dinosaur* (Harper & Row)
· ————	*Sammy the Seal* (Harper & Row)
· Huber et al.	*It Happened One Day* (Harper & Row)
· Hurley	*Dan Frontier and the Wagon Train* (Benefic)
· McClintock	*A Fly Went By* (Random House)
· McKee	*Come Along* (Houghton Mifflin)
· ————	*On We Go* (Houghton Mifflin)
Morrison	*Yours Till Niagara Falls* (Scholastic)
· Norman	*Johnny Appleseed* (Coward, McCann)
· ————	*A Man Named Columbus* (Coward, McCann)
· Committee of Authors	*Operation Alphabet* (Grades 1–4) (Noble & Noble)
* · Rambeau	*Jim Forest and Dead Man's Peak* (Field Pub.)
· Seuss	*The Cat in the Hat* (Random House)
· Shane and Hester	*Storyland Favorites* (Laidlaw)
· Stolz	*Emmett's Pig* (Harper & Row)
· Wasserman	*Sailor Jack and the Target Ship* (Benefic)

THIRD GRADE

Author	Title
* · Agle and Wilson	*Three Boys and a Mine* (Scribner's)
* · Allen	*Great Moments in American History* (Follett)

* · ————	*Ten Great Moments in Sports* (Follett)
* · Anderson	*Friday, the Arapaho Indian* (Harper & Row)
* · ————	*Squanto and the Pilgrims* (Harper & Row)
* · Anderson and Johnson	*Pilot Jack Knight* (Harper & Row)
Anglund	*The Brave Cowboy* (Harcourt, Brace)
· Austin, ed.	*John Paul Jones* (Garrard)
· ————	*Samuel F .B. Morse* and many other biographies (Garrard)
* · Bammon and Whitehead	*The Lost Uranium Mine* (Benefic)
· Battle	*Jerry Goes to the Circus* (Benefic)
· Beals	*Chief Black Hawk* (Harper & Row)
· Berry	*Leif the Lucky* (Garrard)
· Bishop	*The Five Chinese Brothers* (Coward, McCann)
* · ————	*Lafayette* (Garrard)
· Bulla	*Down the Mississippi* (Scholastic)
· ————	*Star of Wild Horse Canyon* (Scholastic)
* · Carmer	*Henry Hudson* (Garrard)
* · Coleman et al.	*Submarine Rescue* (Field Publications)
· Colver	*Abraham Lincoln* (Garrard)
* · Dagliesh	*The Smiths and Rusty* (Scribner's)
· Dolch, ed.	*Aesop's Stories, adapted* (Garrard)
————	*Andersen Stories* (Garrard)
————	*Ivanhoe* (Garrard)
* ————	*Robin Hood Stories* (Garrard)
* · Eisner	*Buried Gold* (Follett)
* ————	*Mystery of Broken Wheel Ranch* (Follett)
* · Epstein	*George Washington Carver* (Garrard)
* · Friedman	*Dot for Short* (Morrow)
* · Haywood	*Betsy's Little Star* (Morrow)
* · ————	*Eddie and Luella* (Morrow)
· Huber et al.	*After the Sun Sets* (Harper & Row)
· Hurley	*Dan Frontier, Sheriff* (Benefic)
· Johnson and Jacobs	*Treat Shop* (Charles E. Merrill)
* · Latham	*Samuel F. B. Morse* (Garrard)
Leeming and Miller	*Riddles, Riddles, Riddles* (Watts)
· LeGrand	*Why Cowboys Sing in Texas* (Abingdon)
Mellon	*A Treasure Chest of Humor* (Hart)
* Rambeau	*Jim Forest and Lone Wolf Gulch* (Field Pub.)
————	*The Mystery of Morgan Castle* (Field Pub.)
Rey	*Curious George* (Houghton Mifflin)
* · Seylar	*Mary Elizabeth and Mr. Lincoln* (Follett)
· Shane and Hester	*Doorways to Adventure* (Laidlaw)
· West	*The Happy Hollisters* (Doubleday)

* · Wilkie   *Daniel Boone* (Garrard)
  · Witty et al.   *Fun and Frolic* (Heath)

FOURTH GRADE

SHORT STORIES AND SELECTIONS

Author	*Title*
* · Bamman and Whitehead	*City Beneath the Sea* (Benefic)
* Bunce, ed.	*O. Henry's Best Stories* (Globe)
* · Coleman et al.	*Frogmen in Action* (Field Publications)
* · Commager	*First Book of the American Revolution* (Watts)
Durr, Windley and Yates	*Kaleidoscope* (Houghton Mifflin)
** · Heavey and Stuart	*Teen-Age Tales*, Bks. A & B (Heath)
· Huber et al.	*It Must Be Magic* (Harper & Row)
· Johnson and Jacobs	*Magic Carpet* (Charles E. Merrill)
· Kottmeyer, ed.	*Cases of Sherlock Holmes* (Webster, McGraw-Hill)
* · ———	*Greek and Roman Myths* (Webster, McGraw-Hill)
Monson and Johnston	*Martin Mooney Mysteries* (Educators Publishing Service)
· Russell et al.	*Roads to Everywhere* (Ginn)

SUPPLEMENTARY READING

· Anderson	*Blaze Finds the Trail* (Macmillan)
Atwater	*Mr. Popper's Penguins* (Little, Brown)
Beatty	*Blitz* (Houghton Mifflin)
· Bechdolt	*Oliver Becomes a Weatherman* (Scholastic)
Bjorklund	*Rodeo Roundup* (Doubleday)
Bloch	*Leave It to Herbert* (Scholastic)
· Cleary	*Henry Huggins* (Morrow)
———	*Otis Spofford* (Morrow)
Collodi	*Pinocchio* (Random House)
** · Dagliesh	*The Davenports Are at Dinner* (Scribner's)
* · Guthridge	*Tom Edison* (Bobbs-Merrill)
· Haywood	*"B" is for Betsy* and others (Harcourt, Brace)
———	*Eddie's Pay Dirt* (Scholastic)
· Higgins	*Stephen Foster* (Bobbs-Merrill)
· Holland	*No Children, No Pets* (Knopf)
* · Ketcham	*Baby Sitter's Guide by Dennis the Menace* (Holt)
———	*Dennis the Menace* (Holt)

* · Kottmeyer, ed.	*King Arthur and His Knights* (Webster, McGraw-Hill)
* · ———	*Robin Hood Stories* (Webster, McGraw-Hill)
* · ———	*Trojan War* (Webster, McGraw-Hill)
Krasilovsky	*The Man Who Didn't Wash His Dishes* (Doubleday)
Lauber	*Clarence the T.V. Dog* (Coward, McCann)
Lewellen	*T.V. Humphrey* (Knopf)
· Lindgren	*Pippi Longstocking* (Viking)
* · MacGregor	*Miss Pickerell and the Geiger Counter* (Whittlesey House)
* · ———	*Miss Pickerell Goes to Mars* (Whittlesey House)
* · Monsell	*Susan Anthony* (Bobbs-Merrill)
Morrison, ed.	*Yours till Niagara Falls* (Scholastic)
Preston, ed.	*Barrel of Laughs* (Scholastic)
* · Rambeau	*The Mystery of the Missing Marlin* (Field Pub.)
Seuss	*If I Ran the Zoo* (Seuss)
———	*Yertle the Turtle* (Seuss)
* · Snow	*Samuel Morse* (Bobbs-Merrill)
* · Stevenson	*Booker T. Washington* (Bobbs-Merrill)
* · ———	*Clara Barton* (Bobbs-Merrill)
* · ———	*George Carver* (Bobbs-Merrill)
** · Stevenson	*Treasure Island*, adapted (Scott, Foresman)
* · Van Riper	*Lou Gehrig* (Bobbs-Merrill)
* · ———	*Will Rogers* (Bobbs-Merrill)
* · Wagoner	*Louisa Alcott* (Bobbs-Merrill)
* · Weil	*Franklin Roosevelt* (Bobbs-Merrill)
West	*The Happy Hollisters and the Mystery of the Totem Faces* (Doubleday)
* · Wilson	*Annie Oakley* (Bobbs-Merrill)
* · ———	*Ernie Pyle* (Bobbs-Merrill)
Winterfeld	*Castaways of Lilliput* (Harcourt, Brace)
———	*Arrow Book of Jokes and Riddles* (Scholastic)
———	*Betty Crocker Junior Baking Book* (General Mills)
Withers, ed.	*A Rocket in My Pocket* (poems) (Harcourt, Brace)
Wyndham	*Candy Stripers* (Scholastic)

SIMPLIFIED CLASSICS

* Defoe	*Robinson Crusoe* (Garrard)
* · ———	*Robinson Crusoe* (Random House)
** · Hugo	*Les Misérables* (Globe)
* · Kottmeyer, ed.	*Robin Hood* (Webster, McGraw-Hill)
· Moderow	*Six Great Stories* (Scott, Foresman)
* · Swift	*Gulliver's Stories* (Garrard)

FIFTH GRADE

SHORT STORIES AND SELECTIONS

Author	*Title*
* · Abrashkin	*Danny Dunn and the Homework Machine* (Scholastic)
· Cook	*Golden Book of the American Revolution* (Simon & Schuster)
Durham et al.	*Directions 1* (Houghton Mifflin)
———	*Directions 2* (Houghton Mifflin)
· Johnson and Jacobs	*Enchanted Isles* (Merrill)
Kramer	*Arrow Book of Ghost Stories* (Scholastic)
· Larrick, ed.	"*Rivers of the World*": *The Mississippi* (Garrard)
———	"*Rivers of the World*": *The St. Lawrence* (Garrard)
Olsen et al	*Breaking Loose* (Noble & Noble)
———	*Playing It Cool* (Noble & Noble)
** · Strang et al.	*Teen-Age Tales*, Bks. 1–5

SUPPLEMENTARY READING

** · Baker	*Juarez of Mexico*, adapted (Webster, McGraw-Hill)
** · ———	*Simon Bolivar*, adapted (Webster, McGraw-Hill)
** Becker	*Chimp in the Family* (Scholastic)
* Bowman	*Pecos Bill* (Whitman)
· Brooks	*Freddy the Detective* (Scholastic)
* Butterworth	*The Enormous Egg* (Little)
** · Doyle	*Cases of Sherlock Holmes*, adapted (Webster, McGraw-Hill)
** Edmonds	*The Matchlock Gun* (Dodd)
Freeman	*Fun with Chemistry* (Random House)
———	*Fun with Cooking* (Random House)
Green	*Simple Tricks for the Young Magician* (Hart)
** · Harkins	*Punt Formation* (Morrow)
** · Jackson	*Squeeze Play* (Crowell)
** Lawson	*Ben and Me* (Little)
* Lewellen	*Tee Vee Humphrey* (Knopf)
* · Lindgren	*Mio My Son* (Scholastic)
* · Longstreth	*Elephant Toast* (Scholastic)
* · McCloskey	*Homer Price and the Donuts* (Viking)
———	*Centerbury Tales* (Viking)
* · Moody	*Little Britches* (Norton)
** · Piersall and Hirshberg	*Fear Strikes Out* (Little)

Pinkerton	*The First Overland Mail* (Random House)
Stewart	*To California by Covered Wagon* (Random House)
· Travers	*Mary Poppins* (Harcourt, Brace)
** · Tucker	*Dan Morgan* (Wheeler)
** Villiers	*Windjammer's Story* (Scholastic)
· Williams and Abrashkin	*Danny Dunn and the Anti-Gravity Paint* (Whittlesey House)
** · Wilson	*Herbert* (Knopf)
* · _____	*Snowbound in Hidden Valley* (Scholastic)
** · Winwar	*Napoleon and the Battle of Waterloo* (Random House)

SIMPLIFIED CLASSICS

** · Dickens	*A Tale of Two Cities* (Webster, McGraw-Hill)
** · Hugo	*Les Misérables* (Globe)
** · Melville	*Moby Dick* (Sanborn)
** · Poe	*The Gold Bug and Other Stories* (Webster, McGraw-Hill)
Sandrus	*Eight Treasured Stories* (Scott, Foresman)
* · Twain	*Tom Sawyer* (Scott, Foresman)
Verne	*Around the World in Eighty Days* (Scott, Foresman)
** · Wallace	*Ben Hur* (Webster, McGraw-Hill)

SIXTH GRADE

SUPPLEMENTARY READING

** · Alcott	*Little Women* (Little)
* · Boylston	*Clara Barton* (Scholastic)
** · _____	*Sue Barton, Student Nurse* (Little)
* · Brink	*Caddie Woodlawn* (Macmillan)
* · Cleary	*Fifteen* (Scholastic)
** de Kruif	*Microbe Hunters* (Harcourt, Brace)
** · Felsen	*Hot Rod* (Dutton)
* · Fisher	*Understood Betsy* (Holt)
** Forbes	*Mama's Bank Account* (Harcourt, Brace)
Freedman	*Mrs. Mike* (Coward, McCann)
* · Friedman	*The Janitor's Girl* (Morrow)
* · Garfield	*Follow My Leader* (Viking)
* Holberg	*Restless Johnny: The Story of Johnny Appleseed* (Crowell)
* · Kjelgaard	*Big Red* (Holiday House)
* · _____	*Irish Red* (Holiday House)
** · Leighton	*The Story of Florence Nightingale* (Grosset & Dunlap)

* ·	Lovelace	*Heaven to Betsey* (Crowell)
** ·	Malkus	*The Story of Winston Churchill* (Grosset & Dunlap)
** ·	Price	*The Story of Marco Polo* (Grosset & Dunlap)
*	Smith	*The Hundred and One Dalmations* (Viking)
* ·	Wilson	*Herbert* (Knopf)

SIMPLIFIED CLASSICS

*	Coolidge	*Hercules and other Tales from Greek Myths* (Houghton Mifflin)
** ·	Dickens	*David Copperfield* (Scott, Foresman)
** ·	Eliot	*Silas Marner* (Scott, Foresman)
** ·	Hugo	*Les Misérables* (Laidlaw)
** ·	Kipling	*Captains Courageous* (Scott, Foresman)
** ·	Melville	*Moby Dick* (Scott, Foresman)
**	Shakespeare	*Julius Caesar* (Globe)
* ·	Swift	*The Story of Lemuel Gulliver in Lilliput Land,* adapted (Sanborn)
	Twain	*Huckleberry Finn* (Scott, Foresman)
* ·	_____	*The Prince and the Pauper* (Globe)
** ·	_____	*Tom Sawyer* (Scott, Foresman)
**	Wyss	*Swiss Family Robinson* (Globe)

SEVENTH GRADE

SHORT STORIES AND SELECTIONS

SUPPLEMENTARY READING

	Author	*Title*
**	Burnett	*The Secret Garden* (Lippincott)
** ·	Cavanna	*Angel on Skis* (Morrow)
**	Doss	*The Family Nobody Wanted* (Little)
** ·	Du Jardin	*Double Date* (Lippincott)
**	DuMaurier	*Rebecca* (Doubleday)
** ·	Emery	*First Love, True Love* (Westminster)
** ·	Farley	*The Black Stallion* (Random House)
**	Garst	*Crazy about Horses* (Hastings)
	Gipson	*Old Yeller* (Harper & Row)
	Godden	*The Green Gage Summer* (Viking)
**	Hilton	*Goodbye, Mr. Chips* (Grosset & Dunlap)
** ·	Meader	*Sparkplug of the Hornets* (Harcourt, Brace)
**	Whitney	*Mystery on the Isle of Skye* (Westminster)
**	Wiggin	*Rebecca of Sunnybrook Farm* (Houghton Mifflin)

Appendix B

SIMPLIFIED CLASSICS

**	Blackmore	*Lorna Doone* (Globe)
** ·	Bronte	*Jane Eyre* (Globe)
**	Defoe	*Robinson Crusoe* (Sanborn)
** ·	Dickens	*Oliver Twist* (Laidlaw)
** ·	Homer	*The Odyssey* (Globe)
** ·	Scott	*Ivanhoe* (Globe)
** ·	Sewell	*Black Beauty* (Globe)
** ·	Stevenson	*Treasure Island* (Globe)

EIGHTH GRADE

SUPPLEMENTARY READING

	Author	Title
** ·	Daly	*Seventeenth Summer* (Dodd)
** ·	Forbes	*Johnny Tremain* (Houghton Mifflin)
**	Forester	*The African Queen* (Modern Library)
**	Frank	*Diary of Anne Frank* (Doubleday)
	Godden	*Episode of Sparrows* (Viking)
** ·	Harkins	*Son of the Coach* (Holiday House)
**	Hersey	*Hiroshima* (Knopf)
**	Heyerdahl	*Kon Tiki* (Rand McNally)
**	Hilton	*Lost Horizon* (Grosset & Dunlap)
**	Hunt	*Conquest of Enerest* (Grosset & Dunlap)
**	Knight	*Lassie Come Home* (Winston)
**	Lederer and Burdick	*The Ugly American* (Norton)
** ·	London	*White Fang* (Grosset & Dunlap)
**	Lord	*A Night to Remember* (Holt)
**	MacLean	*Guns of Navarone* (Doubleday)
** ·	Meader	*T Model Tommy* (Harcourt, Brace)
**	Michener	*The Bridge at Toko-Ri* (Random House)
**	Montgomery	*Anne of Green Gables* (Grosset & Dunlap)
**	Moore	*The Baby Sitter's Guide* (Crowell)
**	Remarque	*All Quiet on the Western Front* (Little)
**	Salinger	*Catcher in the Rye* (Grosset & Dunlap)
**	Smith	*A Tree Grows in Brooklyn* (Harper & Row)
**	Steinbeck	*Of Mice and Men* (Bantam)
**	———	*The Pearl* (Viking)
**	———	*The Short Reign of Pippin IV* (Viking)
**	Verne	*Twenty Thousand Leagues under the Sea* (Scribner's)
**	Wells	*War of the Worlds* (Harper & Row)

SIMPLIFIED CLASSICS

**	Austen	*Pride and Prejudice* (Globe)
**	Dickens	*A Tale of Two Cities* (Laidlaw)
**	Dumas	*The Count of Monte Cristo* (Globe)
**	Eliot	*Silas Marner* (Globe)
**	————	*The Mill on the Floss* (Globe)
**	Hawthorne	*The Scarlet Letter* (Globe)
**	Twain	*Connecticut Yankee* (Globe)

APPENDIX C

Workbooks, Games, and Devices

Devices for Teaching Sight Vocabulary

Title	Level
Basic Sight Vocabulary Cards (Garrard)	2–3
Flash-X (EDL Laboratories, Huntington)	1–6
Go Fish (Remedial Education Press)	1
Grab: junior, senior, advanced (Dorothea Alcock)	1–5, according to set
Group Word Teaching Game (Garrard)	1–3
My Crossword Puzzle Book, 13 vols., 1–2 (Primary Educ. Svc.)	2 plus
Picture Word Cards (Garrard)	1
Pocket-Tac (Reading Inst. of Boston)	1–3
Rolling Phonics (Scott, Foresman)	1–3
The Rolling Reader (Scott, Foresman)	1–3
Sight Phrase Cards (Garrard)	2 plus
Take (Garrard)	3 plus

Workbooks for Practice in Word Analysis

Author	Title	Level
Hargrave and Armstrong	*Building Reading Skills* (McCormick-Mathers)	1–6
Kottmeyer	*Conquests in Reading* (Webster, McGraw-Hill)	2–4

Stone et al.	*Eye and Ear Fun Books*, I–IV (Webster, McGraw-Hill)	1–4
Feldmann and Merrill	*Learning about Words* (Teachers College)	3
(Committee of Authors)	*Operation Alphabet* (Noble & Noble)	Primer–4
Boning	*Phonic Analogies* (Dexter & Westbrook)	1
Krane	*Phonics Is Fun*, 1, 2, 3 (Modern Curriculum Press)	1–3
Makar	*Primary Phonics* (Educator's Publishing Service)	1
Smith	*Symbol Tracking* (Ann Arbor Pub.)	Preprimary
Weinberg	*Word Analysis* (Macmillan)	4–8
Durrell	*Word Analysis Practice* (Harcourt, Brace)	4–6
Smith	*Word Tracking* (Ann Arbor Pub.)	1–3

Workbooks and Materials for Comprehension, Vocabulary, and Spelling

Author	*Title*	*Level*
Bereiter et al.	*Catching On* (Open Court)	2–6
Foster	*Developing Reading Skills*, A–D (Laidlaw)	4–7
Scope	*Dimensions, Across and Down, Wide World* (Scholastic)	5
Robinson et al.	*EDL Study Skills Library*	4–9
Wyatt et al.	*Kaleidoscope Readers* (Field Educ. Publishers)	4–8
Stone et al.	*New Practice Readers*, Bks. A–G (Webster, McGraw-Hill)	2–7
Anderson and Kinchelue	*Reader's Digest Advanced Reading Skill Builders* (Reader's Digest)	7,8
Wagner et al.	*Reader's Digest Reading Skill Builders*, Bks. II–VI; two at each level (Reader's Digest)	High 2– high 6
Liddle	*Reading for Concepts*, Books A–H (Webster, McGraw-Hill)	3–9

Strong	*Sentence Combining* (Random House)	
Boning	*Specific Skills Series* (Barnell Loft)	2–9
Parker	SRA *Reading Laboratories* (Sci. Rsch. Ass.). Boxes of reading booklets at various levels	3–11
Scope	Scope Activity Kit (Scholastic) *Sports* *Frauds and Hoaxes* *Television*	4
Scope	Scope Skills-Building Programs (Scholastic) *Chillers and Thrillers* *Sprint* *Trackdown* *Jobs in Your Future*	4–5
Scope	Scope Visuals (Scholastic) Vocabulary Building Getting Applications Right	4
Pauk	*Six-Way Paragraphs* (Jamestown Publications)	6–11
McCall and Crabbs	*Standard Test Lessons in Reading,* Bks. A–E (Teachers College)	3–12

High School and College Levels

Author	Title	Level
Blake, K.	*College Reading Skills* (Prentice-Hall)	College
Williston, G.	*Comprehension Skills Series* (Jamestown Publishers)	J.H.S.– College
Schumacher et al.	*Design for Good Reading* (A,B,C,D) (Harcourt, Brace)	9–12
Schmidt, B. et al.	*Developing Reading Proficiency* (Merrill)	H.S.– College
Brown, J.	*Efficient Reading,* Revised Editions, Forms A & B (Heath)	H.S.– College
Miller, L.	*Increasing Reading Efficiency* (Holt)	H.S.– College
Milan, D.	*Modern College Reading* (Scribner's)	H.S.– College
Miller, L.	*Personalizing Reading Efficiency* (Burgess)	H.S.– College

SRA	*Rate and Power Builders* SRA III A	H.S.–College
Fry, E.	*Reading Drills* (Jamestown Publishers)	7–10
Brown, J.	*Reading Power* (Heath)	H.S.
Spargo, E.	*Selections from the Black* (Jamestown Publishers) 3 Levels	7–College
Spargo, E., and Williston, G.	*Timed Readings* (Jamestown Publishers) 8 Levels	7–College
Spargo, E.	*Topics for the Restless* (Jamestown Publishers) 3 Levels	7–College
Spargo, E.	*Voices from The Bottom* (Jamestown Publishers) 3 Levels	7–College

Plays

Author	Title	Level
Burbank, A. S., and Crossley, B.	*Popular Plays for Classroom Reading* (Plays Inc.)	5–6
Various Authors	*Story Plays* (Harcourt, Brace)	3–4
Scholastic	*Twelve Angry Men and Other Plays* (Scholastic Magazine)	3–4

Activity Books

Author	Title	Level
Arnold, W. C.	*Fun with Next to Nothing* (Scholastic)	2
Wyler, R., Ames, G., and Chernoff, G. T.	*Magic Secrets* (Scholastic)	3
	Just a Box (Scholastic)	2
Schneider	*Let's Find Out about Heat, Weather and Air* (Sholastic)	3

Dictionaries

Pyramid Primary Dictionary Series
(Pyramid Publications)
Macmillan Dictionary for Children
(Macmillan)
Thorndike-Barnhart Dictionaries
(beginning, intermediate, junior,
advanced levels) Scott-Foresman
Webster's New World Dictionary
(Prentice-Hall)
*Clear and Simple Thesaurus
Dictionary* (Grosset & Dunlap)

Spelling

Author	*Title*
Mersand and Griffith	*Spelling Your Way to Success* (Barrons Educational Series)
Gallagher, R., and Colvin, J.	*Words Most Often Misspelled and Mispronounced* (Pocket Books)
Johnson, Eric	*Improve Your Own Spelling* (McGraw-Hill)

Teacher References

Author	*Title*
Morgan, F.	*An Approach to Writing Through Perception* (Harcourt, Brace)
Barkan, J. et al.	*Teachers Manual for Searching for Values, A Film Anthology* (Learning Corp. of America)
Barks, W.	*Reading Skills Checklist and Activities* (Center for Applied Research)
Silver, A., and Hagin, R.	*Search and Teach* (Walker Educational Books)
Leavitt, H. D., and Sohn, D. A.	*Stop, Look, and Write* (Bantam)
Dodd, A. W.	*Write Now, Insights into Creative Writing* (Globe)

Petty, W., and   *Slithery Snakes and other Aids to*
  Bowen, M.   *Children's Writing* (Appleton,
                        Century, Crofts)

Mueser, A.,   *Reading Aids through Grades,*
  Russell, D., Karp, E.   Revised Ed. (Teachers College
                        Press)

Suggestions for Teacher-Devised Games

Dot Game[1]

The teacher can mimeograph a "dot picture" as in common "dot booklets," using consonants or blends for each dot. The sounds are pronounced, and the children draw a line for all the dots of the corresponding sound.

The Guessing Game[2]

After 35 words or so are learned, a guessing game that is a favorite with most children can be played. For example, the teacher wants to practice learning the sight words *found, shall, the, you,* and *put.* The children already know Pat and Polly, who are characters in their reader, and they easily recognize the words *sees, dog, jump, book,* and *down.* The teacher writes the following sentences on the blackboard:

> Polly *found* it.
> Polly sees *the* dog.
> Can *you* jump?
> *Put* Pat's book down.
> I *shall* go.

The words to be practiced are underlined. First the children read together all five sentences. The teacher then says, "I am thinking of one of the underlined words. Who can guess the word I am thinking?" The children take turns coming to the blackboard, pointing to the word they have chosen, and saying, "Is it the word 'the'?" If it is, he becomes the leader and is allowed to think of a word while the others guess. The children take turns for as long as desirable. (It is important that the child who guesses points to the chosen word, so that the teacher is certain that he had not thought one word and mistaken it for another of the underlined words.)

---

1. Devised by Stanley Hoffman.
2. Nila B. Smith, *Learning to Recognize Words.* Out of print.

Appendix C

Learning Letters and Letter Sounds by Using Children's Initials[3]

When children are not too familiar with letters or letter sounds, the teacher can take small cards (about 3 x 5) and print a letter of the alphabet on each one in capital and lower-case form. The teacher then asks the child whose initials she holds up to stand. Also, whenever there is a reason to line up, the teacher can have the children take their places as she holds up their initials. Later when the letters are better known, the teacher can ask the child who sits in front of or next to the child whose initials are held to stand. Still later, just the sounds of the pupil's initials might be used.

Tick-tack-toe

A tick-tack-toe frame is drawn on the blackboard or a piece of paper, and a list of words to be practiced is placed in full sight. Two individuals or two teams can play. The players choose who is to go first and who shall have the X's and O's. The pupil then says one of the words. If he is correct, he may place his mark next to the word and in any box he chooses in the tick-tack-toe frame. (A mark is placed next to a word only to designate that it has already been chosen.) Another pupil then chooses a word and puts his mark in front of it and in the box he chooses. The game continues until one player gets three like marks in a row.

3. Adapted by Helen O'Keefe of the Bellows School, Mamaroneck, N.Y., from D. Durrell, *Improving Reading Instruction* (Tarrytown-on-Hudson, N.Y.: World Book Co., 1956).

APPENDIX D

Selected Paperback Books[1]

Preprimer

Author	*Title*
Einsel	*Did You Ever See?* (Scholastic)
	"Did you ever see a cat . . . bat?," plus 13 other absurd animal situations. An amusing book that lets children guess at ryhmes. 35-word vocabulary.
Krauss	*The Happy Egg* (Scholastic)
	Delightful picture story about how a happy egg hatches out as a happy baby bird. 33-word vocabulary.

The following four books are intended as an introduction not only to books but to basic concepts which relate to the young child's limited but expanding experience. (Wonder)

De Caprio	*One, Two* 30-word vocabulary
Seymour	*Big Beds and Little Beds* 33-word vocabulary
	The Tent 15-word vocabulary
Stephens	*Jumping* 34-word vocabulary

Following are the titles of six 24-page books illustrated with photographs of real children. The vocabulary and sentence structure are derived from the oral language of six-year-olds. (Chandler)

1. We wish to acknowledge the diligence and competency with which Elaine Kaplan and Yvette Parker compiled this list of paperbacks. Each book was carefully read and assessed before it was considered elegible for inclusion. We are also grateful to Cathy Lipkin and Peggy Schwarz for their additional contributions to this list.

Carillo, ed.   *Swings, Slides, Trucks and Cars to Ride, Bikes, Supermarket,* and *Let's Go!*

Primer

Author   *Title*

Each of the following three books has a brief text set in large, easy-to-read type, enabling the young reader to grasp easily the concept being presented. (Wonder)

DeCaprio   *Bus from Chicago*   49-word vocabulary
Jardine   *Up and Down*   50-word vocabulary
Seymour   *On the Ranch*   30-word vocabulary
Smith et al.   *Who Can* (New MacMillan Reading Program)

First Grade

Author   *Title*

Bethell   *Barney Beagle Plays Baseball* (Wonder)
               Amusing story of a dog who wants to be a true friend to his young master.
Cook   *The Little Fish That Got Away* (Scholastic)
               The traditional fish story with a surprise twist. Minimum, easy-to-read text.
Kessler   *Mr. Pine's Mixed-Up Signs* (Wonder)
               Amusing tale of what happens when Mr. Pine, the sign painter, loses his glasses.
Potter and   *First Fairy Tales* (Merrill)
   Harley   Contains 18 stories and 117 two-color illustrations. (Also for second grade.)
Smith et al.   *Lost and Found* (New MacMillan Reading Program)

Second Grade

Author   *Title*

Bulla   *Eagle Feather* (Scholastic)
               Exciting adventure story of a modern Navajo Indian boy. Authentic picture of Indian life.

———————   *Old Charlie* (Scholastic)
Realistic tale, told with humor and suspense, of how two young brothers think of an ingenious solution to save a beloved old horse.

Burton   *Katy and the Big Snow*
Katy is a big red snowplow.

Clarke   *Congo Boy* (Scholastic)
Action-filled African folk tale: a boy earns his own hunting spear through an act of generosity.

Compere   *Story of Thomas Alva Edison, Inventor* (Scholastic)
The life of the great inventor, combining biography, history, adventure, and science for very young readers.

Freeman   *A Book of Real Science* (Scholastic)
Basic concepts of physical science (heat, light, electricity, sound, gravity) invitingly presented in terms within a young child's experience and understanding.

Halpern   *Stranger than Fiction* (Globe)

Littledale   *The Magic Fish* (Scholastic)
Lively retelling of the folk tale about a poor fisherman, his greedy wife, and a magic fish who grants wishes.

Moore   *Lucky Book of Riddles* (Scholastic)
Gay illustrations add to the delight of these easy-to-read riddles.

Potter   *Giants and Fairies* (Merrill)
Contains 20 stories and 63 two-color illustrations.

Stanek   *How We Use Maps and Globes* (Benefic)
Basic social studies skills are introduced and developed. Colorful and interesting illustrations amplify the subject matter.

Udry   *Let's Be Enemies*
Two best friends decide to be enemies.

Wyler and Ames   *Magic Secrets* (Scholastic)
23 magic tricks—some very easy, some harder. Pictures all the way.

No listed Author   *Jack and the Beanstalk* (Scholastic)

Retold for younger children with all the original gusto and flavor.

Third Grade

Author	*Title*

Bemelmans   *Madeline* (Scholastic)
The delightful modern classic about the smallest of "twelve

little girls in two straight lines" in Miss Clavel's boarding school.

Bishop — *The Five Chinese Brothers* (Scholastic)
Clever folk tale of look-alike brothers who outwit an executioner. Ideal bridge from "read-to-me" to "read-it-myself."

Branley and Vaughan — *Mickey's Magnet*
A boy learns about magnets and how to make one. A magnet is included.

Bridwell — *Clifford* series
About a girl and her oversized dog.

Bulla — *Ghost Town Treasure* (Scholastic)
Three children on an exciting search for gold in a canyon near a "ghost town" uncover a cave full of natural marvels. Large type, easy to read.

Colver — *Abraham Lincoln* (Scholastic)
Warmly told, straightforward biography of Lincoln as a boy, as a man, and as a president.

Davidson — *The Adventures of George Washington* (Scholastic)
Exciting biography covering Washington's adventurous life —from the French and Indian War all the way to the presidency.

Elting and Folsom — *If You Lived in the Days of the Wild Mammoth Hunters* (Scholastic)
Easy-to-read archaeology about life in prehistoric days.

Hoban — *Bread and Jam for Frances* (Scholastic)
What happens when a little badger named Frances is allowed a steady diet of her favorite bread and jam. There is a series of Frances books.

Holl — *Magic Tales* (Merrill)
Contains 19 stories and 48 two-color illustrations.

Krasilovsky — *The Man Who Didn't Wash His Dishes*
The tale of a man who liked to eat but not to do the dishes.

Larom — *Bronco Charlie: Rider of the Pony Express* (Scholastic)
Eleven-year-old Charlie Miller braves many obstacles to bring the mail through in true Pony Express tradition.

Lobel — *Frog and Toad Together*
Frog and Toad Are Friends
Funny simple stories.

McGovern — *If You Lived in Colonial Times*
Very well organized and clear.
If You Sailed on the Mayflower
The Pilgrims First Thanksgiving

Moore — *Johnny Appleseed* (Scholastic)
Skillful blend of fact and legend distinguishes this moving biography of America's beloved historical figure.

Parish	*Amelia Bedelia*
	Play Ball, Amelia Bedelia
	What happens when Amelia tries to play baseball. Very funny.
Peterson	*The Littles* (Scholastic)
	The Littles are tiny people who live in the walls of the Bigg's house. Of course their greatest fear is mice.
Rey	*Curious George Rides a Bike* (Scholastic)
	More monkey business as Curious George sets off on a new bike and runs head on into a traveling circus.
Rey	*Pretzel*
	The enchanting story of the problems of being the longest dog in the world.
Slobodkina	*Caps for Sale* (Scholastic)
	Based on charming folk tale. Peddler of caps runs into trouble when monkeys steal his wares.
Ward	*The Biggest Bear* (Scholastic)
	Johnny and his pet bear get into a beehive of mischief.
Williams and Abrashkein	*Danny Dunn and the Anti-Gravity Paint*
	A science fiction story that is factual and funny.

The following twelve books are historically accurate biographies which have particular appeal for children of all ages. (Dell)

Colver	*Abraham Lincoln*
———	*Florence Nightingale*
Epstein	*George Washington Carver*
Graff	*George Washington*
———	*Helen Keller*
Graves	*Benjamin Franklin*
———	*Eleanor Roosevelt*
———	*John F. Kennedy*
Kaufman	*Thomas Alva Edison*
Latham	*Sam Houston*
Parlin	*Amelia Earhart*
Patterson	*Frederick Douglass*

Fourth Grade

Author	*Title*
Becker	*A Chimp in the Family* (Scholastic)
	A comical chimp wreaks havoc in a pet-shop owner's household. Includes health tips for youngsters.

Buckley and Jones	*Our Growing City* (Holt)
Cleary	*Henry Huggins* (Scholastic)
	Eight-year-old Henry and his dog, Ribsy, get into hilarious predicaments.
Cavanah	*Abe Lincoln Gets His Chance*
	A story of young Lincoln based on his own, his family's, and his friends' recollections.
Humphreville	*Harriet Tubman: Flame of Freedom* (Houghton Mifflin)
	Emphasizes her childhood traits of character that led to adult achievement.
Katz et al.	*Real Stories* Book 1 (Globe)
Lauber	*Junior Science Book of Icebergs and Glaciers* (Scholastic)
Lofting	*Doctor Doolittle Tales* (Scholastic)
	Selections from *Doctor Doolittle, a Treasury*. The beloved animal doctor's search for the Pushmi-Pullyu in Africa, plus adventures on Spidermonkey Island.
————	*Story of Doctor Doolittle* (Dell)
	A little old doctor who has so many animal pets all over his house that his patients won't visit him—becomes the animals' own doctor, able to speak their languages and cure their sufferings.
Moody	*Riders of the Pony Express* (Dell)
	This authentic account vividly recreates the life of the young men and boys who carried the mail almost 2,000 miles in ten days and nights of merciless riding over mountains, across deserts, and through the heart of hostile Indian country.
O'Donnell, McElaney, and Taylor	*Secrets of the Animal World* (Scholastic)
	Facts—curious, amazing and funny—about dozens of diverse creatures. Sure to entice the book-shy youngster.
Peterson	*How to Write Codes and Send Secret Messages*
Ripley	*Matthew Henson: Arctic Hero* (Houghton Mifflin)
	Part of a series about men and women who have made world history, emphasizing childhood traits of character that led to adult achievement.
Schneider	*Let's Find Out about Heat, Weather and Air* (Scholastic)
	Basic scientific facts, plus easy experiments with heat, cold, air.
Wyler	*Arrow Book of Science Riddles* (Scholastic)
	Provocative riddles and their sound scientific explanations. A wealth of science information in a visually attractive format.
Zim	*Alligators and Crocodiles* (Scholastic)
	Fact-filled, picture-filled book recommended for high interest science reading and vocabulary building.

Fifth Grade

Author	Title
Ames and Wyler	*First Days of the World* (Scholastic) Clearly written, beautifully illustrated first book about the beginnings of our planet and the life on it.
Atwater	*Mr. Popper's Penguins* (Scholastic) Adventures of Mr. Popper and his Antarctic guests.
Corbett	*The Lemonade Trick* (Scholastic) Kerby's strange chemistry set produces magic, miracles, mayhem, and mirth.
Garfield	*Follow My Leader* (Scholastic) Engrossing story, written with sympathy and humor, of a young boy's adjustment to blindness with the help of his Seeing Eye Dog.
Gelman	*Young Baseball Champions* (Scholastic) Exciting, straightforward biographies of Willie Mays, Hank Aaron, Mickey Mantle, seven more major leaguers who reached stardom.
Glemser	*Radar Commandos* (Scholastic) True, action-filled story about a French teenage boy who, at great risk, brings vital information to the Allies in World War II.
Hickok	*Story of Helen Keller* (Scholastic) Story of her triumph over handicaps.
Irving	*Hurricanes and Twisters* (Scholastic)
Kramer, ed.	*Arrow Book of Ghost Stories* (Scholastic) Nine selected tales.
Lauber	*Science Book of Volcanoes* (Scholastic)
Lindgren	*Pippi Longstocking* Popular tale of a "wild" girl.
Mann	*My Dad Lives in a Downtown Hotel* (Scholastic) A young boy has to cope with the problem of his parents getting a divorce.
McGovern, ed.	*Aesop's Fables* (Scholastic) The timeless classic beautifully retold in modern language for middle grade readers.
Ravielli	*Wonders of the Human Body* (Scholastic) Facts about the human machine. Drawings.
Rinkoff	*Member of the Gang* (Scholastic) Story of a black boy's search for identity.
Rood	*Bees, Bugs, and Beetles* (Scholastic)
Selsam	*The Birth of an Island* (Scholastic)
Silverberg	*The Lost Race of Mars* (Scholastic)

In the year 2017 on Mars, a scientist's two children try to find the survivors of a lost civilization.

Spyri — *Heidi* (Scholastic)
The heart-warming classic about a Swiss mountain girl.

Sterling — *The Story of Caves* (Scholastic)

Thorne — *Story of Madame Curie* (Scholastic)
Life of the eminent scientist.

Verral — *Rocket Genius* (Scholastic)
Life of rocket pioneer Robert Goddard and his many contributions to the space age.

Weiss — *Mixups and Fixups* (Scholastic)
Twelve fun-filled animal yarns.

Sixth Grade

Author	*Title*

Alcock — *Run, Westy, Run* (Archway)
Realistic account of what happens when a boy runs away continually in spite of all adult authorities. There are no easy solutions—he has to work out his own problems.

Bakeless — *Spies of the Revolution* (Scholastic)
Thirteen exciting stories of espionage during the American Revolution.

Baldwin — *Go Tell It on the Mountain* (Noble & Noble)
The noted writer's first novel illuminates three generations of one family by recounting one day in their lives.

Burdick and Wheeler — *Fail-Safe* (Noble & Noble)
The terrifying account of a global "accident" that is all too possible.

Clarke — *The Challenge of the Sea* (Dell)
Mr. Clarke takes the reader to the world beneath the seas, recording what we know and what we hope to learn and offering imaginative accounts of what tomorrow may bring.

Clayton — *Martin Luther King: The Peaceful Warrior* (Archway)
A moving biography, which tells the story of his childhood in Atlanta, his career as one of the greatest Negro leaders of our time, and his tragic assassination.

Craig — *Robinson Crusoe* (Educators Publishing Service)
This high interest story captures the student's attention, and the use of phonetically regular words helps to improve his reading ability.

Doyle — *Great Stories of Sherlock Holmes* (Dell)
Twelve of Sherlock Holmes's most famous adventures.

Fleming *Chitty Chitty Bang Bang, The Magical Car* (Scholastic)
Humorous story of a magic car which is usually getting it's owner out of trouble.

Forbes *Johnny Tremain* (Dell)
Set in Boston of 1775 and follows the young apprentice from a tragic accident in the silversmith's shop to his dramatic involvement as a patriot in the exciting days just before the American Revolution.

Katz et al. *Real Stories*, Book 2 (Globe)

Kjelgaard *Big Red* (Scholastic)
Tales of an Irish Setter.

Meadowcraft *By Secret Railway* (Scholastic)
Two boys, one white, one Negro, and their adventures in 1860 with the South-to-North "Underground Railway."

Neville *It's Like This, Cat* (Scholastic)
Newberry Award winner about a big-city teenage boy's adventures and problems.

Offit *Soupbone* (Archway)
Fast-paced effervescent baseball story which will delight and amuse young fans.

Parks *A Choice of Weapons* (Noble & Noble)
An engrossing account of the early struggles of the award-winning *Life* staff photographer.

Potter and Robinson *Myths and Folk Tales around the World* (Globe)

Rankin *Daughter of the Mountains* (Archway)
Momo journeys from the high mountain passes of Tibet down to the plains of India in search of her little dog. Vivid characterizations and descriptions.

Serraillier *Selected Stories from the Enchanted Island* (Scholastic)
Seven stories based on Shakespeare's plays, retold in Serraillier's crisp, modern style.

Smiley et al. *Gateway English Series* (Macmillan)
Anthologies created with educationally disadvantaged students and reluctant readers in mind. Settings, characters, and situations are meaningful to today's young people.

Smith *A Tree Grows in Brooklyn* (Noble & Noble)
The classic American novel of a young girl's coming of age.

Speevack *The Spider Plant* (Archway)
A story strong in human values—the detailed and convincing picture of an admirable Puerto Rican family new to New York City and life in a large housing project.

Sperry *Call It Courage* (Scholastic)
Legend of a young Polynesian boy who is determined to conquer his cowardice—or die!

Spiegler et al.   *Mainstream Books* (Merrill)

These five anthologies, packed with dynamic and vital literature, will encourage all students to find both enjoyment and enlightenment in their reading. The level of the selections is low enough for the reluctant readers, while the interest level is high enough for the good readers. A partial list of authors includes: Stephen Crane, Langston Hughes, Carl Sandburg, Lorraine Hansberry, Ogden Nash, and Isaac Asimov.

Sterling   *Mary Jane* (Scholastic)

The first Negro girl to attend an integrated junior high, Mary Jane finds she is not really alone.

Sullivan   *Pioneer Astronomers* (Scholastic)

The dramatic moments of discovery of 18 outstanding astronomers—from Copernicus to modern times.

———   *Pioneer Germ Fighters* (Scholastic)

Outstanding work of 12 scientists who conquered some of mankind's most deadly diseases.

Times 4 (Noble & Noble)

Four spell-binding science fiction tales: *The Time Machine* by H. G. Wells; *A Thief in Time* by Robert Sheckley; Mack Reynolds' *Business, As Usual*; Jack Finney's *The Face in the Photo.*

Verne   *Around the World in Eighty Days* (Dell)

The adventures of Phineas Fogg and his valet Passepartout on their fantastic trip around the world.

Wood   *The Life and Words of John F. Kennedy* (Scholastic)

Well-written biography; memorable photographs, quotations.

Favorite Stories From Basil Readers and Anthologies

We have examined a variety of readers in order to simplify the teachers' task in locating suitable stories for children functioning at readability levels one through six. At the early levels, we have emphasized myths, folklore, and other old-time favorites because children of all ages enjoy them; furthermore, many of the other stories with controlled vocabulary which are found in the basal readers are not generally appealing to the older child. Since identical stories are often included in many different readers, only a small sampling has been chosen from each one. At the upper levels, humorous stories, biographical sketches, classics, and adventure tales were selected because these have proven to be the preference of many children.

FIRST GRADE

Reader	Story
Basic Reading Series (Lippincott)	The Deer and the Hunter
	The Goose That Laid the Golden Egg
	The Ox and the Frog (1^2)
	The Shepherd Boy (1^1)
I Know a Story (Harper & Row)	The Boy Who Went to the North Wind
	The Gingerbread Boy
	Mr. Vinegar
More Fun with Our Friends (Scott, Foresman)	Why Tom-Tom Ran
Sky Blue (Heath)	Mr. Wind and Mr. Sun
Sunny and Gay (Bobbs-Merrill)	The Funny Birthday Wish
	The Little Fish

SECOND GRADE

Reader	Story
Basic Reading Series (2^1) (Lippincott)	The Emperor's New Clothes
	The Golden Touch
	Kit Carson
	The Magic Pot
Basic Reading Series (2^2) (Lippincott)	Florence Nightingale
	Jenny Lind
Come Along (Houghton Mifflin)	Curious George
	The Five Brothers
	Katy and the Big Snow
	Katy No Pocket
Enchanted Gates (Macmillan)	The Tiger and the Cherry Tree
	The Ugly Duckling
	Why the Sea Is Salt
Foolish and Wise (Bobbs-Merrill)	Foolish Jack
Friends Old and New (Scott, Foresman)	Small Mouse Reads
It Happened One Day (Harper & Row)	The Donkey and His Band
	Jack and the Beanstalk
	Lazy Jack
	The Monkey and the Bananas
	The Old Woman and the Fox
	The Twelve Sillies

287

More Friends Old and New (Scott, Foresman)	*A Clever Fox*
	The Man Who Kept House
	A New Kettle
	The Quarrel
On We Go (Houghton Mifflin)	*Noodle*
	Snipp and His Brothers
	The Story of a Clown
Shining Bridges (Macmillan)	*The Brave Potter*
	A Dollar for a Donkey
	Nothing-At-All
Storyland Favorites (Laidlaw)	*The Bear, the Man and the Fox*
	The Fox and the Crow
	Gudbrand on the Hill
	The Lion and the Mouse
	Snow White and Rose Red
	The Wind and the Sun
We Are Neighbors (Ginn)	*Mike Mulligan and the Steam Shovel*
	The Old Woman and the Fox
	Stone Soup

THIRD GRADE

Reader	*Story*
After the Sun Sets (Harper & Row)	*Brier Rose*
	Cinderella
	East of the Sun and West of the Moon
	The Princess on the Glass Hill
	Snip the Tailor
Basic Reading Series (Lippincott)	*Abe Lincoln and the Borrowed Book*
	Camels Come to America
	Pinocchio
	The Story of Heidi
Better than Gold (Macmillan)	*How Boots Fooled the King*
	How the Wise Man Caught the Thief
	Gone Is Gone
	Gray Legs
	A Penguin in the House
	Weighing an Elephant
Climbing Higher (Houghton Mifflin)	*The Apple of Contentment*
	The Fast Sooner Hound
	The Stupid Thief
Doorways to Adventure (Laidlaw)	*Chi-Wee Runs a Race*
	Joseph and His Brothers
	Robert Fulton
	A Story from Bambi
	Waukewa's Eagle

Finding New Neighbors (Ginn)	*The Horse Who Lived Upstairs* *The King's Contest* *The Princess Who Always Believed What She Heard* *The Traveling Musicians*
Friends Far and Near (Ginn)	*My Dog Rinty* *The Three Feathers* *The Top of the World* *Toto of the South Seas*
Fun All Around (Bobbs-Merrill)	*The Camel and the Jackal* *The Missing Donkey* *Santa's Mistake*
Looking Ahead (Houghton Mifflin)	*The Little Horse That Raced a Train* *The Magic Shoes* *The Stonecutter*
Meadow Green (Heath)	*Blaze and the Forest Fire* *Hansel and Gretel* *Rapunzel*
More Roads to Follow (Scott, Foresman)	*Foji and the Fog* *It's a Wolf* *Pippi Is a Thing Finder* *The Plate of Pancakes* *Sequoyalis Talking Leaves*
Roads to Follow (Scott, Foresman)	*Betsy and Ellen Go to Market* *Eddie and the Goat*

FOURTH GRADE

Reader	*Story*
Basic Reading Series (Lippincott)	*Alexander Fleming* *Clara Barton* *Louis Pasteur* *Rikki Tikki Tavi* *Voyages of Dr. Doolittle*
The Magic Word (Macmillan)	*The Great Houdini* *The Oak and the Reed* *The Rooster and the Pearl* *The Seven Sticks* *That Spot*
Open Highways (Scott, Foresman)	*The Radish Cure* *Tower to the Moon*
Paths to Follow (American Book Co.)	*The Golden Touch* *King of Baseball* *The Miracle Miler* (Glenn Cunningham)
Peacock Lane (Heath)	*Chanticleer and the Fox* *Ferdinand Magellan* *The Flight of Icarus*

	The Magic Carpet
	Onion Boy's Adventure
Roads to Everywhere	Kintu
(Ginn)	The Brahman and the Tiger
	The Brave Little Tailor
	The Five Chinese Brothers
	The Steadfast Tin Soldier
	The Stonecutter
	When Totaram Washed the Elephant
Shining Hours	An Army of Two
(Bobbs-Merrill)	The Left Over Hat
	The Mighty Candle
	The Monkeys Scream at Crocodiles
Ventures	Charlotte
(Scott, Foresman)	The Day We Made the Electric Thinker
	Gallons of Guppies
	Many Moons
Winding Hills	Columbus
(Random House)	The Horse from Nowhere
	John Billington, Friend of Squanto
	Story of Wild Horse Canyon
	The Wonderful Weaver

FIFTH GRADE

Reader	*Story*
Basic Reading Series	The Blind Toy-Maker
(Lippincott)	A Dog Named Spike
	George Washington Carver
	Pygmalion and Galatea
	Watson Meets Holmes
Beyond the Horizon	A Captive in Lilliput
(Bobbs-Merrill)	The Fourth Day
	Trojan Horse
	The Wolf Pit
Bold Journey	Herbert's Oral Composition
(Macmillan)	I Get a Colt to Break In
Frontiers to Explore	Daniel Boone's Daughter
(American Book Co.)	The Happy Prince
	The Old Woman and the Traveler
Kings and Things	The Black Stallion and the Red Mare
(American Book Co.)	The Fountain of Youth
	Pandora and the Secret Box
	24 Hours on an Ice Pan
Open Highways	The Case of the Scattered Cards
(Scott, Foresman)	The Magic Sandals

Silver Web (Heath)	*Charlotte's Web*
	First under the North Pole
	Riding the Pony Express
	The Story or Dr. Doolittle
Sky Lines	*The Bell of Atri*
(Houghton Mifflin)	*The Discovery of the North Pole*
	Story Treasures
Trails to Treasure	*Amelia Earhart*
(Ginn)	*Balto's Race against Death*
	A Famous Ride
	The Heaps of Yellow Jacks
	Henry Can Fix It (Henry Ford)
	Mozart the Wonder Boy
	Paul's Great Flapjack Griddle
Vistas (Scott, Foresman)	*A Dog and a Glacier*
	Royal Banquet
	Time Cat
Wider than the Sky	*Aladdin and the Wonderful Lamp*
(Harcourt, Brace)	*The Emperor's New Clothes*
	Miguel
	The Princess and the Pea
	Robin Hood
	The Six Horsemen

SIXTH GRADE

Reader	*Story*
Basic Reading Series	*After Twenty Years*
(Lippincott)	*Galileo*
	The Great Mountains
	John F. Kennedy

APPENDIX E

Word Lists

The Basic Sight Vocabulary of 220 Words[1]

a	big	down	goes
about	black	draw	going
after	blue	drink	good
again	both	eat	got
all	bring	eight	green
always	brown	every	grow
am	but		
an	buy	fall	had
and	by	far	has
any		fast	have
are	call	find	he
around	came	first	help
as	can	five	her
ask	carry	fly	here
at	clean	for	him
ate	cold	found	his
away	come	four	hold
	could	from	hot
be	cut	full	how
because	did	funny	hurt
been	do	gave	I
before	does	get	if
best	done	give	in
better	don't	go	into

1. E. W. Dolch, *Teaching Primary Reading* (Champaign, Ill.: Garrard Press, 1960), p. 255. Reprinted by permission. Copyright 1960 by E. W. Dolch.

is
it
its

jump
just

keep
kind
know

laugh
let
light
like
little
live
long
look

made
make
many
may
me
much
must
my
myself

never
new
no
not
now

of

off
old
on
once
one
only
open
or
our
out
over
own

pick
play
please
pretty
pull
put

ran
read
red
ride
right
round
run

said
saw
say
see
seven
shall
she

show
sing
sit
six
sleep
small
so
some
soon
start
stop

take
tell
ten
thank
that
the
their
them
then
there
these
they
think
this
those
three
to
today
together
too
try
two

under
up
upon
us
use

very

walk
want
warm
was
wash
we
well
went
were
what
when
where
which
white
who
why
will
wish
with
work
would
write

yellow
yes
you
your

The 95 Most Common Nouns[2]

apple

baby
back
ball
bear
bed
bell
bird
birthday
boat
box
boy
bread
brother

cake
car
cat
chair
chicken
children
Christmas
coat
corn
cow

day
dog
doll
door
duck

egg
eye

farm
farmer
father
feet
fire
fish
floor
flower

game
garden
girl
good-bye
grass
ground

hand
head
hill

home
horse
house

kitty

leg
letter

man
men
milk
money
morning
mother

name
nest
night

paper
party
picture
pig

rabbit
rain
ring
robin

Santa Claus
school
seed
sheep
shoe
sister
snow
song
squirrel
stick
street
sun

table
thing
time
top
toy
tree

watch
water
way
wind
window
wood

2. Ibid., p. 296.

APPENDIX F

Publishers' Names and Addresses

Abingdon Press
201 8th Ave. S.
Nashville, Tenn. 37202

Addison-Welsey Publishing Co., Inc.
Reading, Mass. 01867

Dorothea Alcock
107 N. Elspeth Way
Covina, Calif. 91722

Allyn & Bacon
470 Atlantic Ave.
Boston, Mass. 02110

American Book Co.
450 W. 33 St.
New York, N.Y. 10001

American Federation of Teachers
716 North Rush St.
Chicago, Ill.

American Guidance Service, Inc.
Publishers' Building
Circle Pines, Minn. 55014

Ann Arbor Science Publishers
Drawer 1425
Ann Arbor, Mich. 48106

Appleton-Century-Crofts, Inc.
292 Madison Ave.
New York, N.Y. 10017

Archway Press, Inc.
48 W. 48 St.
New York, N.Y. 10036

Armed Forces Institute
Madison, Wisconsin 53703

Augsburg Publishing House
426 S. Fifth St.
Minneapolis, Minn. 55415

Avelon Hill Game Co.
4517 Harford Rd.
Baltimore, Md. 21214

Bantam Books, Inc.
666 Fifth Ave.
New York, N.Y. 10019

Barnell Loft
Baldwin, N.Y.

Barron's Educational Services
113 Crossways Park Dr.
Woodbury, N.Y. 11797

Basic Books, Inc.
10 E. 53 St.
New York, N.Y. 10022

Behavioral Publications, Inc.
72 Fifth Ave.
New York, N.Y. 10011

Behavioral Research
Palo Alto, Calif. 94302

Benefic Press
10300 W. Roosevelt Rd.
Westchester, Ill. 60153

Benziger
8701 Wilshire Blvd.
Beverly Hills, Calif. 90211

Berkley Publishing Corp.
200 Madison Ave.
New York, N.Y. 10016

William C. Brown Co.
2460 Kerper Blvd.
Dubuque, Iowa 52001

Brunner/Mazel, Inc.
19 Union Square West
New York, N.Y. 10003

The Bobbs-Merrill Co., Inc.
4300 W. 62 St.
Indianapolis, Ind. 46206

Burgess Publishing Co.
7108 Ohms Lane
Minneapolis, Minn. 55435

California Test Bureau
Del Monte Research Park
Monterey, Calif. 93940

Cambridge Book Co.
488 Madison Ave.
New York, N.Y. 10022

Cambridge University Press
32 E. 57 St.
New York, N.Y. 10022

Chandler Publishing Co.
124 Spear St.
San Francisco, Calif. 94105

College Skills Center
101 W. 31 St.
New York, N.Y. 10001

Columbia University Press
562 W. 113 St.
New York, N.Y. 10025

Consulting Psychologists Press
577 College Ave.
Palo Alto, Calif.

Continental Publishing Co.
10866 Bluffside Dr.
North Hollywood, Calif. 91604

Council for Basic Education
725 15th St., N.W.
Washington, D.C. 20005

Coward, McCann & Geoghegan, Inc.
200 Madison Ave.
New York, N.Y. 10016

Arthur C. Croft Publications
100 Garfield Ave.
New London, Conn. 06320

Thomas Y. Crowell Co., Inc.
666 Fifth Ave.
New York, N.Y. 10019

The John Day Co., Inc.
62 W. 45 St.
New York, N.Y. 10036

Dell Publishing Co., Inc.
1 Dag Hammarskjold Plaza
New York, N.Y. 10017

Dexter & Westbrook Ltd.
958 Church St.
Baldwin, N.Y. 11510

Doubleday & Co., Inc.
245 Park Ave.
New York, N.Y. 10017

F. A. Davis Company
1915 Arch St.
Philadelphia, Pa. 19103

E. P. Dutton & Co.
201 Park Ave. S.
New York, N.Y. 10003

Educational Developmental Labs
Huntington, N.Y. 11743

Educational Technology Publications
Englewood Cliffs, N.J. 07632

Educational Testing Service
Rosedale Rd.
Princeton, N.J. 08540

Educators Publishing Service
75 Moulton St.
Cambridge, Mass. 02138

Essay Press
P.O. Box 2323
La Jolla, Calif. 92037

Field Educ. Pub., Inc.
609 Mission St.
San Francisco, Calif. 94105

Follett Publishing Co.
1010 W. Washington Blvd.
Chicago, Ill. 60607

W. H. Freeman and Co., Publishers
660 Market St.
San Francisco, Calif. 94104

Garrard Publishing Co.
1607 N. Market St.
Champaign, Ill. 61820

Geigy Pharmaceuticals
550 Morris Ave.
Summit, N.J. 07901

Ginn & Co.
191 Spring St.
Lexington, Mass. 02173

Globe Book Co., Inc.
175 Fifth Ave.
New York, N.Y. 10010

Goodyear Publishing Co., Inc.
15113 Sunset Blvd.
Pacific Palisades, Calif. 90272

Grosset & Dunlap, Inc.
51 Madison Ave.
New York, N.Y. 10010

Grune & Stratton, Inc.
111 Fifth Ave.
New York, N.Y. 10003

Guidance Associates of Delaware
1526 Gilpin Ave.
Wilmington, Del. 19806

Harcourt, Brace, & Jovanovich, Inc.
757 Third Ave.
New York, N.Y. 10017

Harper & Row, Publishers
10 E. 53 St.
New York, N.Y. 10022

Harr, Wagner
(See Field Pub.)

Hart Publishing Co., Inc.
15 W. Fourth St.
New York, N.Y. 10012

Harvard University Press
79 Garden St.
Cambridge, Mass. 02138

D.C. Heath & Co.
125 Spring St.
Lexington, Mass. 02173

Hogarth Press, Ltd.
40-42 William IV St.
London, W.C. 2, England

Holt, Rinehart and Winston, Inc.
383 Madison Ave.
New York, N.Y. 10017

Houghton Mifflin Co.
1 Beacon St.
Boston, Mass. 02107

Indiana University Press
Tenth and Morton Sts.
Bloomington, Ind. 47401

Inst. Research on
Exceptional Children
Urbana, Ill. 61801

International Reading Association
Newark, Delaware 19711

International Universities Press
239 Park Ave. S.
New York, N.Y. 10003

Appendix F

Jamestown Publishers
Providence, R.I.

Johns Hopkins University Press
Baltimore, Md. 21218

Charles A. Jones Publishing Co.
4 Village Green, S.E.
Worthington, Ohio 43085

Jossey-Bass, Inc., Publishers
615 Montgomery St.
San Francisco, Calif. 94111

Kendall/Hunt Publishing Co.
2460 Kerper Blvd.
Dubuque, Iowa 52001

Alfred A. Knopf, Inc.
201 E. 50 St.
New York, N.Y. 10022

Laidlaw Bros.
Thatcher and Madison Sts.
River Forest, Ill. 60305

Language Research Associates
Chicago, Illinois

J. B. Lippincott Co.
E. Washington Square
Philadelphia, Pa. 19105

Little, Brown & Co.
34 Beacon St.
Boston, Mass. 02106

Liveright
500 Fifth Ave.
New York, N.Y. 10036

Longman, Inc.
72 Fifth Ave.
New York, N.Y. 10011

Lyons & Carnahan
407 E. 25 St.
Chicago, Ill. 60616

The M.I.T. Press
28 Carleton St.
Cambridge, Mass. 02142

McCormick-Mathers Publishing Co.
450 W. 33 St.
New York, N.Y. 10001

McGraw-Hill Book Co.
1221 Avenue of the Americas
New York, N.Y. 10020

David McKay Co., Inc.
750 Third Ave.
New York, N.Y. 10017

Macmillan, Inc.
866 Third Ave.
New York, N.Y. 10022

G. & C. Merriam Co.
47 Federal St.
Springfield, Mass. 01101

Charles E. Merrill Publishing Co.
1300 Alum Creek Drive
Columbus, Ohio 43216

Modern Curriculum Press
13900 Prospect Rd.
Cleveland, Ohio 44136

William Morrow & Co., Inc.
105 Madison Ave.
New York, N.Y. 10016

C. V. Mosby Co.
11830 Westline Industrial Drive
St. Louis, Mo. 63103

National Council of
   Teachers of English
1111 Kenyon Rd.
Urbana, Ill. 61801

N.Y.C. Board of Education
110 Livingston St.
Brooklyn, N.Y. 11201

Noble & Noble, Publishers, Inc.
1 Dag Hammarskjold Plaza
New York, N.Y. 10017

North-Holland Publishing Co.
52 Vanderbilt Ave.
New York, N.Y. 10017

W. W. Norton & Co., Inc.
500 Fifth Ave.
New York, N.Y. 10036

Open Court Publishing Co.
1058 Eighth St.
La Salle, Ill. 61301

The Orton Society
Towson, Maryland 21204

Oxford Book Co., Inc.
11 Park Place
New York, N.Y. 10007

Partners in Publishing
Box 50347
Tulsa, Oklahoma 74150

Personnel Press
191 Spring St.
Lexington, Mass. 02173

Plays, Inc.
8 Arlington St.
Boston, Mass. 02116

Pocket Books
630 Fifth Ave.
New York, N.Y. 10020

Portal Press
605 Third Ave.
New York, N.Y. 10016

Prentice Hall, Inc.
Englewood Cliffs, N.J. 07632

Primary Education Service
8217 S. Halstead St.
Chicago, Ill.

The Psychological Corp.
757 Third Ave.
New York, N.Y. 10017

Psychological Test Specialists
Box 1441
Missoula, Montana 59801

G. P. Putnam's Sons
200 Madison Ave.
New York, N.Y. 10016

Queen's Printer
171 Slater St.
Ottawa, Canada K1A 059

Rand McNally & Co.
8255 Central Park Ave.
Skokie, Ill. 60076

Raven Press
1140 Avenue of the Americas
New York, N.Y. 10036

Random House, Inc.
201 E. 50 St.
New York, N.Y. 10022

Reader's Digest Assn.
Pleasantville, N.Y. 10570

Reading Institute of Boston
116 Newbury St.
Boston, Mass. 02116

Remedial Education Press
2138 Bancroft, N.W.
Washington, D.C. 20008

Rotterdam University Press
Heemraadssingel 112, Postbus 1474,
    N1-3003
Rotterdam, Netherlands

Benjamin H. Sanborn & Co.
221 E. 20 St.
Chicago, Ill. 60616

Schocken Books, Inc.
200 Madison Ave.
New York, N.Y. 10016

Scholastic Book Services
50 W. 44 St.
New York, N.Y. 10036

Science Research Associates
259 E. Erie St.
Chicago, Ill. 60611

Scott, Foresman & Co.
1900 E. Lake Ave.
Glenview, Ill. 60025

Charles Scribner's Sons
597 Fifth Ave.
New York, N.Y. 10017

Silver Burdett Co.
250 James St.
Morristown, N.J. 07960

Simon & Schuster, Inc.
630 Fifth Ave.
New York, N.Y. 10020

Slossen Educational Publishers
140 Pine St.
East Aurora, N.Y. 14052

Steck-Vaughn Co.
Box 2028
Austin, Texas 78767

Syracuse University Press
1011 E. Water St.
Syracuse, N.Y. 13210

Teachers College Press
1234 Amsterdam Ave.
New York, N.Y. 10027

Charles C. Thomas, Publisher
301-27 E. Lawrence Ave.
Springfield, Ill. 62717

University of Chicago Press
5801 Ellis Ave.
Chicago, Ill. 60637

University of Illinois Press
Urbana, Ill. 61801

University Park Press
Chamber of Commerce Bldg.
Baltimore, Md. 21202

The Viking Press, Inc.
625 Madison Ave.
New York, N.Y. 10022

George Wahr Publishing Co.
316 S. State St.
Ann Arbor, Mich. 48108

Walker Educational Books
720 Fifth Ave.
New York, N.Y. 10019

Ward Lock Educational Ltd.
116 Baker St.
London W1, England

Franklin Watts, Inc.
730 Fifth Ave.
New York, N.Y. 10019

Wayne State University Press
5980 Cass St.
Detroit, Mich. 48202

Webster Publishing
Manchester Rd.
Manchester, Mo. 63011

Heni Wenkart
4 Shady Hill Sq.
Cambridge, Mass. 02138

Albert Whitman & Co.
560 W. Lake St.
Chicago, Ill. 60606

John Wiley & Sons, Inc.
605 Third Ave.
New York, N.Y. 10016

The H. W. Wilson Co.
950 University Ave.
Bronx, N.Y. 10452

John H. Winston Co.
1010 Arch St.
Philadelphia, Pa. 19107

Wonder-Treasure Books
51 Madison Ave.
New York, N.Y. 10010

World Book Co.
See Harcourt, Brace & Jovanovich

York Press
101 E. 32 St.
Baltimore, Md. 21218

Name Index

Subject Index

Academic requirements, high school, 247

Activity books, 273

Achievement, analysis of, 82–90

Alexia, 26

Anxiety, 51–52

Assignments, high school, 247

Attitudes toward reading: compelling stories and, 69–72; of older students, 202

Auditory discrimination, 16, 133–34; of short vowel sounds, 135–36

Basic sight vocabulary, 292–93

Bibliotherapy, 68–69

Blending of sounds, 134, 136–37; maturational factors and, 16

Brain-damaged children, 29

Brain-injured children, 29

Bright students, underachievement by, 236–53

Causative factors, 10–22; constitutional, 11–12; cultural, 20; educational, 19–20; emotional, 12–13; intellectual, 19; interaction of, 21–22; neurological-developmental, 13–18; physical, 11–12

Cerebral dominance, 16–18, 41–43

Classroom libraries, 157–58

Classroom teachers: comprehension taught by, 177–78; evaluation by, 79–99

Collaboration, psychotherapeutic principle of, 64

College students: comprehension and study skills of, 192–96; expressive writing by, 197–99; workbooks for, 272–73

Common nouns, 294

Compelling stories, change in attitude through, 69–72

Compound words, 142

Comprehension, 168–74; adjusting reading rate and, 175; finding main idea and important details for, 173–74; following directions and, 174; individualized factual and fictional materials for, 171–73; in oral reading, 155–56; supplementary reading for, 181–82; taught in classroom, 177–78; of textbooks, 169–70; workbooks for, 271–72

Constitutional factors, 11–12; learning and, 54

Context, 145

Cultural factors, 20

Curiosity, 51–52

Devices for teaching word recognition, 124–25, 270

Developmental dyslexia, 26

Developmental factors, 13–18

Developmental lag, 33

Diagnosis, 79–114; analysis of reading achievement for, 82–90; background information for, 80, 101–2; of educational factors, 105–7; intelligence and, 80–81, 103; of physical factors, 103; making recommendations in relation to, 113–14; of neurological factors,